FEATURE LOGICS, INFINITARY DESCRIPTIONS AND GRAMMAR

T0345351

CSLI
Lecture Notes
No. 44

FEATURE LOGICS, INFINITARY DESCRIPTIONS AND GRAMMAR

Bill Keller

CENTER FOR THE
STUDY OF LANGUAGE
AND INFORMATION

CSLI was founded early in 1983 by researchers from Stanford University, SRI International, and Xerox PARC to further research and development of integrated theories of language, information, and computation. CSLI headquarters and the publication offices are located at the Stanford site.

CSLI/SRI International **CSLI/Stanford** **CSLI/Xerox PARC**
333 Ravenswood Avenue   Ventura Hall   3333 Coyote Hill Road
Menlo Park, CA 94025   Stanford, CA 94305   Palo Alto, CA 94304

Library of Congress Cataloging-in-Publication Data
Keller, Bill, 1958–
    Feature logics, infinitary descriptions, and grammar / Bill Keller.
       p.   cm. — (CSLI lecture notes ; no. 44)
    Includes bibliographical references and index.
    ISBN 1-881526-26-7 (cloth) — ISBN 1-881526-25-9 (paper)
    1. Computational linguistics. 2. Language and logic. 3. Grammar, Comparative and general. I. Title. II. Series.
P98.K4 1993
410'.285--dc20   93-20668
                                                        CIP

To my parents

Contents

Preface

The work presented in this book is a revised version of the author's doctoral thesis, which was submitted to the School of Cognitive and Computing Sciences (COGS) at the University of Sussex in April 1991. The book is primarily concerned with computational linguistics — an area of research which thrives at the intersection of computer science, linguistics and logic. COGS has provided an ideal environment for pursuing research of an essentially interdisciplinary nature. Indeed, the research reported in this book owes a great deal to the presence in COGS of expertise in each of these different fields. But it has also benefited greatly from the spirit of the place and the idea that there is much to be be discovered at the interfaces between what are often regarded as distinct disciplines.

A good deal of the work carried out in revising the text for publication has been concerned with updating and extending the coverage of the survey of feature logics contained in chapter 2. In the past couple of years since the thesis was deemed to be 'finished' (is a thesis ever finished?) further work in this area has been reported. Efforts have have been made to incorporate newer developments (e.g. Carpenter's work on typed feature structures) as well as to provide a more consistent presentation of the material at a technical level. To this end, both the account of Johnson's work on attribute-value structures and Smolka's work on the language of feature terms have been re-worked and expanded to provide detail comparable to that found in the section on Rounds-Kasper logic.

Inevitably, choices have had to be made concerning what material to include in chapter 2 and what to pass over or cover only briefly. Without sufficient technical detail, a survey of feature logics would fail to be illuminating; with too much detail it would be overly long. An attempt has thus been made to steer a course between these two extremes and to select that work which is of undoubted theoretical or practical importance, or which has direct relevance to the rest of the material contained in this book.

Both the introductory and concluding chapters have also undergone considerable revision in order to provide a clearer statement of goals and results. On the other hand, chapters 3, 4 and 5 are substantially unchanged from the thesis, although very little of the text has not been scrutinized with an eye to clarification and, where necessary, correction. Some of the proofs which appeared in the thesis have also been re-worked in order to make them easier going on the reader.

There are many people who have contributed to the work reported in this book. I am particularly indebted to my thesis supervisor, Gerald Gazdar, whose advice was invaluable throughout the time it took to complete the research. I feel that I learned a great deal in this time, and I hope that at least some of the clarity he imparted to my thinking has found its way into the final manuscript. I would also like to thank my thesis examiners, Ewan Klein and Yoshido Suzuki, who made a number of constructive suggestions for improving the text.

A number of people have taken the time to read and comment on the work reported here, mostly without my asking directly. I am grateful for the interest they have expressed in my work as well as for the suggestions they have made. In particular, I would like to thank Patrick Blackburn, whose work on feature logics from a modal perspective has been inspiring; Mark Johnson for pointing out an error in my account of the treatment of negation in the Rounds-Kasper framework; and David Weir, who helped sharpen my understanding of TAG and other 'mildly context-sensitive' grammar formalisms. An anonymous referee provided me with comments and criticisms on the draft which was sent to CSLI, and these proved extremely useful in deciding how to go about the daunting task of revising the text for publication. While working in COGS I have also benefited from the advice and support of fellow researchers. Special thanks in this respect go to Lynne Cahill, Roger Evans, Robert Gaizauskus and Lionel Moser.

A small band of people volunteered to take on the arduous task of proof-reading. I am especially grateful to Raymond Wilson, who carefully read through the entire text. In addition, several postgraduate students in COGS read individual chapters. Thanks are due to Chris Cockayne, Catherine Longhurst, Anne Malchow, Alexandra Payne, Ben Shanks, Georgina Spary and Jane Sumnall. Of course, I am solely responsible for any errors which may remain.

Finally, I wish to thank Moira Wilson. The work on this book would have taken a good deal longer to complete had it not been for her support and tolerance over the past few years.

Chapter 1

Introduction

During the last decade or so, a number of new approaches to natural language grammar have appeared that share a remarkably similar view of the problems of linguistic description and the representation of linguistic objects. The new approaches may be characterized as being *constraint-based*, and have developed a notion of record- or frame-like data items called *feature structures* that play a key role in the representation of linguistic information. Feature structures provide for the representation of linguistic objects in terms of hierarchical sets of feature labels and associated values, and support a computationally efficient pattern-matching and information-combining operation called *unification*. Unification can be understood as a process of 'merging' two compatible feature structures to produce a new structure containing all of the information present in the original pair (but no more than this). In many grammar formalisms, feature structure unification is the primary mechanism for verifying constraints on the well-formedness of linguistic objects, giving rise to the term *unification-based grammar*. Examples of unification-based grammar formalisms include Functional Unification Grammar (FUG) (Kay (1979, 1985)), PATR (Shieber et al. (1983), Shieber (1984a)), Head-Driven Phrase Structure Grammar (HPSG) (Pollard and Sag (1987)), Unification Categorial Grammar (UCG) (Calder et al. (1988), Zeevat et al. (1987)), Categorial Unification Grammar (CUG) (Uszkoreit (1986)), Feature Structures Based Tree Adjoining Grammar (FTAG) (Vijay-Shanker (1987), Vijay-Shanker and Joshi (1988)), Dependency Unification Grammar (DUG) (Hellwig (1988)), Regular Unification Grammar (RUG) (Carlson (1988)) and Tree Unification Grammar (TUG) (Popowich (1988, 1989)). A number of other formalisms employ feature structures to

1

represent linguistic objects, but place less emphasis on the notion of unification. These include, most notably, Lexical Functional Grammar (LFG) (Kaplan and Bresnan (1982)) and Generalized Phrase Structure Grammar (GPSG) (Gazdar et al. (1985)).

For work in natural language processing, a sound theoretical understanding of the mathematical and computational properties of feature structures and their constraint languages is of vital importance. To this end, a number of researchers in computational linguistics have recently developed and investigated logical languages for describing and reasoning about feature structures. Such *feature logics* embody abstract theoretical models of feature structures and their description languages. A feature logic provides a precise framework within which the properties of feature structures and the languages used to describe them may be studied, free from the details of concrete grammar formalisms.

The work described in this book builds on and extends previous work on feature logics. There are two broad contributions to the study of feature logics and their application to the formalization of grammar contained in the following chapters. First, taking the feature logic originally introduced by Rounds and Kasper (1986) as a point of departure, this language is extended to allow for certain kinds of infinitary operators on descriptions. More specifically, descriptions of paths in feature structures are generalized to regular expressions over feature labels, and the properties of the resulting language are investigated. This extension is motivated in part by the linguistically useful device of *functional uncertainty*, proposed by Kaplan and Zaenen (1986) within the framework of LFG for the succinct description of unbounded dependencies in natural languages. One contribution of the present work is to provide a formal treatment of the functional uncertainty mechanism within the framework of Rounds-Kasper logic.

Second, it is shown that the combination of regular path expressions and description negation results in a language with considerable expressive power. In particular, it is possible to make universal statements about the values of certain classes of paths within a feature structure. The ability to capture generalizations about features and their values provides the power needed to encode grammars. A further contribution of the present work therefore, has been to demonstrate the feasibility of representing entire grammars in a uniform logical language with a precise formal semantics.

The idea of providing a completely logical treatment of grammar is appealing for several reasons. Logic offers a uniform basis for representing grammatical information or knowledge, and a rigorous foundation for proving properties of particular grammar formalisms. In addition, methods developed in automated theorem proving can yield efficient processing algorithms (both parsers and generators) for formalisms based on logic. The seminal work of Colmerauer (1978), and the concepts of logic programming developed by Kowalski (1974), have given rise to a tradition of *logic grammar*, in which the first order predicate calculus is employed as a basis for linguistic description. Examples of approaches to natural language grammar based on the predicate calculus include the Definite Clause Grammar (DCG) formalism described by Pereira and Warren (1980), Pereira's (1983, 1981) Extraposition Grammar (XG), McCord's (1985) Modular Logic Grammar (MLG), the work of Dahl and her colleagues (Dahl and Abramson (1984), Dahl and McCord (1983)) and the LFP grammar formalism introduced more recently by Rounds (1988). Work in this tradition has emphasized a view of grammar as a branch of proof theory. That is to say, a grammar comprises a set of axioms, and showing that a sentence belongs to the language described by the grammar amounts to a formal proof that a particular theorem follows from these axioms. Moreover, for grammar formalisms based on the definite clause subset of first order logic, general theorem proving techniques such as resolution can provide practical parsing algorithms: "parsing as deduction" (Pereira and Warren 1983).

The approach taken in this book emphasises a view of the connection between grammar and logic which is complementary to that adopted in the tradition of logic grammar. The view is taken that a feature logic is first and foremost a language for describing particular kinds of structures representing linguistic objects or knowledge. Furthermore, a grammar can be understood as a definition of a class of objects representing structural information about the expressions in a language. In the present work, such a definition is expressed as a logical description which is interpreted in a space of feature structures. A particular feature structure is well-formed with respect to a given grammar just in case it satisfies (in the sense of model-theory) the corresponding description. The notion of 'grammaticality as satisfiability' adopted here is reminiscent of the approach to natural language grammar found in the framework of Arc-Pair Grammar (APG) introduced by Johnson and Postal (1980). Whereas the APG framework is formulated in terms of first order logic however, the present work draws on more recent logical models of grammar, and in particular the feature logic of Rounds and Kasper.

1.1   Outline of this Book

The remainder of the present chapter deals with the nature of constraint-based grammar and feature structures in an informal way. Section 1.2 provides a brief overview of the most important characteristics of constraint-based approaches to grammar, and section 1.3 gives an intuitive account of the notion of a feature structures. The importance of providing explicit, formal models of feature structures and their description language is then discussed in section 1.4.

Chapter 2 presents a detailed survey and comparison of recent work on feature logics, and provides the technical background for subsequent chapters. There is an initial discussion of the denotational model of feature structures and descriptions proposed by Pereira and Shieber (1984) as a basis for the formal semantics of unification-based grammar formalisms. Problems relating to the treatment of negative and disjunctive descriptions of feature structures within this framework provide some motivation for the logical perspective on feature structures and their description languages adopted in subsequent work. The next several sections describe a number of different approaches to the formalization of feature structures and their description languages. Section 2.2 introduces the feature logic of Rounds and Kasper, which provided the first theoretically satisfying treatment of disjunctively specified feature structures. Extensions of the feature logic introduced by Rounds and Kasper are also discussed: the formal treatment of description negation, typed feature structures, and the treatment of recursive information.

This is followed by an account of the constraint language L_C (Category Logic) developed by Gazdar et al. as part of a meta-theoretical framework for the formalization of the notion of a syntactic category. Johnson's Attribute-Value Logic, and the language of feature terms proposed by Smolka are described in sections 2.4 and 2.5 respectively.

Chapter 3 introduces the language of *Regular Rounds-Kasper logic*, a rather natural extension of the logic of Rounds and Kasper in which descriptions of paths in feature structures are generalized to regular expressions over feature labels. To provide some motivation for this extension, the chapter begins with an overview of the phenomenon of unbounded dependency, and the device of functional uncertainty proposed by Kaplan and Zaenen. The language of Regular Rounds-Kasper logic (**RRK**) is defined formally in section 3.3 and investigated in the sections which follow. Two computational problems concerning descriptions in the language **RRK** are considered. Firstly, it is shown that the *logical equivalence problem* for descriptions in **RRK** is PSPACE hard, and secondly that the *satisfiability problem* for descriptions is decidable subject to an acyclicity restriction on feature structures.

In chapter 4 the language **RRK** is extended to incorporate description negation. The motivation for introducing negative constraints stems from the observation that regular path expressions can be used to express existential quantification over feature values within a feature structure. The introduction of description negation makes possible the expression of universal statements about features and their values. It is shown that the language of *Regular Rounds-Kapser logic with Negation* (**NRRK**) subsumes the constraint language L_C introduced by Gazdar et al., which employs two modal operators on formulas to permit the formulation of constraints that apply 'recursively', to successively embedded levels of structure. The chapter concludes with a demonstration that the satisfiability problem for **NRRK** is undecidable, and this result is related to the ability of **NRRK** descriptions to capture generalizations about structures involving re-entrancy.

In chapter 5 the language **NRRK** is viewed as a 'stand alone' formalism for representing grammars. A grammar is understood as a definition of a collection of objects or structures representing linguistic information about strings, and it is shown that such a definition may be expressed in **NRRK** as a single logical description which captures a generalization about the well-formedness of nodes in constituent-structure trees (suitably encoded in feature structures). Thus, a feature structure is taken to represent a well-formed parse tree for a grammar just in case it satisfies the corresponding logical description. It is shown that **NRRK** is sufficiently expressive to encode the descriptive devices employed in a number of different grammar formalisms: simple Context-Free Grammar, ID/LP Grammar, the unification-based formalism PATR, Categorial Grammar and Tree Adjoining Grammar.

Finally, chapter 6 draws a number of conclusions from the work described in this book, and indicates briefly some directions for future work.

1.2   Constraint-Based Grammar Formalisms

This section provides a non-technical overview of the common characteristics of the constraint-based grammar formalisms. The constraint-based grammar formalisms have evolved relatively independently, and accordingly been shaped by rather different design objectives and theoretical positions. On the one hand, unification-based formalisms such as PATR and FUG were designed primarily as general, computational tools to facilitate the task of implementing natural language processing systems. As such, they impose few (non-trivial) constraints on the kinds of linguistic descriptions which can be written down. Formalisms such as GPSG and LFG, on the other hand, were designed to serve as formal realizations of particular theoretical frameworks, and accordingly embody restrictive statements of 'universal grammar'. Despite their different origins, and their distinctive and often innovatory features however, the constraint-based grammar formalisms share a number of important characteristics. The most important of these are briefly summarised below. An excellent introduction to unification-based approaches to grammar is provided by Shieber (1986a). Sells (1985) and Horrocks (1987) provide introductions to GPSG and LFG, and compare these formalisms to the Government-Binding (GB) framework (Chomsky 1981).

- *Declarativism*. The constraint-based grammar formalisms characterize the relationship between natural language expressions and the information they carry (both syntactic and semantic) without reference to particular models of linguistic processing. In this sense, constraint-based grammars may be contrasted with the procedural formalisms which were predominant in computational linguistics during the 1970s (e.g. the Augmented Transition Network (ATN) formalism due to Woods (1970)). It is now generally recognized that declarative formalisms for describing grammars offer particular advantages over inherently procedural models of language (see Kaplan (1989), Keller (1992)). In particular, declarative formalisms are more perspicuous, they allow for greater flexibility in experimenting with alternative implementation strategies, and in principle they are neutral with respect to parsing and generation.

- *Surface Orientation/Context-Free Skeleton*. Constraint-based grammar formalisms provide a direct characterisation of the surface form of natural language expressions. Typically, they make use of a context-free 'skeleton' grammar (either phrase-structure rules or a categorial component) in order to describe the hierarchical structure and left-to-right order of strings. In this sense, constraint-based grammars are to be contrasted with transformational models of grammar in which surface form is derived from deep structures by means of transformational rules.

- *Feature Structures*. An important characteristic of constraint-based grammar formalisms is the use of hierarchical systems of features and values known as feature structures to represent linguistic objects. Feature structures are related to the record structures of computer science and the frames (Minsky 1975) of artificial intelligence. The notion of a feature structure plays an important role in this book, and a preliminary, informal account of the main concepts is therefore presented in the following section. The next chapter describes a number of formal models of feature structures and their description languages.

- *Constraint Languages*. In order to characterize the well-formedness of linguistic objects constraint-based grammar formalisms employ specialized languages for expressing propositions about features and their values. Constraint languages are used to capture syntactic phenomena such as agreement, subcategorization and unbounded dependencies, and account for much of the notational elegance of the formalisms.

1.3   Feature Structures

Feature structures are mathematical objects which are employed in many contemporary grammar formalisms in order to represent or model linguistic objects. For example, in GPSG feature structures are used to represent syntactic categories, while in LFG they are used to encode information about deep grammatical relations and the predicate-argument structure of strings. In many unification-based grammar formalisms (e.g. FUG, PATR and HPSG) feature structures are used to model all kinds of linguistic information: semantic, syntactic, phonological and so on. In some formalisms feature structures are utilized alongside more traditional notions of constituent structure, while in others they are the only structures used to represent linguistic objects.

The precise details of what constitutes a feature structure may vary from formalism to formalism. However, there exists a central core of ideas which can be presented in abstraction from any particular approach. Thus, in its most general form, a feature structure can be regarded as consisting of a set of *features*, where each feature comprises a *feature label* (or *attribute*) paired with a *feature value*. Each feature label is a simple symbol (e.g. number, person or agr) which uniquely identifies or names a particular feature. Feature values, on the other hand, may be either *simple*, or *complex*. A simple value is just an atomic symbol (e.g. singular, plural, 3, or nom); a complex value is an embedded feature structure.

A feature structure may be pictured in matrix form as shown for example in (1).

$$(1) \quad \begin{bmatrix} \text{cat} & \text{NP} \\ \text{agr} & \begin{bmatrix} \text{number} & \text{singular} \end{bmatrix} \end{bmatrix}$$

Intuitively, the feature structure in (1) may be regarded as representing a noun phrase (i.e. the value of **cat** is the atomic symbol **NP**) which is singular in number. The feature label **agr** (for 'agreement') has a complex value: an embedded feature structure which contains a single feature specification indicating in this case that **number** is **singular**.

In mathematical terms, feature structures are certain kinds of labelled, directed graphs. The feature structure shown in matrix form in (1) may be pictured graphically as shown below:

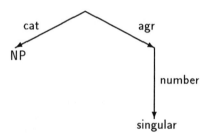

The relationship between these two ways of presenting feature structures should be clear. On the whole, in this book it will be convenient to make use of the matrix presentation for feature structures.

In the unification-based grammar formalisms, feature structures are regarded as inherently *partial* representations of linguistic objects. That is, given a particular feature structure, it is always possible to add further information in the form of additional feature specifications. For example, the feature structure shown in (2) below contains all of the features of (1), but has in addition information about **person** (namely, that it have the value 3).

$$(2) \quad \begin{bmatrix} \text{cat} & \text{NP} \\ \text{agr} & \begin{bmatrix} \text{number} & \text{singular} \\ \text{person} & 3 \end{bmatrix} \end{bmatrix}$$

It is natural to relate feature structures according to the amount of information they contain. Intuitively, one feature structure may be said to *subsume* another if the latter contains just as much information about feature labels and their values as the former (possibly more). For example, the feature structure given previously in (1) subsumes that shown in (2) above. Conversely, the feature structure in (2) is more specific than or *extends* that given in (1). In addition, it is generally assumed that there exists a completely uninformative, or most general feature structure which subsumes all other feature structures.

On the other hand, it is not always the case that two feature structures are related by subsumption in this way. For example, the feature structure shown in (3) below neither subsumes nor extends the feature structure given in (1).

$$(3) \quad \begin{bmatrix} \text{cat} & \text{NP} \\ \text{agr} & \begin{bmatrix} \text{person} & 3 \end{bmatrix} \end{bmatrix}$$

Although the feature structures in (1) and (3) are not related by subsumption there is a clear sense in which the information they contain is compatible. Intuitively, both feature structures can be taken to represent different aspects or views of the *same* linguistic object. In this case, the feature structures may be *unified*. Unification is an operation which takes two compatible feature structures and 'merges' them, to produce a new feature structure which is more specific than either but as general as possible. The unification of the feature structures in (1) and (3) above is in fact that shown in (2). It may be noted that this feature structure contains all of the information contained in (1) and (3) separately, but no more than this. Equivalently, the feature structure in (2) is the most general feature structure which is subsumed by both (1) and (3).

Two feature structures may also be incompatible in the sense that they disagree about certain features and their values. Compare for example the feature structure given in (4) below with that given previously in (1). Under the assumption that distinct, atomic feature values cannot be unified, then the two feature structures contain conflicting information about the value of the feature label **number**. More specifically, in (1) the feature label **number** has the atomic value **singular**, while in (4) is has the atomic value **plural**.

$$(4) \quad \begin{bmatrix} \text{cat} & \text{NP} \\ \text{agr} & \begin{bmatrix} \text{number} & \text{plural} \\ \text{person} & 3 \end{bmatrix} \end{bmatrix}$$

In this case the unification operation is not defined and may be said to *fail*.

There is a second operation on feature structures which is in some sense the dual of unification. The *generalisation* operation takes two feature structures and produces a new feature structure which is more general than either, but as specific as possible. Generalisation is always defined (i.e. it never fails). For example, the generalisation of (2) and (4) is the feature structure in (3). Note that this feature structure contains all of the information which is common to both (2) and (4) but no less than this.

Finally, an important property of feature structures is that they may be *re-entrant*. That is to say, different feature labels may *share* the same value. Another way of thinking about this is to consider the values of these labels to have been unified. Re-entrancy in feature structures provides an elegant means of capturing syntactic phenomena such as agreement, and will be indicated by co-indexing shared values as shown for example in (5).

$$(5) \quad \begin{bmatrix} \text{cat} & \text{S} \\ \text{agr} & \boxed{1}\begin{bmatrix} \text{person} & 3 \end{bmatrix} \\ \text{subject} & \begin{bmatrix} \text{agr} & \boxed{1} \end{bmatrix} \end{bmatrix}$$

In (5) the two **agr** feature labels have exactly the same value: namely, the feature structure which appears as the value of **agr** in the outermost feature matrix. This feature structure is annotated with a co-indexing box $\boxed{1}$ which also appears as the value of the second **agr** label, indicating that the value is shared by both feature labels. In order to see more clearly what is going on, it is convenient to picture the matrix in (5) as a graph:

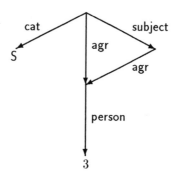

As the graph presentation makes clear, there is a single feature value which is common to both labels. It is important to distinguish this kind of value sharing from those cases where two feature labels simply happen to have informationally equivalent values. The difference is best explained in terms of a distinction between *token-identity* and a weaker notion of *type-identity*. In the first case there is a single value or token, whereas in the latter case there are different tokens of the same type. For example, the feature structure shown in (6) below differs from that given previously in (5) in that the values of the two **agr** labels are merely type-wise identical.

$$
(6) \quad
\begin{bmatrix}
\text{cat} & \text{S} \\
\text{agr} & \begin{bmatrix} \text{person} & 3 \end{bmatrix} \\
\text{subject} & \begin{bmatrix} \text{agr} & \begin{bmatrix} \text{person} & 3 \end{bmatrix} \end{bmatrix}
\end{bmatrix}
$$

The feature structure in (6) provides less information about features and values than that shown in (5). Thus in terms of the subsumption relation on feature structures, (6) subsumes (5).

1.4   Formal Models of Feature Structures

The preceding section has provided an intuitive account of the nature of feature structures and partial information. In order to ensure that this account is coherent however, it is necessary to formulate mathematically precise definitions of the key notions. Formalization is actually important for several reasons.

- Formalization provides the basis for establishing hard results about the mathematical properties of systems which employ feature structures. In the absence of a suitable formal framework it is impossible to prove or refute anything.

- However plausible an intuitive account may seem, the user of a particular formalism can never be entirely sure that it does not mask subtle inconsistencies or is not deficient in some respect. The process of formalization can serve to reveal such inconsistencies.

- From the perspective of computational linguistics, formalization is a prerequisite of implementation. Computational linguists require systems for representing and reasoning about linguistic information which are formal enough to be implemented on a computer.

The development of suitable, formal models of feature structures has already shed much light on the mathematical foundations and computational properties of constraint-based grammar formalisms. First, formalization has helped to clarify fundamental conceptual issues concerning the status of feature structures. For example, it has turned out to be important to distinguish between feature structures on the one hand, and descriptions of these structures on the other. At an intuitive level, it may not be immediately clear why this distinction needs to be made. Indeed, for certain formalisms (e.g. FUG) the two notions are conflated. Unfortunately, failure to distinguish between feature structures and their descriptions leads to problems in the treatment of negative or disjunctive information. Thus, it is by no means clear how to provide a formally satisfying account of negative or disjunctive feature values. By contrast, such constraints are readily incorporated into a suitable description language in terms of Boolean combinations of more basic constraints.

Second, formalization has brought into focus the important notion of partial information. The treatment of 'partiality' has important consequences for the interpretation of feature structure descriptions in general, and the treatment of negative descriptions in particular. In fact, two rather different views of feature structure and partial information have emerged.

From a unification-based or 'information-processing' perspective, a feature structure may be viewed as representing just that information which is available about a linguistic object at a particular point in a computation. As noted in the previous section, it is possible to define a natural relation on feature structures according to the amount of information they contain (*subsumption*), together with appropriate notions of compatibility and incompatibility of information and operations such as unification. Regarding feature structures as inherently partial objects presents certain difficulties in the treatment of negative constraints on these structures however. More specifically, the fact that a given feature structure *fails* to satisfy a given description does not imply that it satisfies the negation of that description. The reason is that the amount of available information may grow as a computation proceeds (i.e. through unification) so that absence of information must be viewed as a possibly transitory state of affairs. This has led some researchers to explore non-classical interpretations of negative constraints on feature structures (Moshier and Rounds (1987), Dawar and Vijay-Shanker (1989, 1990)).

Alternatively, it is possible to view feature structures as complete or 'totally-instantiated' representations of linguistic objects. This approach has been adopted in the work of both Johnson (1988) and Smolka (1988, 1989). Here, the notion of partial information is located entirely in the relationship between feature structures and descriptions. That is to say, descriptions provide partial information about feature structures in the sense that they pick out sets of admissible structures (which in turn encode complete information about linguistic objects). In this case however, the presence or absence of features and values within a given feature structure simply indicates the presence or absence of certain attributes of the corresponding linguistic object. Negative descriptions thus present no special difficulties, and may be interpreted in terms of the absence of particular features and values.

Finally, formalization has led to insights into the problems of implementing constraint-based grammar formalisms for efficient parsing and generation of natural languages. As a case in point, many constraint-based grammar formalisms make use of disjunctive descriptions of feature structures. In FUG, for example, a grammar is actually specified as one large disjunctive constraint. Disjunctive constraints are also to be found in the *Feature Co-occurrence Restrictions* (FCRs) of GPSG and the lexical entries of LFG, and HPSG allows for disjunctively specified feature values. Practical algorithms for computing with disjunctive descriptions of feature structures are therefore of some interest to workers in computational linguistics.

The formal framework of Rounds and Kasper (1986) has allowed a close examination of the computational complexity of processing disjunctive descriptions. In fact, it can be shown that determining the consistency of such descriptions is an NP-complete problem. This has suggested to some researchers that the use of disjunctive information in constraint-based formalisms should be restricted in some way (see e.g. Ramsay (1987)). On the other hand, the performance of algorithms for computing with disjunctive information can be significantly improved in practice by delaying expansion to disjunctive normal form as far as possible. This insight has led to the development of reasonably efficient methods for handling disjunction such as those proposed by Kasper (1987b) and Eisele and Dörre (1988, 1990).

Thus, attempts to formulate precise definitions of the intuitive notions 'feature structure' and 'description' have served to clarify important issues in the specification and implementation of constraint-based grammar formalisms. A number of different formal frameworks are surveyed and compared in the following chapter.

Chapter 2

A Survey of Feature Logics

Constraint-based approaches to grammar employ special-purpose languages for describing linguistic objects in terms of features and their values. A key idea is that a grammar associates with each word or phrase a set of descriptions or constraints which must be solved in order to determine grammaticality. As the sophistication of constraint-based approaches to grammar has grown, so has the need for a rigorous, mathematical treatment of their description languages. A suitable formalization should serve to facilitate comparison of existing grammar formalisms and suggest ways in which they can be extended and improved. From the perspective of computational linguistics, the implementation of constraint-based grammars requires efficient algorithms for solving sets of constraints. A formal account of descriptions is an essential step in demonstrating the correctness of such algorithms, and may yield more efficient processing strategies.

Historically, the calculus of partially ordered record types developed by Aït-Kaci (1984, 1986) provided the first well worked out account of unification on partially-specified data objects. Aït-Kaci's calculus was designed to model the notions of subsumption and unification in inheritance-based knowledge representation formalisms such as semantic networks and frame-based languages like KL-ONE (Brachman and Schmolze (1985)). Unfortunately, Aït-Kaci did not distinguish between the domain of descriptions and the data objects themselves, with resultant technical difficulties in the treatment of negative and disjunctive information. More specifically, it is difficult to provide a satisfactory account of negative or disjunctive data objects.

Pereira and Shieber (1984) described the first linguistically motivated account of constraints and unification as a basis for the semantics of a variety of unification-based grammar formalisms. In contrast to Aït-Kaci, Pereira and Shieber took care to distinguish between the domain of grammatical representations (feature structures) and the domain of descriptions. However, their denotational model of descriptions suffered from being limited to purely conjunctive descriptions. Once again, extending the approach to account for negative and disjunctive descriptions is not straightforward.

More recently, researchers in computational linguistics have adopted a logical perspective on grammatical representations and their descriptions. From this perspective descriptions are just formulas of a logical language which express propositions about features and their values. Over the past several years, a number of such languages have been developed and the properties of their associated logics investigated. The aim of the present chapter is to provide a survey of these *feature logics* and to compare and contrast the different approaches. As a point of departure, the chapter begins with a discussion of the denotational model of descriptions developed by Pereira and Shieber, and outlines the problem of incorporating negative and disjunctive descriptions into this model. Next, section 2.2 introduces the feature logic originally developed by Rounds and Kasper (Rounds and Kasper (1986), Kasper and Rounds (1986), Kasper (1987a), Kasper and Rounds (1990)) which provided the first formally satisfying account of disjunctive descriptions. A number of linguistically-motivated extensions of Rounds-Kasper logic are also discussed: the treatment of negation, types and inheritance, and the logical treatment of grammar.

Section 2.3 describes the constraint language L_C (Category Logic) introduced by Gazdar et al. (1988). Category Logic is similar to the language of Rounds and Kasper logic, but was developed primarily as a tool for specifying the category systems of various grammar formalisms. The most notable feature of Category Logic is the inclusion of two modal operators on formulas which allow for the expression of general or recursive constraints on features and values.

Section 2.4 provides an account of Johnson's (1988) Attribute-Value logic. In contrast to the unification-based view adopted by Rounds and Kasper, Johnson regards feature structures (attribute-value structures) as completely specified objects. Johnson's attribute-value languages are relational and describe sets of grammatical objects in terms of constraints amongst variables. Significantly, this approach leads to a simple, classical treatment of description negation.

The language of feature terms introduced by Smolka (1988, 1989) is described in section 2.5. Like Johnson's attribute-value descriptions, Smolka's feature terms are interpreted as set-denoting expression and negation is treated classically. However, Smolka does not restrict the domain of interpretation for feature terms to feature structures, but adopts instead an 'open worlds' model-theoretic semantics for descriptions which is similar to the standard interpretation of the first-order predicate calculus. Feature structures constitute one possible domain of interpretation for the logic, and Smolka shows that this interpretation is canonical in the sense that all of the important properties of feature terms can be determined with respect to this interpretation alone.

2.1   A Denotational Model of Descriptions

In the unification-based grammar formalisms, feature structures are understood as inherently partial representations of linguistic objects. At the same time however, there is an important sense in which descriptions of feature structures are also partial. A given description provides information about the possible values of certain feature labels, but equally it leaves other aspects of a feature structure completely unconstrained. The denotational model of feature structure descriptions introduced by Pereira and Shieber (1984) captures this notion of partial information. The approach draws on the mathematical theory of domains developed by Scott (1982) as the basis for a precise specification of the meaning of programming languages. A particular attraction of domain theory in this context is that it provides the mathematical tools needed for talking about partial information.

2.1.1   Feature Structures and Descriptions

Feature structures can be understood as partial functions from a domain of features labels F to a domain of features values V. Values in V may be either simple constants (elements of a domain of atomic values A) or else embedded feature structures. Thus, the domain of values is given as the solution to the following recursive domain equation:

$$V \simeq [F \to V] + A$$

Elements of the domain V can be regarded as trees (either finite or infinite) with branches labelled by elements of F, and terminals labelled by constants in A. Interior nodes correspond to embedded feature structures (i.e. complex values). When defined, the value of a feature label f in a complex value v is given by $v(f)$: the result of applying the partial function v to f. The result of applying an atomic value to a feature label is not defined. A *path* is a finite sequence of feature labels in F^*. When defined, the value of a path $p = f_1 \ldots f_n$ in a complex value v is obtained as $(\cdots v(f_1)\cdots)(f_n)$.

In order to talk about feature structures, unification-based formalisms employ systems of constraints on features and values. Consider for example the following typical grammar rule which is written in the unification-based formalism PATR:

$$S \quad \rightarrow \quad NP \ VP$$
$$\langle S \ head \rangle = \langle VP \ head \rangle$$
$$\langle S \ head \ subject \rangle = \langle NP \ head \rangle$$

The PATR rule can be regarded as consisting of two parts: an ordinary context-free phrase structure rule and a set of equational constraints amongst features and their values (so-called *path equations*). The context-free part of the rule describes the way in which strings are concatenated to form larger strings. In this example, a string of category S is to be formed by concatenating strings of categories NP and VP in that order. Each constituent mentioned in the rule is associated with a feature structure from V, and the path equations describe the way in which these feature structures are related. Thus, the first equation in the rule states that the value of **head** in the feature structure associated with S is identical to the value of **head** in the feature structure associated with VP. The second equation states that the value of the path **head subj** in the feature structure associated with S is the same as the value of **head** in the feature structure associated with NP.

More precisely, a *path equation* is a formula $x = y$, where x and y may be either paths or constants. For p a path and a a constant, the equation $p = a$ holds of a feature structure v just in case p is defined in v and has the atomic value a. On the other hand, for p and q paths, an equation $p = q$ holds of a feature structure v just in case both p and q are defined in v and have the same value. Intuitively, a description of a feature structure is a set of path equations of this kind. Because of the need to capture the important properties of partiality and compatibility of descriptions however, it is not possible to identify descriptions with arbitrary sets of path equations. Rather, descriptions are taken to be sets of equations which are both *consistent* and *deductively closed* as explained below.

The notion of *consistency* for sets of path equations is defined in terms of two different ways in which path equations may make incompatible statements about features and values. First of all, two path equations $p = a$

and $p = b$ (where a and b are distinct constants) make incompatible statements about the value of the path p. The presence of two equations of this form signifies an attempt to unify distinct atomic values: a *constant clash*. Secondly, two path equations $pq = a$ and $p = b$ are incompatible because the path p is simultaneously required to have both a simple and a complex value: a *constant/complex clash*. A set of path equations which contains either a constant clash or a constant/complex clash is inconsistent. More generally, an arbitrary set of path equations is consistent just in case its deductive closure does not contain clashes of either kind, where the notion of deductive closure is defined as follows.

Let d be a finite set of path equations. The *deductive closure* of d is the smallest set of path equations d' such that $d \subseteq d'$ and d' is closed under the following rules of inference:

Trivial Reflexivity: $$\frac{}{\epsilon = \epsilon}$$ (ϵ is the null path)

Restricted Reflexivity: $$\frac{pq = x}{p = p}$$

Symmetry: $$\frac{x = y}{y = x}$$

Transitivity: $$\frac{p = x, \ x = q}{p = q}$$

Substitutivity: $$\frac{p = q, \ pr = x}{qr = x}$$

The rules of inference capture the reflexivity, symmetry, transitivity and substitutivity of path equality. By modelling feature structure descriptions as deductively closed sets of path equation the problem of *implicit* information can be ignored. Two descriptions are equivalent just in case they are the same set of path equations.

Pereira and Shieber make use of Scott's (1982) information systems construction in order to define an abstract domain D which characterises the collection of feature structure descriptions. In fact, the domain D corresponds to the set of all consistent and deductively closed sets of path equations ordered by set inclusion. This domain is a meet semi-lattice with bottom element the description $\{\epsilon = \epsilon\}$: i.e. the set containing only the 'trivial' path equation. Given that the trivial equation holds of any feature structure, the bottom element of D corresponds to the least informative feature structure description. The inclusion ordering on descriptions in D

corresponds to the notion of subsumption for feature structure descriptions. For two descriptions d and d' in D, d *subsumes* d' just in case $d \subseteq d'$, in which case d' contains at least as much information as d about features and values. Furthermore, the *unification* of two feature structure descriptions is obtained by taking the deductive closure of their union. If the resulting set of path equations is inconsistent (i.e. it is not an element of D) then unification is said to *fail*.

2.1.2   The Problem of Negation and Disjunction

The denotational model of feature structures provides a satisfactory account of subsumption and unification for sets of constraints which apply purely *conjunctively*. Although this is sufficient for the purposes of modelling the descriptive apparatus of the PATR formalism, constraint-based grammar formalisms typically employ description languages which have considerably more expressive power. In particular, the ability to express disjunctive and negative constraints on features and values appears to be desirable. For example, disjunction is an integral part of the FUG formalism, where a grammar actually consists of a single disjunctive description.

The linguistic application of negative and disjunctive descriptions has been pointed out by Karttunen (1984). For example, in English, regular verbs in the present tense have just two morphological forms: one form which is used in the 3rd person singular (i.e. *loves*), and another which is used in the 1st and 2nd person singular, and the plural (*love*). Given this, it seems that a natural way of characterising a present tense verb form such as *love* is by means of a single negative constraint; namely, that *love* is not 3rd person singular. Similarly, the ability to express disjunctive descriptions can be motivated on linguistic grounds. For example, the German definite article *die* is used with nouns which are *either* feminine singular *or* plural, and which have *either* nominative *or* accusative case.

Karttunen presents an operational interpretation of negative and disjunctive information by showing how the basic unification operation is modified to cope with these new kinds of constraint[1]. To accommodate negative constraints, the operation (Negate A B) is used to ensure that two feature structures A and B can never become alike. If A and B contain conflicting information about the value of some feature, then Negate does nothing.

---

[1] Actually, Karttunen considers only disjunctive specifications of feature *values* (so-called *value disjunction*).

Otherwise it adds the negative constraint $\neg B$ to A and the negative constraint $\neg A$ to B. The idea is that any attempt to unify A with a feature structure C should succeed only if all of the negative constraints on A (and all of those on C) are satisfied.

The case of disjunctive constraints is more complex. In general the result of unifying disjunctive specifications is a disjunction of *tuples* of compatible feature structure descriptions. Each tuple is consistent in the sense that its elements can be unified, although unification cannot be performed immediately. For example, if A and B are incompatible, but C is compatible with either A or B, then the result of unifying the disjunction $\{A\ B\}$ with C is the complex disjunction $\{(A\ C)\ (B\ C)\}$. The description C cannot simply be unified with A since this would render it incompatible with B. Likewise, C cannot be unified with B. Instead therefore, both A and B acquire the *positive* constraint C. Later unification operations can cause certain of the tuples to become inconsistent, in which case they are eliminated. When only a single tuple remains its elements are finally unified. If all of the tuples in a disjunction become inconsistent, then unification fails.

The interpretation of negative and disjunctive constraints on feature structures poses a number of problems for the denotational model of feature structure descriptions developed by Pereira and Shieber. Consider first of all the case of disjunctive specifications of feature structures. It is clear that a disjunctive description cannot be encoded simply as a consistent and deductively closed set of path equations. As noted above, a set of equational constraints provides purely conjunctive information about features and values. Rather, it appears that disjunctive information must be encoded in terms of sets of descriptions. Technically, this requires disjunctive descriptions to be modelled as elements of some suitable power domain of the domain D of 'ordinary' feature structure descriptions. As Rounds and Kasper (1986) point out, such a specification would be difficult to use in proving the correctness of any implementation of disjunctive constraints.

Problems also arise in regard of the interpretation of negative constraints on feature structures. First of all, the intended interpretation of a negative constraint 'agreement is not 3rd person singular' is presumably that *either* agreement is not 3rd person *or* agreement is not singular. In general, it appears that negative constraints may give rise to disjunctive specifications. More seriously, the presence of negative constraints on features and values cannot be adequately accounted for by the absence of the corresponding positive information. The fact that a given feature structure description does not require that a particular feature label has a particular value cannot be taken to imply that the feature label *does not* have that value. Indeed, this is one of the hallmarks of partial information. Information about features and values may 'grow' as additional constraints are taken into account during a computation (i.e. through unification). In the context of partial information the theoretical treatment of negative constraints is particularly problematic, and a number of alternative approaches to negative information are described in the course of this chapter.

2.1.3   Summary

The denotational model of feature structure descriptions due to Pereira and Shieber provides a precise account of purely conjunctive constraints on feature structures. For certain linguistic applications however, the ability to express negative and disjunctive conditions is desirable. Unfortunately, extending the model to account for negative and disjunctive constraints on feature structures presents a number of difficulties. These difficulties provide some motivation for the logical approaches to feature structures and their descriptions discussed in the following sections.

2.2   Rounds-Kasper Logic

This section introduces the language of feature structure descriptions originally developed by Rounds and Kasper (Rounds and Kasper (1986), Kasper and Rounds (1986), Kasper (1987a), Kasper and Rounds (1990)). On this approach, descriptions of feature structures are expressed as formulas of a propositional logic which is interpreted in the domain of feature structures. The approach extends the denotational model of Pereira and Shieber by providing a precise account of disjunctive descriptions. Consider for example the feature matrix shown in figure 2.1, in which braces ({ and }) are used to group alternative feature structure specifications. The feature matrix can be understood as stating that agreement is either feminine, singular or else plural, and that the value of case is either nominative or accusative.

The basic insight of Rounds-Kasper logic is that a feature matrix such as that shown in figure 2.1 can also be represented in linear form by a logical formula like that shown below:

agr : ((gender : fem ∧ number : sing) ∨ number : plur) ∧ case : (nom ∨ acc)

In the logical representation, each feature is described by a formula $l : \phi$, where l is a feature label (e.g. **agr, gender, number** etc.) and ϕ is a formula

$$\left[\begin{array}{ll} \text{agr} & \left\{ \begin{array}{l} \left[\begin{array}{ll} \text{gender} & \text{fem} \\ \text{number} & \text{sing} \end{array} \right] \\ \left[\begin{array}{ll} \text{number} & \text{plur} \end{array} \right] \end{array} \right\} \\ \text{case} \quad \{\text{nom acc}\} \end{array} \right]$$

Figure 2.1: A disjunctively specified feature matrix

representing the feature value. Atomic feature values are represented by simple symbols such as **fem**, **plur** and **nom** and complex descriptions are built up using the boolean connectives $\wedge$ and $\vee$ in a standard way. For example, the description **case** : (**nom** $\vee$ **acc**) states that the feature label **case** may have either of the atomic values **nom** or **acc**.

2.2.1   The Domain of Feature Structures

The domain of feature structures is defined with respect to two sets of primitive symbols:

1. a non-empty set L of *feature labels*; and

2. a non-empty set A of *atomic values*.

In the following, feature labels in L will be denoted by l (possibly with subscripts) and atoms in A will be denoted by a, b, c.

Definition 2.1 A *feature structure* (over L and A) is a tuple $\mathcal{A} = \langle Q, q_0, \delta, \pi \rangle$ where:

- Q is a non-empty, finite set of *states*.

- $q_0 \in Q$ is the *start state*.

- $\delta : (Q \times L) \to Q$ is a partial *transition function*.

- $\pi : Q \to A$ is a partial *assignment function* such that $\forall q \in Q, \forall l \in L$ if $\pi(q)$ is defined, then $\delta(q, l)$ is undefined.

$$\begin{bmatrix} \text{cat} & \text{S} \\[4pt] \text{agr} & \boxed{1} \begin{bmatrix} \text{number} & \text{sing} \\ \text{person} & 3 \end{bmatrix} \\[12pt] \text{subj} & \begin{bmatrix} \text{agr} & \boxed{1} \end{bmatrix} \end{bmatrix}$$

Figure 2.2: Matrix notation for the feature structure of example 2.2

A feature structure can be conveniently viewed as a labelled, directed graph in which nodes correspond to states, and there is an edge from q to q' with label l just in case $\delta(q, l) = q'$. This means that each node has at most one outgoing edge with a particular label l. In addition, terminal nodes of the graph (i.e. nodes with no outgoing edges) may be decorated by elements of the set A of atomic values.

Example 2.2 Suppose that cat, subj, agr, number and person are feature labels in L and that S, sing and 3 are atomic values in A. The feature matrix pictured in figure 2.2 may be formalized as a feature structure $\mathcal{A} = \langle Q, q_0, \delta, \pi \rangle$ where $Q = \{q_0, q_1, q_2, q_3, q_4, q_5\}$ and δ and π are completely specified by:

1. $\delta(q_0, \text{cat}) = q_1$ $\qquad \delta(q_0, \text{agr}) = q_2$ $\qquad \delta(q_0, \text{subj}) = q_3$
   $\delta(q_2, \text{number}) = q_4$ $\quad \delta(q_2, \text{person}) = q_5$ $\quad \delta(q_3, \text{agr}) = q_2$

2. $\pi(q_1) = \text{S}$ $\qquad\qquad \pi(q_4) = \text{sing}$ $\qquad\qquad \pi(q_5) = 3$

The partial transition function δ may be extended to a partial function $\delta^* : (Q \times L^*) \to Q$ from state-path pairs to states as follows: if p is the empty path then $\delta^*(q, p) = q$; otherwise, if $p = lp'$ is a non-empty path then $\delta^*(q, p) = \delta^*(\delta(q, l), p')$. Let $\mathcal{A} = \langle Q, q_0, \delta, \pi \rangle$ be a feature structure, and let q and q' be states in Q. If $\delta^*(q, p) = q'$ for some path p then the state q' is said to be *reachable* from the state q. The feature structure $\mathcal{A} = \langle Q, q_0, \delta, \pi \rangle$ is called *connected* if every state of $\mathcal{A}$ is reachable from the start state q_0 (i.e. for every $q \in Q$, there exists some path p such that $\delta^*(q_0, p) = q$). It will be required that feature structures are connected in this sense.

It is useful to be able to talk about the value of a given path with respect to a particular feature structure. Let $\mathcal{A} = \langle Q, q_0, \delta, \pi \rangle$ be a feature structure. The *path set* of the feature structure $\mathcal{A}$ is defined as that set of paths $Paths(\mathcal{A}) = \{p \in L^* | \delta(q_0, p) \text{ is defined}\}$. The value of a given path $p \in Paths(\mathcal{A})$ in the feature structure $\mathcal{A}$ (written $\mathcal{A}/p$) is then defined as:

$$\mathcal{A}/p = \langle Q', \delta^*(q_0, p), \delta', \pi' \rangle$$

where $Q' \subseteq Q$ is that subset of the states of $\mathcal{A}$ which are reachable from the new start state $\delta^*(q_0, p)$, and δ' and π' are the restrictions of δ and π respectively to states in Q'. It is easy to check that $\mathcal{A}/p$ is a feature structure. In addition, the *Nerode relation* $\mathcal{N}_\mathcal{A}$ of $\mathcal{A}$ is that equivalence relation on paths in $Paths(\mathcal{A})$ given by:

$$p\mathcal{N}_\mathcal{A}p' \Leftrightarrow \delta^*(q_0, p) = \delta^*(q_0, p')$$

One agreeable consequence of the definition of a feature structure given above is that it captures an important distinction between type- and token-identity for feature values. Intuitively, two feature values are type-wise identical simply if they represent the same information about features and values. Token-identity for feature values is a stronger condition which requires that the values are actually the same object. Clearly, token-identical feature values are type-identical, but the converse is not in general true. According to the above definitions, the values of two different paths in a feature structure $\mathcal{A}$ are token-identical just in case they cause a transition to the same state (equivalently, they belong to the same Nerode-equivalence class). For example, in the feature structure of example 2.2, the paths **agr** and **subj agr** share the same value because both paths result in a transition to the state q_2.

In the unification-based formalisms, feature structures are viewed as inherently *partial* representations of linguistic objects. Given any feature structure $\mathcal{A}$, it is always possible to find another feature structure $\mathcal{B}$ which is a more specific or informative representation than $\mathcal{A}$. In this case, $\mathcal{A}$ is said to *subsume* $\mathcal{B}$. The following definition shows that there is a close connection between the notion of subsumption and the existence of feature structure homomorphisms (Moshier and Rounds 1987).

Definition 2.3 (*Subsumption*) Let $\mathcal{A} = \langle Q, q_0, \delta, \pi \rangle$ and $\mathcal{A}' = \langle Q', q'_0, \delta', \pi' \rangle$ be two feature structures. Then $\mathcal{A} \sqsubseteq \mathcal{A}'$ ($\mathcal{A}$ *subsumes* $\mathcal{A}'$, $\mathcal{A}'$ *extends* $\mathcal{A}$) just in case there exists a mapping $h : Q \to Q'$ which meets the following conditions:

- $h(q_0) = q'_0$

- if $\delta(q, l)$ is defined, then $\delta'(h(q), l) = h(\delta(q, l))$

- if $\pi(q)$ is defined, then $\pi'(h(q)) = \pi(q)$

It is easy to see that the subsumption relation is reflexive: for any feature structure $\mathcal{A}$, simply choose h as the identity function on the states of $\mathcal{A}$. Furthermore, subsumption is clearly transitive: if h is a homomorphism from $\mathcal{A}$ to $\mathcal{B}$ and h' a homomorphism from $\mathcal{B}$ to $\mathcal{A}'$, then the composition of h and h' is a homomorphism from $\mathcal{A}$ to $\mathcal{A}'$.

Two feature structures $\mathcal{A}$ and $\mathcal{B}$ are said to be (*subsumption*) *equivalent* if $\mathcal{A} \sqsubseteq \mathcal{B}$ and $\mathcal{B} \sqsubseteq \mathcal{A}$, and they are *incomparable* if neither $\mathcal{A} \sqsubseteq \mathcal{B}$ nor $\mathcal{B} \sqsubseteq \mathcal{A}$. It should be noted that equivalent feature structures are not necessarily identical. The reason, of course, is that they may yet differ with respect to their state sets. Thus, the subsumption relation $\sqsubseteq$ is only a *preorder* on the domain of feature structures. For this reason it is sometimes considered more convenient to work in the space of subsumption equivalence classes of feature structures, which admits a weak partial ordering induced by the relation $\sqsubseteq$. The resulting space is a meet semi-lattice, with a bottom element the equivalence class of one-state feature structures having no labels or values.

Two feature structures $\mathcal{A}$ and $\mathcal{A}'$ are called *compatible* just in case there exists a third feature structure $\mathcal{B}$ such that $\mathcal{A} \sqsubseteq \mathcal{B}$ and $\mathcal{A}' \sqsubseteq \mathcal{B}$. The feature structure $\mathcal{B}$ is said to be a *unifier* for $\mathcal{A}$ and $\mathcal{A}'$. Intuitively, the existence of a unifier shows that the feature structures do not contain conflicting information about features and their values. Compatible feature structures can therefore be regarded as different representations or views of the same linguistic object. The unifier $\mathcal{B}$ is called *minimal* just in case $\mathcal{B}'$ is a unifier for $\mathcal{A}$ and $\mathcal{A}'$ implies $\mathcal{B} \sqsubseteq \mathcal{B}'$. The main result concerning the subsumption ordering on feature structures is captured by the following theorem (see Rounds and Kasper (1986) and Moshier (1988)).

Theorem 2.4 (Unification) *Minimal unifiers exist for compatible pairs of feature structures.*

In many constraint-based grammar formalisms, feature structure unification provides the primary means of combining linguistic information and verifying sets of constraints. Feature structure unification can be efficiently implemented, and practical algorithms which run in almost linear time have been described by Aït-Kaci (1984), and Moshier (1988).

As a final point, it may be noted that the definition of a feature structure given above allows for the possibility of cycles. More formally, a feature structure $\mathcal{A} = \langle Q, q_0, \delta, \pi \rangle$ is *cyclic* if there exists a state q of $\mathcal{A}$ and a non-empty path p such that $\delta^*(q, p) = q$, and otherwise $\mathcal{A}$ is *acyclic*. Rounds and Kasper originally considered only acyclic feature structures, although Moshier (1988) relaxes this restriction and provides an efficient unification algorithm for feature structures with cycles. Johnson (1988, pp.19–20) suggests that cyclic feature structures might be linguistically useful in the analysis of the filler-gap dependencies of relative clauses. Moreover, there are practical reasons for studying cyclic structures. In particular, it is possible for cycles to arise during the unification process, and any implementation must be able to handle such cases robustly.

2.2.2   The Language of Rounds-Kasper Logic

The language of Rounds-Kasper logic (**RK**) is parameterized with respect to the set of feature labels L and the set of atoms A. The set of well-formed formulas or descriptions of **RK** is defined as the smallest set which contains:

- $\top$

- $\bot$

- a for any $a \in A$

- $l : \phi$ for $l \in L$ and ϕ a description

- $(\phi \wedge \psi)$ for ϕ, ψ descriptions

- $(\phi \vee \psi)$ for ϕ, ψ descriptions

- $(p_1 \doteq p_2)$ for $p_1, p_2 \in L^*$.

To ease readability, brackets will be omitted when no ambiguity can arise from doing so. In addition, it will be assumed that the 'labelling operator' (':') has higher precedence than the logical connectives '$\wedge$' and '$\vee$'. Consequently, the description $p : \phi \wedge p' : \psi$ is unambiguous and distinct from $p : (\phi \wedge p' : \psi)$.

The special descriptions $\top$ and $\bot$ are included to model the 'trivial description' and the 'inconsistent description' respectively. Informally, the description $\top$ is satisfied by any feature structure, whereas the description $\bot$ is never satisfiable. Atoms in A describe atomic feature values, while a description of the form $l : \phi$ states that the feature label l is defined and has a value which satisfies the description ϕ. A *path equation* $(p_1 \doteq p_2)$ is used to assert that the values of the paths p_1 and p_2 are token-identical[2].

Example 2.5 Suppose that cat, agr, number, person and subj are feature labels in L and that S, sing, plur and 3 are atomic feature values in A, then the following are well-formed descriptions:

1. (cat : S ∧ agr : ((number : sing ∧ person : 3) ∨ number : plur))

2. (cat : S ∧ (agr $\doteq$ subj agr))

Intuitively, both of the above descriptions are satisfied by the feature structure of example 2.2. More formally, the conditions under which a feature structure $\mathcal{A} = \langle Q, q_0, \delta, \pi \rangle$ satisfies a description ϕ (written $\mathcal{A} \models \phi$) are defined as follows:

- $\mathcal{A} \models \top$;

- $\mathcal{A} \not\models \bot$;

- $\mathcal{A} \models a \Leftrightarrow \pi(q_0) = a$.

- $\mathcal{A} \models l : \phi \Leftrightarrow \mathcal{A}/l$ is defined and $\mathcal{A}/l \models \phi$;

- $\mathcal{A} \models (\phi \vee \psi) \Leftrightarrow \mathcal{A} \models \phi$ or $\mathcal{A} \models \psi$;

- $\mathcal{A} \models (\phi \wedge \psi) \Leftrightarrow \mathcal{A} \models \phi$ and $\mathcal{A} \models \psi$.

- $\mathcal{A} \models (p_1 \doteq p_2) \Leftrightarrow p_1 \mathcal{N}_{\mathcal{A}} p_2$.

A description ϕ of **RK** is said to be *satisfiable* if $\mathcal{A} \models \phi$ for some feature structure $\mathcal{A}$, and otherwise ϕ is said to be *unsatisfiable*.

From an information-processing perspective, an important result concerning the satisfaction relation $\models$ is that it is *monotonic* with respect to the subsumption relation. That is to say, if $\mathcal{A} \models \phi$ and $\mathcal{A} \sqsubseteq \mathcal{B}$ then it follows that $\mathcal{B} \models \phi$. This result shows that as more information is added to a feature structure, previously verified constraints will continue to hold. Consequently, partial information about a linguistic object available from

---

[2]The presentation of the logic given here thus differs slightly from that in (1987a), where a statement of the form $[\langle p_1 \rangle, \langle p_2 \rangle, \ldots, \langle p_n \rangle]$ is used to assert the Nerode equivalence of the paths $p_1, p_2, \ldots, p_n$.

different sources can be combined efficiently through unification as a computation proceeds. The interpretation of the description language also reveals that conjunction of descriptions corresponds to feature structure unification. Rounds and Kasper (1986) have shown that there is a close correspondence between feature structures and non-disjunctive descriptions (i.e. descriptions with no occurrences of $\vee$). Specifically, for any satisfiable, nondisjunctive description ϕ it is possible to find a feature structure $\mathcal{A}$ such that $\mathcal{B} \models \phi$ implies that $\mathcal{A} \sqsubseteq \mathcal{B}$ (the proof is by induction on the structure of descriptions). The feature structure $\mathcal{A}$ is called a *most general satisfier* for ϕ and is clearly unique up to subsumption equivalence.

Of course, for an arbitrary description ϕ (one possibly containing disjunctions) there will not in general exist such a unique most general satisfier. However, it is not difficult to show that there exists a finite set of subsumption-incomparable feature structures $\{\mathcal{A}_1, \ldots, \mathcal{A}_n\}$ satisfying ϕ, such that $\mathcal{B} \models \phi$ implies that $\mathcal{A}_i \sqsubseteq \mathcal{B}$ for some $i \in \{1, \ldots, n\}$. To see this, it may be noted that the set of most general satisfiers for a disjunctive description $(\phi \vee \psi)$ can be obtained by taking the subsumption-minimal elements in the union of the sets of feature structures which satisfy ϕ and ψ separately. Because any description contains only a finite number of disjunctions, this set can contain only a finite number of subsumption-incomparable feature structures.

Two descriptions ϕ and ψ are said to be (*logically*) *equivalent* (written $\phi \simeq \psi$) just in case they have the same set of satisfying feature structures. For example, it is clear that the following equivalences hold:

(7)   a. $a \wedge b \simeq \bot \; (a \neq b)$

         b. $a \wedge l : \phi \simeq \bot$

         c. $l : (\phi \wedge \psi) \simeq l : \phi \wedge l : \psi$

The first two equivalences ensure that conjoining descriptions of incompatible feature structures results in an unsatisfiable description (unification failure). Equivalence (7a) states that distinct atomic values do not unify (a *constant clash*) while (7b) states that atomic values and complex values do not unify (*a constant/complex clash*). The equivalence in (7c) shows that feature labels distribute over conjunctions. Intuitively, the unification of two feature structures defined for the same feature label l can succeed only if it is possible to unify the values for l.

A complete axiomatisation of the logical behaviour of feature structures can be given in the form of a calculus of logical equivalences for descrip

Equivalences for Boolean Lattices with $\bot$ and $\top$:

$$\phi \vee \bot \simeq \phi \qquad\qquad\qquad\qquad (\textit{Top and Bottom})$$
$$\phi \wedge \bot \simeq \bot$$
$$\phi \vee \top \simeq \top$$
$$\phi \wedge \top \simeq \phi$$
$$\phi \vee \psi \simeq \psi \vee \phi \qquad\qquad\qquad\qquad (\textit{Commutativity})$$
$$\phi \wedge \psi \simeq \psi \wedge \phi$$
$$(\phi \vee \psi) \vee \chi \simeq \phi \vee (\psi \vee \chi) \qquad\qquad (\textit{Associativity})$$
$$(\phi \wedge \psi) \wedge \chi \simeq \phi \wedge (\psi \wedge \chi)$$
$$\phi \vee \phi \simeq \phi \qquad\qquad\qquad\qquad (\textit{Idempotence})$$
$$\phi \wedge \phi \simeq \phi$$
$$(\phi \vee \psi) \wedge \phi \simeq \phi \qquad\qquad\qquad (\textit{Absorption})$$
$$(\phi \wedge \psi) \vee \phi \simeq \phi$$
$$(\phi \vee \psi) \wedge \chi \simeq (\phi \wedge \chi) \vee (\psi \wedge \chi) \qquad (\textit{Distributivity})$$
$$(\phi \wedge \psi) \vee \chi \simeq (\phi \vee \chi) \wedge (\psi \vee \chi)$$

Equivalences for Descriptions and Labels:

$$l : \bot \simeq \bot \qquad\qquad\qquad\qquad (\textit{Unification Failure})$$
$$l : \phi \wedge l : \psi \simeq l : (\phi \wedge \psi) \qquad\qquad (\textit{Distribution of Labels})$$
$$l : \phi \vee l : \psi \simeq l : (\phi \vee \psi)$$
$$(lp_1 \doteq lp_2) \simeq l : (p_1 \doteq p_2)$$
$$a \wedge b \simeq \bot \text{ for all } a, b \in A \text{ with } a \neq b \qquad (\textit{Constant Clash})$$
$$a \wedge l : \phi \simeq \bot \qquad\qquad\qquad (\textit{Constant/Complex Clash})$$

Equivalences for Path Equations:

$$(\epsilon \doteq \epsilon) \simeq \top \qquad\qquad\qquad\qquad (\textit{Trivial Reflexivity})$$
$$(p_1 p_2 \doteq p_3) \simeq (p_1 p_2 \doteq p_3) \wedge (p_1 \doteq p_1) \qquad (\textit{Restricted Reflexivity})$$
$$p_1 : \top \simeq (p_1 \doteq p_1)$$
$$(p_1 \doteq p_2) \simeq (p_2 \doteq p_1) \qquad\qquad\qquad (\textit{Symmetry})$$
$$(p_1 \doteq p_2) \wedge (p_2 \doteq p_3) \simeq (p_1 \doteq p_2) \wedge (p_2 \doteq p_3) \wedge (p_1 \doteq p_3) \quad (\textit{Transitivity})$$
$$(p_1 \doteq p_2) \wedge p_1 : \phi \simeq (p_1 \doteq p_2) \wedge p_2 : \phi \qquad (\textit{Restricted Substitutivity})$$
$$(p_1 \doteq p_2) \wedge (p_3 \doteq p_2 p_4) \simeq (p_1 \doteq p_2) \wedge (p_3 \doteq p_1 p_4)$$

Figure 2.3: A calculus of logical equivalences for descriptions of **RK**

tions. The calculus shown in figure 2.3 differs only in minor respects from that presented by Kasper (1987a). The key to showing completeness for this calculus is the existence of a *disjunctive normal form* (DNF) result for descriptions. Kasper shows that the equivalences can be used to transform any satisfiable description into DNF (or to $\perp$ if the description is not satisfiable). Unfortunately, any algorithm for computing DNF will require exponential time in the worst case. Moreover, Kasper demonstrates that satisfiability for propositional formulas in conjunctive normal form (a well-known NP-complete problem) is linear-time reducible to satisfiability of feature structure descriptions. It follows that satisfiability for arbitrary descriptions is also NP-complete.

Although this result indicates that the worst-case complexity of any unification algorithm for disjunctive descriptions is prohibitive, it is notable that average time-complexity can be improved by delaying expansion to DNF. On the basis of this observation, Kasper (1987b) has developed a practical unification algorithm for disjunctive descriptions which works by removing any inconsistent disjuncts before a description is expanded. In this algorithm, ordinary feature structure unification is used to test for inconsistent disjuncts in a description, but the results of successful unifications are discarded. This is a potential source of inefficiency, because essentially the same test may need to be performed many times in the course of unifying two descriptions involving disjunction. Eisele and Dörre (1988) present an alternative unification algorithm for disjunctive descriptions which saves the results of test unifications which may eventually contribute to a solution. However, their algorithm is restricted to descriptions involving only disjunctive feature values. A more general algorithm which makes use of a novel device of named disjunction has also been described by Eisele and Dörre (1990).

2.2.3   Partial Information and the Treatment of Negation

This section considers the problems which arise when the language of **RK** is extended to incorporate negative descriptions of feature structures. The linguistic motivation for introducing some form of description negation has already been discussed in section 2.1.2. In particular, negation can provide for the succinct encoding of lexical entries. For example, consider the following description which might form part of a lexical entry for the regular verb *love*:

(8)   cat : verb $\wedge$ form : *love* $\wedge$ agr : $\neg$(person : 3 $\wedge$ number : sing)

The description simply states that *love* is a verb which is not 3rd person singular. Intuitively, this is just an economical way of saying that *love* is either 1st or 2nd person singular, or 1st, 2nd or 3rd person plural. However, the precise interpretation of negative descriptions of this kind is problematic from the perspective of information growth. Note that a classical account of description negation would require simply that $\mathcal{A} \models \neg\phi$ just in case $\mathcal{A} \not\models \phi$. For example, the feature structure shown below satisfies the description given in (8) simply because it lacks any specification for the feature label **person**.

$$(9) \quad \begin{bmatrix} \text{cat} & \text{V} \\ \text{form} & \textit{love} \\ \text{agr} & \begin{bmatrix} \text{number} & \text{sing} \end{bmatrix} \end{bmatrix}$$

As already noted, in unification-based formalisms feature structures are regarded as inherently partial objects. A feature structure represents just that information available about a linguistic object at a particular point in a computation. This information may grow as a computation proceeds and additional constraints are taken into account. Unfortunately, the classical account of description negation results in a failure of monotonicity. The feature structure shown in (9) has many extensions in which **person** is defined and has the atomic value 3, and these extensions do not satisfy (8). Thus it is possible to have $\mathcal{A} \models \phi$ and $\mathcal{A} \sqsubseteq \mathcal{B}$ but $\mathcal{B} \not\models \phi$. In computational terms, this means that the processing of negative constraints on feature structures cannot be freely interleaved with feature structure unification. Pereira (1987) points out that monotonicity must be preserved if feature structure unification is to provide a computationally efficient method of combining partial information about linguistic objects.

Moshier and Rounds (1987) have proposed an alternative to the classical treatment of description negation that is based on the semantics of intuitionistic logic (Kripke 1965). On this approach, the classical satisfaction relation is replaced by the model-theoretic notion of *forcing* (Fitting 1969). Given a set of feature structures $\mathcal{K}$, they define a relation $\Vdash_{\mathcal{K}}$ (read 'forces in $\mathcal{K}$') between feature structures in $\mathcal{K}$ and descriptions. The idea is that $\mathcal{A} \Vdash_{\mathcal{K}} \phi$ holds just in case every extension of $\mathcal{A}$ in the set $\mathcal{K}$ satisfies ϕ. In the case of description negation, the appropriate clause in the definition of the forcing relation is given by:

$$\mathcal{A} \Vdash_{\mathcal{K}} \neg\phi \Leftrightarrow \forall \mathcal{B} \in \mathcal{K} \text{ if } \mathcal{A} \sqsubseteq \mathcal{B} \text{ then } \mathcal{B} \nVdash_{\mathcal{K}} \phi$$

In other words, a feature structure $\mathcal{A}$ satisfies a negated description $\neg\phi$ just in case no *extension* of $\mathcal{A}$ (in the set $\mathcal{K}$) satisfies the description ϕ. In contrast to the classical treatment of negation, the intuitionistic semantics preserves monotonicity: information about features and their values may grow without invalidating previously verified constraints. While the forcing construction appears to provide a satisfactory account of description negation however, the approach also raises a number of questions. Consider first the specification of the set of feature structures $\mathcal{K}$ as required in the definition of the forcing relation. As Moshier and Rounds point out, if $\mathcal{K}$ is simply taken to be the set of all feature structures, then the resulting interpretation of negative constraints is too strong. For example, it turns out that a description such as that shown in (10) will never be satisfied:

(10) $\neg(\mathsf{cat} : \mathsf{V} \wedge \mathsf{case} : \top)$

Intuitively, the description in (10) might be used to state that verbs are not specified for case. Clearly however, any feature structure which satisfies cat : V but lacks a specification for case has an extension in which case is defined. It follows that no feature structure will satisfy (10).

For this reason, Moshier and Rounds actually require that $\mathcal{K}$ be some proper subset of the set of all feature structures. The intention is that this subset should represent the class of all 'legal' or 'permissible' feature structures with respect to some given 'theory of grammar'. Thus, the set $\mathcal{K}$ contains just those feature structures to which descriptions are intended to apply. The problem now is that the apparatus introduced by Moshier and Rounds provides no sensible means of defining what is meant by 'legal' or 'permissible' in this context.

One possible solution to this problem is to introduce an explicit notion of *typing* for feature structures. The set $\mathcal{K}$ might then be identified with the set of all feature structures which are well-typed in some sense. This idea has been investigated by Carpenter (1990, 1992) and is discussed in the following section. Alternatively, Gazdar et al. (1988) have developed a logical language for specifying general constraints on feature structures as part of a formal framework for reconstructing the category systems of a variety of grammatical frameworks. This approach is described in section 2.3.

Although a strong, intuitionistic treatment of negation appears natural in the context of partial information, it is not clear that the forcing relation provides the most appropriate interpretation of negative constraints on feature structures. Kasper (1988) has described a unification procedure for negative and conditional descriptions as part of an extension of Functional Unification Grammar. The unification algorithm distinguishes between feature structures which *satisfy* a given description, those which are merely *compatible* with it and those which are *incompatible* with, or contradict the description. Kasper's semantics for description negation is entirely classical, but negation is restricted to descriptions which do not contain path equations. This means that it is possible to localize the effects of negation as simple negative constraints on atomic values or the existence of feature labels. As a result, although the satisfaction relation is not monotonic with respect to subsumption, Kasper's algorithm retains the order-independent properties of unification algorithms for descriptions without negation.

Langholm (1989) considers a simple approach to negation in which each state of a feature structure is associated with a set of feature labels which must be *undefined* at that state. On this approach, a feature structure may be defined as a structure $A = \langle Q, q_0, \delta, \pi, v \rangle$, where v is a function from states in Q to subsets of L, such that $l \in v(q)$ implies that $\delta(q, l)$ is undefined. In this case, $A \models \neg l : \phi$ just in case either $l \in v(q_0)$ or $\delta(q_0, l)$ is defined but $A/l \models \neg \phi$. In addition, $A \models \neg(\phi \wedge \psi)$ if and only if $A \models \neg \phi$ or $A \models \neg \psi$ (and similarly for the case of negated descriptions involving disjunction). Langholm's treatment of negation is monotonic given a suitably revised definition of subsumption, but it is not as powerful as general negation in that it provides no treatment of negated atomic feature values. That is, in order to retain monotonicity it is also necessary to rule out descriptions of the form $\neg a$ where a is an atomic value.

Dawar and Vijay-Shanker (1989, 1990) have proposed an alternative to the intuitionistic treatment of description negation that is based on Kleene's (1952) strong three-valued logic. As in Kasper's unification algorithm, each description ϕ is associated with three distinct sets of feature structures: a set *Tset* of feature structures which satisfy ϕ; a set *Fset* of feature structures which contradict ϕ; and a set *Uset* of feature structures which neither satisfy nor contradict ϕ. A feature structure A satisfies a negated description $\neg \phi$ just in case A belongs to the *Fset* associated with the formula ϕ. The resulting system is again monotonic and is shown to be computationally no harder than Rounds-Kasper logic.

Finally, Carpenter (1990) has investigated *path inequalities* as a restricted form of classical description negation. A path inequality is a description $(p_1 \not\approx p_2)$ and is used to state that the values of the paths p_1 and p_2 can never be identified (i.e. unified). In order to provide an interpretation for descriptions of this kind, Carpenter extends the notion of a feature structure to include explicit information about inequalities between states. An *inequated feature structure* may be defined as a tuple $\mathcal{A} = \langle Q, q_0, \delta, \pi, \not\approx \rangle$ where $\langle Q, q_0, \delta, \pi \rangle$ is an ordinary feature structure, and $\not\approx \subseteq Q \times Q$ is a symmetric and anti-reflexive inequality relation on states. If $q \not\approx q'$, then this is taken to mean that the sub-structures rooted at q and q' represent distinct objects, and any attempt to unify them must fail. In contrast to general description negation, path inequalities are well-behaved in the sense that satisfaction is monotonic with respect to subsumption and that most general unifiers exist for compatible pairs of inequated feature structures.

Of course, path inequalities are a particularly restricted form of negation, and cannot be used to express the sorts of negative constraints on feature structures exemplified by the descriptions in (8) and (10) above. However, Carpenter argues that such constraints are better dealt with by introducing an explicit notion of typing for feature structures, together with conditions on the appropriateness of features. For example, to capture the constraint that verbs are not specified for case (c.f. (10) above) it would be possible to introduce a type **verb** for which the feature label **case** is simply not appropriate. Carpenter's type scheme for feature structures is described in more detail in the following section.

It should be noted that the complications which seem to arise from attempting to incorporate description negation into the framework of Rounds-Kasper logic are due in the main to the unification-based view of feature structures as inherently partial representations of linguistic objects. By contrast, in the work of Johnson (1988, 1991) and Smolka (1988, 1989) descriptions are regarded as constraints on sets of 'complete' or 'totally instantiated' objects. In this context negative information presents no special difficulties and may be treated entirely classically.

2.2.4   Typed Feature Structures and Inheritance

Carpenter (1990, 1992) has introduced an object-oriented type scheme for feature structures based on the use of types in the HPSG formalism (Pollard and Sag (1987)). Carpenter's approach builds on and generalizes earlier work by Calder (1987), King (1989) and Moshier (1988). The types form a multiple inheritance hierarchy allowing information about grammatical objects to be encoded at different levels of abstraction. In addition, Carpenter's type system employs *appropriateness conditions* for features, which are used to model the distinction between features whose values are unknown, and those which are simply irrelevant for a given type.

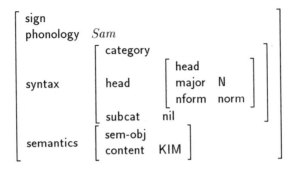

Figure 2.4: An example of an HPSG sign

The linguistic motivation for introducing types stems from the observation that grammatical frameworks typically employ an ontology of different kinds of linguistic objects which have different features. In HPSG for example, an object of type **sign** has features for **phonology**, **syntax**, and **semantics** (see figure 2.4). The value of **syntax** is an object of type **category** which may have features for **head**, **subcat**, and so on. Ultimately, there are basic object types such as **N** or **nil** which have no features of their own.

The benefits of imposing an explicit type discipline on programs are well-known, and many of these benefits carry across in a natural way to implementations of constraint-based grammars:

- users working in untyped systems typically organize data into implicit categories. An explicit type discipline can be used to enforce such conventions, allowing for error detection arising for mis-spellings or misunderstandings of the type system. A tight definition of the different types of permissible data objects leads to better structured, more easily understood and debugged programs;

- multiple inheritance permits information about data objects to be placed at an appropriate level in the type hierarchy, thereby eliminating much redundancy. Moreover, in implementations of constraint-based formalisms type inheritance has run-time benefits: information otherwise encoded by computationally expensive inference steps, or in terms of feature structure unification can be recast as efficient inheritance;

- pre-defined types allow for compact representations of feature structures (e.g. positional, or record-like encodings) and a consequent reduction in access time for feature values. Such representations can be determined once and for all at compile time. Also, once the type of a feature structure is known at run-time, the amount of memory required to represent it is known and can be efficiently allocated.

An *inheritance hierarchy* is defined as a finite set *Type* of type symbols partially ordered by the subsumption relation $\sqsubseteq$. If **sign** and **word** are type symbols in *Type*, then **sign** $\sqsubseteq$ **word** is taken to mean that **sign** is a supertype of **word** (or conversely, that **word** is a subtype of **sign**). In addition, it is required that whenever two types σ and τ have a common subtype, then they have a least such subtype (denoted $\sigma \sqcup \tau$). Finally, an inheritance hierarchy also has a most general or least informative type $\perp$ which is a supertype of every element of *Type*.

A *quasi feature structure* is defined as a tuple $\mathcal{A} = \langle Q, q_0, \delta, \theta \rangle$ where Q, q_0 and δ are as given previously in definition 2.2, and $\theta : Q \rightarrow Type$ is a *total* function from states to types (the *type assignment*). The subsumption relation for quasi feature structures differs from that given previously by taking into account the type information associated with states. The only significant change to be made is in the final condition of definition 2.3 which is replaced by:

$$\theta(q) \sqsubseteq \theta'(h(q)) \text{ for all } q \in Q$$

where θ and θ' are the type assignments of $\mathcal{A}$ and $\mathcal{A}'$. In other words, a quasi feature structure $\mathcal{A}$ subsumes a quasi feature structure $\mathcal{A}'$ just in case $\mathcal{A}'$ provides as least as much information as $\mathcal{A}$ about features and values *including* information about the types of those values.

As noted above, an important motivation for introducing types is to provide for restrictions on features and their values. No such restrictions are imposed by quasi feature structures, which may be defined for any combination of types and features. In the HPSG grammar formalism, Pollard and Sag (1987) introduced a notion of 'appropriateness' in order to model the intuitive distinction between feature labels whose values are simply unknown, and those which should never be defined for a given type. For example, a noun phrase may be lacking relevant information about case, but for a verb phrase case information will never be appropriate. In order to provide a restrictive notion of typing for feature structures, Carpenter presents a formal definition of appropriateness in terms of *appropriateness specifications*:

Definition 2.6 (*Appropriateness*) An *appropriateness specification* is a partial function $Approp : L \times Type \to Type$ from label-type pairs to types which meets (at least) the following conditions:

- (*Minimal Introduction*) for every feature label $l \in L$, there is a most general type $\sigma \in Type$ such that $Approp(l, \sigma)$ is defined.

- (*Upward closure/Right monotonicity*) if $Approp(l, \sigma)$ is defined and $\sigma \sqsubseteq \tau$ then $Approp(l, \tau)$ is defined and $Approp(l, \sigma) \sqsubseteq Approp(l, \tau)$.

The first condition requires the existence of a least type at which a feature label is introduced. This rules out situations in which a feature label is appropriate for two incomparable types, but is not appropriate for any of their supertypes. The second condition has two parts. First, if a feature label is appropriate for a given type, then it is also appropriate for any of its subtypes (upward closure). Secondly, the value of a feature label l appropriate for a type τ is at least as informative as the value of l for any supertype σ of τ at which l is defined (right monotonicity). Taken together, the two conditions ensure that the set of types at which any given feature label is defined forms a principal filter in the inheritance hierarchy. This is necessary in order to provide a well-defined notion of unification for typed feature structures. It should be noted that in Carpenter's type scheme, the *atoms* of Rounds-Kasper logic are modelled most closely by maximal types which are not appropriate for any features.

A well-typed feature structure is now defined as a quasi feature structure in which every feature that is defined both is appropriate and takes an appropriate value:

Definition 2.7 (*Well-typing*) A quasi feature structure $\mathcal{A} = \langle Q, q_0, \delta, \theta \rangle$ is *well-typed* if whenever $\delta(q, l)$ is defined, then $Approp(l, \theta(q))$ is defined and $Approp(l, \theta(q)) \sqsubseteq \theta(\delta(l, q))$

A quasi feature structure $\mathcal{A}$ is *typable* if it has a well-typed extension: that is, there exists a well-typed feature structure $\mathcal{B}$ such that $\mathcal{A} \sqsubseteq \mathcal{B}$. Carpenter shows that any typable feature structure has a minimal well-typed extension which is unique up to subsumption equivalence. Moreover, it is possible to define an effective type inference procedure which takes a quasi feature structure as input and either computes its minimal well-typed extension, or fails if it has no well-typed extensions. The significance of this result is that the type inference procedure yields a notion of well-typed unification. In order to compute the unification of two well-typed feature structures, it is sufficient to compute their 'ordinary' unification and then apply the type inference procedure[3].

Carpenter also considers a more restrictive notion of typing for quasi feature structures in which feature labels that are appropriate are required to be present. A quasi feature structure $\mathcal{A} = \langle Q, q_0, \delta, \theta \rangle$ is *totally well-typed* if it is well-typed and, in addition, if $Approp(l, \theta(q))$ is defined, then $\delta(q, l)$ is also defined. Unfortunately, not every totally typable quasi feature structure has a most general totally well-typed extension. The reason is that appropriateness specifications may involve 'loops' requiring that a feature structure $\mathcal{A}$ of type σ contain a substructure of the same type. In this case, any type inference procedure which attempts to compute the minimal totally well-typed extension of $\mathcal{A}$ may fail to terminate (Franz 1990). On the other hand, restricting attention to loop-free appropriateness specifications yields an effective total type-inference procedure. Moreover, it can be shown that totally well-typed unifiers exist for consistent pairs of totally well-typed feature structures.

Typed feature structures are described by a variant of Rounds-Kasper logic in which type symbols replace atoms as primitive descriptions. In order to accommodate types semantically, the conditions under which a feature structure $\mathcal{A} = \langle Q, q_0, \delta, \theta \rangle$ satisfies a type symbol σ are defined as follows:

$$\mathcal{A} \models \sigma \Leftrightarrow \sigma \sqsubseteq \theta(q_0)$$

It is important to note that $\mathcal{A}$ is not required to be the one state feature structure. Each state of $\mathcal{A}$ has an associated type, even if this is just the most general or least informative type in *Type*. This also means that descriptions such as those shown in (11) below are not necessarily inconsistent:

(11)   a. $\sigma \wedge \tau$

    b. $\sigma \wedge l : \phi$

The description in (11a) is satisfiable just in case there exists a type which is a subtype of both σ and τ. Similarly, the description in (11b) is satisfiable if an object of type σ is appropriate for the feature label l. The primary results of Rounds-Kasper logic carry over to descriptions with type

---

[3]On the other hand, Carpenter (1992, p.92) points out that the inference procedure in combination with the appropriateness conditions is not enough to guarantee that if two feature structures are typable, then so is their unification.

symbols. In particular, the satisfaction relation between feature structures and descriptions is monotonic, and it can be shown that arbitrary descriptions have finite sets of most general satisfiers.

The behaviour of the description language can be given a complete equational axiomatisation by extending the calculus of equivalences for Rounds-Kasper logic given previously in figure 2.3. Pollard (in press) presents a suitable calculus which takes account of joins in the type hierarchy and appropriateness specifications for features and types. For example, if $\sigma \sqcup \tau = \sigma'$, then the calculus includes the equivalence $\sigma \wedge \tau \simeq \sigma'$. In addition, Carpenter presents the following axiom schemes for typed feature structures:

(12)   a. $l : \top \simeq l : \top \wedge \sigma$ (σ is the least type such that $Approp(l, \sigma)$)

   b. $\sigma \wedge l : \top \simeq \sigma \wedge l : Approp(l, \sigma)$ (where $Approp(l, \sigma)$ is defined)

   c. $\sigma \simeq \sigma \wedge l : \bot$ (where $Approp(l, \sigma)$ is defined)

The first equivalence permits an inference from the existence of a given feature label to the least type at which that feature label is defined. The second equivalence allows inferences from a type and the existence of a feature label, to an appropriate value for that feature. Taken together, the equivalences in (12a) and (12b) characterize the logical behaviour of well-typed feature structures. The equivalence in (12c) additionally permits inferences from type information to the existence of appropriate features. In conjunction with the first two equivalences, this axiom schema characterizes the logic of totally well-typed feature structures.

2.2.5   Constraint Systems and Grammars

An important objective of work on feature logics is the provision of a completely logical treatment of grammar. Rounds and Manaster-Ramer (1987) have proposed an extension of Rounds-Kasper logic in order to provide a precise, mathematical formulation of FUG. Their proposal builds on the logic of Rounds and Kasper in two ways. First, the notion of a feature structure is extended to incorporate information about the linear order and hierarchical structure of constituents. Second, their logic makes use of *type variables* in order to model recursion in a grammar.

An *oriented feature structure* is a structure $\mathcal{A} = \langle Q, q_0, \delta, \pi, \alpha, < \rangle$, where $\langle Q, q_0, \delta, \pi \rangle$ is an ordinary feature structure, and α (*ancestor*) and $<$ (*precedence*) are binary relations over the set of states Q. The relation α is required to be a partial order on nodes, while $<$ is transitive and irreflexive (a strict partial order). In addition, the relations α and $<$ obey the following 'non-entanglement' condition:

$$\forall (q, r, s, t) \in Q : (q < r) \wedge (q \alpha s) \wedge (r \alpha t) \Rightarrow (s < t)$$

The value assignment function π is assumed to be a partial function from states in $\mathcal{A}$ to either atomic values in A or terminal symbols in a vocabulary Σ. The idea is that an oriented feature structure can be viewed as a parse tree superimposed on an 'ordinary' feature structure, where states assigned terminal symbols correspond to the leaves of the tree.

In order to describe oriented feature structures, the description language is extended to include two new path operators. Thus, a description $p_1 \alpha p_2$ is used to assert that the state $\delta^*(q_0, p_1)$ is an ancestor of $\delta^*(q_0, p_2)$. Similarly, $p_1 < p_2$ asserts that the value of the path p_1 precedes the value of the path p_2. As a means of expressing recursive information, Rounds and Manaster-Ramer introduce *type variables* as elementary descriptions of the logic. Type variables are interpreted as denoting sets of feature structures and provide for the description of syntactic categories. A grammar is then specified as a system of equations which define the meaning of the type variables in terms of one another. Consider for example the following description (where type variables are written in capitals, terminal symbols in italic script):

S	where	
S	::=	subj : NP $\wedge$ pred : VP $\wedge$ (subj $<$ pred)
NP	::=	form : (*Moira* $\vee$ *Sam*)
VP	::=	pred : V $\wedge$ comp : (NP $\vee$ S) $\wedge$ (pred $<$ comp)
V	::=	form : *knows*

The above description can be viewed as a grammar with start symbol S. Thus, the first equation can be read as stating that a sentence (S) consists of a noun phrase (NP) subject and a verb phrase (VP) predicate, and that the subject precedes the predicate. Because the meaning of the type variable VP is defined with reference to the type variable S, the latter is actually given recursively. Rounds and Manaster-Ramer show that the ability to define the meaning of type variables in this way results in a language with considerable expressive power. Specifically, they show that the satisfiability problem for their logic is undecidable in general.

More recently, Carpenter et al. (1991) have proposed an approach to the specification of constraint-based grammars such as HPSG, in which constraints are expressed in terms of the feature logic analogue of definite clauses. This approach builds on the approach to typed feature structures described in the previous section. The idea is to permit types to be associated with logical descriptions which then constrain the interpretation of those types.

Definition 2.8 (*Constraint Systems*) A *constraint system* Φ associates with each type $\tau \in$ *Type* a feature logic description ϕ_τ.

With respect to a given constraint system Φ, the *inherited constraint* on a type τ is defined as the conjunction of the constraints associated with τ and all of its supertypes. That is, the inherited constraint on τ is given by $\bigwedge_{\sigma \sqsubseteq \tau} \phi_\sigma$. A (well-typed) feature structure $\mathcal{A} = \langle Q, q_0, \delta, \theta \rangle$ satisfies a description ϕ with respect to a constraint system Φ just in case $\mathcal{A} \models \phi$, and every state of $\mathcal{A}$ satisfies the inherited constraint on its associated type. In other words, the maximal substructure rooted at each state q of $\mathcal{A}$ must satisfy $\bigwedge_{\sigma \sqsubseteq \theta(q)} \phi_{\theta(q)}$. The description ϕ can be regarded as a *query*, and a satisfying feature structure $\mathcal{A}$ as a *solution* to ϕ in the system of constraints Φ.

Because the descriptions associated with types can themselves contain occurrences of arbitrary types, constraint systems provide for the recursive description of feature structures. Thus, as in the work of Rounds and Manaster-Ramer, a grammar can be specified as a system of equations that define the meaning of types in terms of one another. Following work by Aït-Kaci (1986) and Aït-Kaci and Nasr (1986), Carpenter et al. provide a method for generating solutions to queries in terms of a re-writing operation on feature structures. The re-writing operation can be understood as applying to the states of a feature structure to 'unify in' a minimal satisfier for the inherited constraint associated with the type attached to that state. This operation is non-deterministic in general, since it may involve a choice between alternative minimal satisfiers. However, it can be shown that the method is complete: every solution to a given query can be effectively generated by rewriting. More specifically, a feature structure $\mathcal{A}$ is a solution to a query ϕ just in case further application of the re-writing operation does not add any more information to $\mathcal{A}$. Moreover, a solution to ϕ is *minimal* if and only if it is a solution obtained by applying the re-writing operation to a minimal satisfier for ϕ.

An implementation of typed constraint systems has been described by Franz (1990). Other work on the implementation of typed unfication grammars has been reported by Emele and Zajac (1990) and Zajac (1992).

2.3   Category Logic

Most grammatical frameworks appeal to the notion of a syntactic category, yet it is rarely given a precise definition. As a result it is often difficult to evaluate and compare different approaches to natural language grammar. For this reason, Gazdar and his colleagues (Gazdar et al. 1988) have introduced a meta-theoretical framework within which the notion of a syntactic category receives a precise, mathematical definition. They define a class of formal objects called *category structures*, which together with a language of constraints on syntactic categories can be used to reconstruct the category systems of various grammatical frameworks.

Syntactic categories are defined inductively as finite, partial functions from *feature labels* in L to *feature values* in V, where a feature value is either *atomic* (an element of a domain of atoms A) or *complex* (a syntactic category). A category can also be viewed as a finite set of feature specifications of the form $\langle l, v \rangle$, where l is a feature label and v a feature value. The *domain Dom(α)* of a syntactic category α is the set of all feature labels in L such that $\alpha(l)$ is defined.

Definition 2.9 (*Category Structures*) A *category structure* is a quadruple $\Sigma = \langle L, A, \tau, \rho \rangle$, where:

- L is a finite set of *feature labels*

- A is a finite set of *atoms*

- $\tau : L \to \{0, 1\}$ is a *type function*

- $\rho : \{l \in L | \tau(l) = 0\} \to \mathcal{P}(A)$ is a *range function*

The type function τ partitions the set of feature labels L into two subsets: a set of atom-valued, or 'type 0' feature labels L^0, and a set of category-valued, or 'type 1' feature labels L^1. In addition, each type 0 feature label l is associated with a range of possible atomic values $\rho(l) \subseteq A$.

A category structure $\Sigma = \langle L, A, \tau, \rho \rangle$ induces a space of 'possible' syntactic categories. Intuitively, the set of categories induced by Σ contains all and only those syntactic categories defined with respect to L and A which respect the constraints imposed by the type and range functions. That is, if α is a category in (the space of categories induced by) Σ, then for any feature specification $\langle l, v \rangle \in \alpha$:

- if $l \in L^0$ then $v \in \rho(l)$

- if $l \in L^1$ then $v \notin A$

In order to reconstruct the category system of a particular grammatical framework it is necessary to further restrict the space of 'possible' categories induced by Σ to include only those categories which are considered to be 'legal' or 'permissible'. Such restrictions are expressed as formulas of a constraint language L_C (Category Logic) which is interpreted in the space of categories induced by Σ. By choosing a suitable set of constraints it is possible to pick out a sub-space of categories modelling the required category system. All and only those categories in Σ which satisfy each of the imposed constraints are considered to be 'legal'.

The language L_C is defined as the smallest set of constraints which contains:

- l for $l \in L$.

- $l : a$ for $l \in L^0$, and $a \in A$.

- $l : \phi$ for $l \in L^1$ and ϕ a constraint.

- $\neg \phi$ for ϕ a constraint.

- $(\phi \wedge \psi)$ for ϕ, ψ constraints.

- $\Box \phi$ for ϕ a constraint.

- $\Diamond \phi$ for ϕ a constraint.

The connectives $\vee$, $\rightarrow$ and $\leftrightarrow$ may be defined in terms of $\neg$ and $\wedge$ in the usual way. Category Logic is similar in many respects to the language of feature structure descriptions introduced by Rounds and Kasper. A constraint of the form l is used to assert the existence of a feature label l; a constraint $l : a$ states that the (type-0) feature label l has the atomic value a; and a constraint $l : \phi$ states that the (type-1) feature label l has a value which satisfies the constraint ϕ. The interpretation of negative and conjunctive constraints is classical. The main innovation in Category Logic is the inclusion of two modal operators $\Box$ and $\Diamond$, which are used to express quantification over feature values within a syntactic category. To provide an interpretation for constraints, a three-place relation may be defined between syntactic categories, category structures and constraints, where $\alpha \models_\Sigma \phi$ is to be read "the category α in Σ satisfies the constraint ϕ". In the case of the modal operator $\Box$, satisfaction is defined as follows:

$$\alpha \models_\Sigma \Box\phi \Leftrightarrow \alpha \models_\Sigma \phi \text{ and } \forall l \in (Dom(\alpha) \cap L^1) : \alpha(l) \models_\Sigma \Box\phi$$

In other words, a category α satisfies a constraint $\Box\phi$ just in case every category value occurring in α (including α itself) satisfies the constraint ϕ. In this way the modal operator $\Box$ permits constraints to apply 'recursively' to successively embedded levels of nested category values. As usual, the modal operator $\Diamond$ is the dual of $\Box$ and has existential force:

$$\alpha \models_\Sigma \Diamond\phi \Leftrightarrow \alpha \models_\Sigma \phi \text{ or } \exists l \in (Dom(\alpha) \cap L^1) : \alpha(l) \models_\Sigma \Diamond\phi$$

Thus, a category α satisfies a constraint $\Diamond\phi$ just in case there is *some* category value in α (possibly α itself) which satisfies the constraint ϕ.

A *category theory* is defined as a pair $\Gamma = \langle \Sigma, C \rangle$, where Σ is a category structure and C is a set of constraints.

Example 2.10 The category system of GPSG (as described in Gazdar et al. (1985)) may be reconstructed as a category theory $\langle \Sigma, C \rangle$ where Σ is given by:

- $L = \{\mathsf{n}, \mathsf{v}, \mathsf{bar}, \mathsf{case}, \ldots, \mathsf{agr}, \mathsf{slash}\}$

- $A = \{0, 1, 2, \ldots, +, \text{-}, \ldots, \mathsf{acc}, \mathsf{nom}\}$

- $\tau = \{\langle \mathsf{n}, 0 \rangle, \langle \mathsf{v}, 0 \rangle, \langle \mathsf{bar}, 0 \rangle, \langle \mathsf{case}, 0 \rangle, \ldots, \langle \mathsf{agr}, 1 \rangle, \langle \mathsf{slash}, 1 \rangle\}$

- $\rho = \{\langle \mathsf{n}, \{+, \text{-}\} \rangle, \langle \mathsf{v}, \{+, \text{-}\} \rangle, \langle \mathsf{bar}, \{0, 1, 2\} \rangle, \ldots, \langle \mathsf{case}, \{\mathsf{acc}, \mathsf{nom}\} \rangle\}$

The set of constraints C comprises all those L_C constraints of the form $\Box\neg(l : \Diamond l)$ where $l \in L^1$ is a type 1 feature label. An instance of a constraint in C for the category theory of GPSG is the following:

$$\Box\neg(\mathsf{slash} : \Diamond\mathsf{slash})$$

This constraint disallows any category in which the feature label **slash** has as its value a syntactic category containing further occurrences of **slash** (at any depth of embedding). As a result, the following set of feature specifications does not constitute a 'legal' category of GPSG even though it clearly belongs to the set of categories induced by the category structure Σ given above:

$$\{\langle n, + \rangle, \langle v, - \rangle, \langle bar, 2 \rangle, \langle slash, \{\langle agr, \{\langle slash, \{\ldots\}\rangle \ldots\}\rangle \ldots\}\rangle \ldots\}\}$$

Gazdar et al. consider a number of computational problems concerning the language L_C. The *checking problem* for syntactic categories is defined as follows: given a category α and a set of L_C constraints C, is α 'legal' with respect to C? In fact, it is possible to solve the checking problem in linear time. On the other hand, they conjecture that the satisfiability problem for L_C is decidable but present no proof. It has been demonstrated by Kracht (1989) that the modal fragment of L_C is in fact the normal modal logic **S4.Grz**[4], which is known to be decidable. Furthermore, Kracht shows that a decision procedure exists for the full logic of category structures. Blackburn and Spaan (1992) have shown that the satisfiability problem for L_C is EXPTIME-complete.

2.4   Attribute-Value Logic

This section describes the account of feature structures and constraints developed by Johnson (1988). Following Rounds and Kasper, Johnson defines a class of formal structures representing linguistic objects (*attribute-value structures*) and develops a logical language for describing these structures. However, Johnson's approach departs from that of Rounds and Kasper in a number of important respects.

- Johnson adopts a view of feature structures as 'complete', or 'totally instantiated' objects. On this view, partial information and unification are not considered to be defining properties of feature structures. As Johnson observes, on the unification-based view, partial information is present in two distinct senses. On the one hand, descriptions of feature structures provide only partial information about features and their values. On the other hand, the feature structures themselves are understood as partial representations or descriptions of linguistic

---

[4]The logic S4 together with the axiom $\Box(\Box(\phi \to \Box\phi) \to \phi) \to \phi$.

objects. Johnson rejects this second source of partial information: feature structures are understood as representing complete information about linguistic objects, while descriptions are partial in the sense that they characterize sets of admissible structures.

- The notion of a feature structure adopted by Johnson is rather broader than that adopted in the Rounds-Kasper framework. In particular, attribute-value structures are not restricted to finite objects, they may be cyclic[5], and no formal distinction is drawn between feature labels (*attributes*) and values. The use of attributes as values is motivated by the treatment of prepositional phrases in LFG (Johnson 1988, p.20)

- Johnson's *attribute-value languages* are relational and employ variables ranging over feature values. The formalism is closely related to the language of function-application expressions used in LFG to describe f-structure, and can be regarded as a variant of the quantifier-free first-order language with equality. The attribute-value languages include general description negation and implication, and these constructions are given a classical interpretation.

Johnson provides the following definition of an attribute-value structure:

Definition 2.11 (*Attribute-Value Structures*) An attribute-value structure is a triple $A = \langle F, C, \delta \rangle$, where:

- F is a set (the *attribute-value elements*);

- C is a subset of F (the *constant elements*); and

- $\delta : F \times F \to F$ is a partial function such that for all $c \in C$ and all $f \in F$, $\delta(c, f)$ is undefined.

Intuitively, attribute-value elements in F represent linguistic objects. Constants in C are special attribute-value elements which have no attributes (i.e. they correspond to atomic values, although as noted above, they may also appear as feature labels). The partial function δ associates with a pair of attribute-value elements a value which may either be a constant element or an attribute-value element with further attributes and values. The function

---

[5] Although the presentation of Rounds-Kasper logic given in section 2.2 allows for cyclic structures, Rounds and Kasper originally restricted their attention to acyclic feature structures.

$$\begin{bmatrix} \text{cat} & \text{S} \\ \text{agr} & \begin{bmatrix} \text{number} & \text{sing} \\ \text{person} & 3 \end{bmatrix}_b \\ \text{subj} & \begin{bmatrix} \text{agr} & \text{b} \end{bmatrix}_c \end{bmatrix}_a$$

Figure 2.5: An attribute-value structure.

δ is partial because not every attribute-value element need have a value on a particular attribute.

Example 2.12 The attribute-value structure pictured in figure 2.5 may be formalised as a structure $\mathcal{A} = \langle F, C, \delta \rangle$ where:

1. $F = \{\text{cat}, \text{subj}, \text{agr}, \text{number}, \text{person}, \text{S}, \text{sing}, 3, \text{a}, \text{b}, \text{c}\}$;

2. $C = F - \{\text{a}, \text{b}, \text{c}\}$;

3. $\delta(\text{a}, \text{cat}) = \text{S}$ $\delta(\text{a}, \text{agr}) = \text{b}$ $\delta(\text{a}, \text{subj}) = \text{c}$
   $\delta(\text{b}, \text{number}) = \text{sing}$ $\delta(\text{b}, \text{person}) = 3$ $\delta(\text{c}, \text{agr}) = \text{b}$

Let A and V be countably infinite, disjoint sets of symbols (the *atoms* and *variables* respectively). The *attribute-value language* over A and V is defined as follows:

1. Terms:
   - x for $x \in V$
   - a for $a \in A$
   - $t_1(t_2)$ for t_1 and t_2 terms

2. Formulas:
   - $\top$
   - $\bot$
   - $t_1 \approx t_2$ for t_1 and t_2 terms
   - $\neg\phi$ for ϕ a formula
   - $(\phi \vee \psi)$ for ϕ and ψ formulas

- $(\phi \wedge \psi)$ for ϕ and ψ formulas

The propositional connectives $\rightarrow$ (implication) and $\leftrightarrow$ (equivalence) are defined in terms of the connectives $\neg$, $\wedge$ and $\vee$ in the usual way. In addition, the notation $(t_1 \not\approx t_2)$ is used as an abbreviation for $\neg(t_1 \approx t_2)$.

Example 2.13 Let A and V be sets of symbols as in the definition of an attribute-value language, where cat, subj, agr, number, S, sing and 3 are atoms in A and x, y and z are variables in V. The following expressions are well-formed formulas of the attribute-value language over A and V:

1. $\mathsf{x(cat)} \approx \mathsf{S} \wedge \mathsf{x(subj)(agr)} \approx \mathsf{y}$

2. $\mathsf{x(subj)} \approx \mathsf{y} \wedge \mathsf{x(agr)} \approx \mathsf{z} \wedge \mathsf{y(agr)} \approx \mathsf{z}$

3. $\mathsf{x(number)} \not\approx \mathsf{sing} \vee \mathsf{x(person)} \not\approx 3$

The first formula of example 2.13 may be interpreted as a description of an attribute-value structure defined for the attributes cat and subj, where cat has as its value the constant element S, and the value of subj is an attribute-value element defined for the attribute agr. The second formula above is actually equivalent to the more compact expression $\mathsf{x(subj)(agr)} \approx \mathsf{x(agr)}$ which describes a structure in which the value of the path subj agr is identical to the value of the attribute agr. Under a suitable interpretation of the variables x, y and z, the first two formulas can be regarded as partial descriptions of the attribute-value structure of example 2.12. The last formula describes an attribute-value structure in which either number is not sing or person is not 3.

Definition 2.14 (*Attribute-Value Models*) An *attribute-value model* is defined as a tuple $\mathcal{M} = \langle F, C, \delta, \varphi, \chi \rangle$, where:

- $\langle F, C, \delta \rangle$ is an attribute-value structure

- φ is a total function from V to F

- χ is an injective function from A to C

The denotation of a term t in a model $\mathcal{M}$ (written $[\![t]\!]^{\mathcal{M}}$) is an element of F. If t is a variable, then $[\![t]\!]^{\mathcal{M}} = \varphi(t)$, and if t is a constant then $[\![t]\!]^{\mathcal{M}} = \chi(t)$. If $t = t_1(t_2)$, then $[\![t]\!]^{\mathcal{M}} = [\![t_1(t_2)]\!]^{\mathcal{M}} = \delta([\![t_1]\!]^{\mathcal{M}}, [\![t_2]\!]^{\mathcal{M}})$ (when this is defined). The satisfaction relation between models and formulas is defined as follows:

- $\mathcal{M} \models \top$

- $\mathcal{M} \not\models \bot$

- $\mathcal{M} \models t_1 \approx t_2 \Leftrightarrow [\![t_1]\!]^{\mathcal{M}}, [\![t_2]\!]^{\mathcal{M}}$ are defined, and $[\![t_1]\!]^{\mathcal{M}} = [\![t_2]\!]^{\mathcal{M}}$

- $\mathcal{M} \models \neg\phi \Leftrightarrow \mathcal{M} \not\models \phi$

- $\mathcal{M} \models (\phi \wedge \psi) \Leftrightarrow \mathcal{M} \models \phi$ and $\mathcal{M} \models \psi$

As noted above, the interpretation of the propositional connectives is entirely classical. In particular, a formula $\neg\phi$ is satisfied by an attribute-value model $\mathcal{M}$ just in case $\mathcal{M}$ does not satisfy ϕ. Johnson presents a sound and complete axiomatization of the valid formulas of an attribute-value language, and describes an algorithm for determining the satisfiability of arbitrary formulas. Deciding satisfiability is shown to be NP-easy by a polynomial-time reduction to the satisfiability problem for formulas of the quantifier-free first-order language with equality. A polynomial-time reduction of the satisfiability problem for propositional logic to satisfiability for formulas of attribute-value logic then shows the latter problem to be NP-complete.

It is notable that in adopting a classical, model-theoretic semantics for descriptions, Johnson is able to offer a simple account of the relationship between feature structures and descriptions. This is particularly evident in the treatment of disjunctive and negative constraints. Although the view of feature structures as partially-specified objects figures strongly in the unification-based grammar formalisms, feature structure unification itself is just one technique for solving linguistic constraints. Johnson's approach suggests that more general constraint-solving techniques can yield algorithms for computing with linguistic descriptions which are at least as efficient as unification-based methods. Moreover, since Johnson adopts a constraint-language which is essentially a restricted subset of classical first order logic (Johnson 1990), algorithms for determining the satisfiability of first-order formulas can be applied directly to constraints on feature structures. The use of first order logic as a language for expressing constraints on feature structures is further investigated in (Johnson 1991). There it is shown that the Schönfinkel-Bernays class of formulas[6] is sufficiently expressive to axiomatize a wide variety of feature structures, including 'set-valued' features.

---

[6]The class of first-order formulas of the form $\exists x_1 \ldots x_n \forall y_1, \ldots, y_m \phi$ where ϕ is a quantifier-free, function-free formula.

2.5   Smolka's Feature Logic

Smolka (1988, 1989) has presented a feature logic which builds on and generalizes the work of Aït-Kaci, and Rounds and Kasper. The expressions
of Smolka's description language are called *feature terms*, and denote sets
of objects in some suitable domain of interpretation. Smolka's approach
generalizes previous work on feature logics in a number of ways:

- *Open world semantics*: Rather than restricting attention to a single domain of interpretation for descriptions (e.g. the feature structures of Rounds-Kasper logic, or Johnson's attribute-value structures)
  Smolka adopts an open-worlds, model-theoretic semantics. Thus, feature structures constitute just one possible domain of interpretation
  for descriptions. On the other hand, the interpretation based on this
  domain is canonical in the sense that it preserves the important notions of consistency, equivalence and subsumption of set descriptions.
  Thus, without loss of generality Smolka's logic can be regarded as a
  formalism for representing and reasoning about feature structures.

- *Negation*: Smolka's logic provides a simple account of general description negation. As in the work of Johnson, descriptions are interpreted
  as denoting sets of 'completely specified' linguistic objects, and negation is treated classically.

- *Sorts*: Smolka extends the description language to include sorts. Sorts
  denote subsets of the domain of interpretation and correspond closely
  to the concepts of terminological languages such as KL-ONE. Collections of *sort definitions* can be used to pick out classes of feature
  algebras, and provide a way of modelling the abstraction mechanisms
  found in many constraint-based grammar formalisms.

2.5.1   Feature Algebras

This section describes the mathematical structures which serve as possible interpretations for Smolka's description language. Rather than fixing a
single domain of interpretation in advance, Smolka considers a whole class
of admissible interpretations for descriptions, called *feature algebras*. Let
L and A be non-empty sets of *feature labels* and *atoms* respectively. The
following definition shows that feature algebras are rather like the usual
interpretations of the first-order predicate calculus:

Definition 2.15 (*Feature Algebras*) A *feature algebra* $\mathcal{I}$ is a pair $(D^{\mathcal{I}}, \cdot^{\mathcal{I}})$ where $D^{\mathcal{I}}$ is the domain of $\mathcal{I}$ and $\cdot^{\mathcal{I}}$ is an *interpretation function* which assigns to each atom $a \in A$ an element $a^{\mathcal{I}} \in D^{\mathcal{I}}$ and to each feature label $l \in L$ a relation $l^{\mathcal{I}} \subseteq D^{\mathcal{I}} \times D^{\mathcal{I}}$ such that the following conditions hold:

- $(d, e) \in l^{\mathcal{I}}$ and $(d, e') \in l^{\mathcal{I}}$ implies $e = e'$

- $a \neq b$ implies $a^{\mathcal{I}} \neq b^{\mathcal{I}}$

- $(d, e) \in l^{\mathcal{I}}$ implies $d \neq a^{\mathcal{I}}$ for each $a \in A$

According to the definition of a feature algebra, feature labels are interpreted as unary, partial functions on the domain $D^{\mathcal{I}}$. Atoms denote unique elements of $D^{\mathcal{I}}$ which are primitive in the sense that they have no features. Let $\mathcal{I} = (D^{\mathcal{I}}, \cdot^{\mathcal{I}})$ be a feature algebra. The interpretation function $\cdot^{\mathcal{I}}$ is extended to paths as follows: if p is the empty path then $p^{\mathcal{I}}$ is the identity function on $D^{\mathcal{I}}$; otherwise, if $p = l_1, \ldots, l_n$ then $p^{\mathcal{I}}$ is the composition of the partial functions $l_1^{\mathcal{I}}, \ldots, l_n^{\mathcal{I}}$ where the function $l_1^{\mathcal{I}}$ is applied first.

A feature algebra is called *canonical* if consistency, equivalence and subsumption of descriptions can be determined with respect to that feature algebra alone. Smolka shows that the set of all feature structures yields a canonical interpretation for his logic. A feature structure is viewed as a finite, rooted, connected and directed graph, with edges labelled by features and terminal nodes decorated by atoms. Smolka provides an elegant definition for feature structures (*feature graphs*) in terms of sets of labelled edges. Let V be a set of symbols disjoint from A (the set of *variables*). Then a labelled edge is a triple xlu where $x \in V$ is a variable, l is a feature label and $u \in A \cup V$ is either an atom or a variable. The notion of a feature graph is defined as follows:

Definition 2.16 (*Feature Graphs*) A *feature graph* G is a pair (u_0, E) where $u_0 \in A \cup V$ (the *root* of G) and E is a finite set of labelled edges such that:

- $u_0 \in A$ implies $E = \emptyset$

- $xlu \in E$ and $xlv \in E$ implies $u = v$ (the graph is determinate)

- $xlu \in E$ implies that E contains edges leading from the root u_0 to the node x (the graph is connected)

Let $G = (x_0, E)$ be a feature graph and l a feature label. If G contains a labelled edge $x_0 l u$, then let G/l denote that maximal subgraph of G with root u. The collection of all feature graphs yields a special feature algebra $\mathcal{F}$ called the *feature graph algebra*:

Definition 2.17 (*Feature Graph Algebra*) The *feature graph algebra* $\mathcal{F}$ is a pair $(D^{\mathcal{F}}, \cdot^{\mathcal{F}})$ such that:

- $D^{\mathcal{F}}$ is the set of all feature graphs

- $a^{\mathcal{F}} = (a, \emptyset)$ for each $a \in A$

- $(G, G') \in l^{\mathcal{F}}$ if and only if G/l is defined and $G/l = G'$

It is not difficult to verify that $\mathcal{F}$ is a feature algebra. In particular, each atom a names a unique feature graph $(a, \emptyset)$ which is undefined for all features in L. Moreover, because feature graphs are determinate, each feature label l denotes a unary, partial function on $D^{\mathcal{F}}$.

2.5.2   Syntax and Semantics of Feature Terms

The description language introduced by Smolka consists of expressions called *feature terms*[7], which denote sets in feature algebras. The language of feature terms is defined as the smallest set which contains:

- $\top$

- $\bot$

- a for $a \in A$

- $l : S$ for $l \in L$ and S a feature term

- $(S \sqcup T)$ for S, T feature terms

- $(S \sqcap T)$ for S, T feature terms

- $\neg S$ for S a feature term

- $p_1 \downarrow p_2$ for p_1, p_2 paths

---

[7]Smolka also considers a more basic relational logic of set descriptions similar to the attribute-value logic of Johnson.

- $p_1 \uparrow p_2$ for p_1, p_2 paths

Feature terms are built up from two special terms $\top$ and $\bot$; atoms in A; function selection (which can be viewed as the inverse of function application); operators for set union ($\sqcup$), intersection ($\sqcap$) and complement ($\neg$); and operators for path agreement ($\downarrow$) and disagreement ($\uparrow$). Path agreements correspond to the path equations of Rounds-Kasper logic and are used to describe structure sharing. Disagreements correspond to the inequations introduced by Carpenter (1990, 1992). An example of a feature term is presented below.

$$(\text{cat} : S \sqcap \text{subj agr} \downarrow \text{pred agr})$$

Informally, this feature term denotes the set of all objects defined for the feature labels **cat**, **subj** and **pred**, where **cat** has the value S, and the paths **subj agr** and **pred agr** are required to share the same (unspecified) value.

The *denotation* of a feature term S in a feature algebra $\mathcal{I}$ (written $[\![S]\!]^{\mathcal{I}}$) is defined as follows:

$$
\begin{aligned}
[\![\top]\!]^{\mathcal{I}} &= D^{\mathcal{I}} \\
[\![\bot]\!]^{\mathcal{I}} &= \emptyset \\
[\![a]\!]^{\mathcal{I}} &= \{a^{\mathcal{I}}\} \\
[\![l : S]\!]^{\mathcal{I}} &= \{d \in D^{\mathcal{I}} | \exists e \in [\![S]\!]^{\mathcal{I}} : (d, e) \in l^{\mathcal{I}}\} \\
[\![S \sqcap T]\!]^{\mathcal{I}} &= [\![S]\!]^{\mathcal{I}} \cap [\![T]\!]^{\mathcal{I}} \\
[\![S \sqcup T]\!]^{\mathcal{I}} &= [\![S]\!]^{\mathcal{I}} \cup [\![T]\!]^{\mathcal{I}} \\
[\![\neg S]\!]^{\mathcal{I}} &= D^{\mathcal{I}} - [\![S]\!]^{\mathcal{I}} \\
[\![p_1 \downarrow p_2]\!]^{\mathcal{I}} &= \{d \in D^{\mathcal{I}} | \exists e \in D^{\mathcal{I}} : (d, e) \in p_1^{\mathcal{I}} \cap p_2^{\mathcal{I}}\} \\
[\![p_1 \uparrow p_2]\!]^{\mathcal{I}} &= \{d \in D^{\mathcal{I}} | \exists e, e' \in D^{\mathcal{I}} : (d, e) \in p_1^{\mathcal{I}}, (d, e') \in p_2^{\mathcal{I}} \text{ and } e \neq e'\}
\end{aligned}
$$

A feature term S is *consistent* if it has a non-empty denotation in some feature algebra (i.e. there exists a feature algebra $\mathcal{I}$ such that $[\![S]\!]^{\mathcal{I}} \neq \emptyset$) and otherwise it is *inconsistent*. Two feature terms S and T are *equivalent* (written $S \simeq T$) just in case $[\![S]\!]^{\mathcal{I}} = [\![T]\!]^{\mathcal{I}}$ for every feature algebra $\mathcal{I}$. Finally, a feature term S *subsumes* a feature term T (written $S \leq T$) just in case $[\![S]\!]^{\mathcal{I}} \supseteq [\![T]\!]^{\mathcal{I}}$ for every feature algebra $\mathcal{I}$. It is notable that consistency, equivalence and subsumption for feature terms are interdefinable:

$$S \text{ is inconsistent} \quad \Leftrightarrow \quad S \leq \bot$$

$$\Leftrightarrow \quad S \simeq \bot$$
$$S \leq T \quad \Leftrightarrow \quad S \sqcap \neg T \text{ is inconsistent}$$
$$S \simeq T \quad \Leftrightarrow \quad S \leq T \text{ and } T \leq S$$

Each of the reductions specified above can be performed in linear time. It follows that the problems of deciding consistency, subsumption and equivalence for feature terms have the same computational complexity. The semantics of feature terms also reveals that path disagreements are actually redundant. More specifically, the following equivalence shows that disagreement can be expressed in terms of path agreement and complement:

$$p_1 \uparrow p_2 \simeq p_1 : \top \sqcap p_2 : \top \sqcap \neg p_1 \downarrow p_2$$

A complement is called *simple* if it has one of the following forms: $\neg a$, $\neg l : \top$ or $\neg p_1 \downarrow p_2$. A feature term which contains only simple complements is called *basic*. Smolka shows that any feature term is linear-time reducible to an equivalent basic feature term. Moreover, for any basic feature term not involving unions (i.e. occurrences of $\sqcup$) it is possible to determine consistency in polynomial time. A feature term is said to be in *disjunctive normal form* (DNF) if it has the form $S_1 \sqcup \ldots \sqcup S_k$, where each S_i $(1 \leq i \leq k)$ is a basic feature term not involving unions. Any basic feature term can be rewritten into DNF by using the following equivalences to push unions up to the top level:

$$(S \sqcap (T \sqcup U)) \quad \simeq \quad (S \sqcap T) \sqcup (S \sqcap U)$$
$$(S \sqcup (T \sqcap U)) \quad \simeq \quad (S \sqcup U) \sqcap (T \sqcup U)$$
$$l : (S \sqcup T) \quad \simeq \quad l : S \sqcup l : T$$

In general, computing the DNF of a feature term S may take time exponential in the size of S. Because determining the consistency of each disjunct can be performed in polynomial time this means that determining the consistency of arbitrary feature terms is NP-easy. The problem can be shown to be NP-hard using Kasper's (1987a) linear-time reduction of satisfiability for propositional formulas in conjunctive normal form to consistency of feature terms. It follows that the consistency problem for arbitrary feature terms is NP-complete. It is worth noting that Kasper's reduction does not depend on the presence of negation (complements) or path disagreements in the description language. In fact, the consistency problem for feature terms without complements or path disagreements is already NP-complete, and their introduction does not make the problem any harder.

2.5.3   Sort Definitions

Smolka considers an extension of the language of feature terms which includes sorts. Sorts denote subsets of the domain of interpretation and correspond closely to the *concepts* of terminological languages such as KL-ONE (Brachman and Schmolze 1985) and its derivatives. In terminological languages concepts may be introduced either as primitives, or they may be structurally defined in terms of other concepts by means of so-called terminological axioms. The idea of introducing defined sorts opens up interesting possibilities. In particular, sets of sort definitions can be used to specify which classes of feature algebras are to be considered in determining consistency, equivalence and subsumption of feature terms.

Syntactically, sorts are just feature terms, and in the following are denoted by s and t. In order to provide an interpretation for feature terms with sorts, it is required that every feature algebra $\mathcal{I}$ assign to every sort s some subset $s^{\mathcal{I}} \subseteq D^{\mathcal{I}}$ of the domain of $\mathcal{I}$. The inclusion of sorts into the description language does not enhance the expressive power of feature terms. Moreover, determining consistency, equivalence and subsumption for feature terms containing sorts is no harder than before. The logical behaviour of sorts is captured by the following equivalence schema:

$$s \sqcap \neg s \simeq \bot$$

On the other hand, the possibility of introducing sorts as 'names' or abbreviations for other feature terms is of greater interest. A *sort equation* may be defined as an expression of the form $s \doteq T$, where s is a sort and T is a feature term. Intuitively, the meaning of a sort equation $s \doteq T$ is that s and T denote the same set of objects. Let $\mathcal{I}$ be a feature algebra. Then $\mathcal{I}$ is said to *satisfy* a sort equation $s \doteq T$ just in case $s^{\mathcal{I}} = [\![T]\!]^{\mathcal{I}}$. Collections of equations can be used to specify admissible classes of feature algebras with respect to which consistency, subsumption and equivalence of feature terms are to be considered. More precisely, a *sort system* may be defined as a finite set of sort equations $\mathcal{E}$ such that $s \doteq S \in \mathcal{E}$ and $s \doteq T \in \mathcal{E}$ implies that $S = T$. If $\mathcal{E}$ contains a sort equation $s \doteq T$, then the sort s is said to be *defined in* $\mathcal{E}$, and T is said to be the *definition of* s (in $\mathcal{E}$). A feature algebra $\mathcal{I}$ is a *model* for a sort system $\mathcal{E}$ just in case $\mathcal{I}$ satisfies each sort equation in $\mathcal{E}$.

Sort systems provide a model for the kinds of abstraction mechanisms employed in many constraint-based grammar formalisms (for example, the *templates* of PATR or the *principles* of HPSG). As an example, consider

the following sort equations which are based on the lexical templates of
PATR (sort symbols are written with initial capitals to distinguish them
from atoms):

Verb $\doteq$ cat : v

Sing3 $\doteq$ agr : (num : singular $\sqcap$ person : three)

Trans $\doteq$ Verb $\sqcap$ subcat : (first : cat : np $\sqcap$ rest : (first : cat : np $\sqcap$ rest : nil))

In any model of the sort equations given above, the sorts Verb, Sing3 and
Trans will behave appropriately as abbreviations for their defining feature
terms. This means that the following feature term can now serve as a
succinct description of the third person singular, transitive verb *loves*:

$$\text{Sing3} \sqcap \text{Trans} \sqcap \text{pred} : love$$

A set of sort equations $\mathcal{E}$ is *noncyclic* if no sort symbol s occurring in $\mathcal{E}$ is
defined in terms of itself. For example, the set of sort equations given above
is noncyclic in this sense. With respect to a noncyclic set of sort equations $\mathcal{E}$
it is decidable whether a feature term S is consistent (that is, whether there
exists a model $\mathcal{I}$ for $\mathcal{E}$ such that $[\![S]\!]^{\mathcal{I}}$ is non-empty). To see this, note that
there is an iterative procedure which replaces sorts in S by their definitions
in $\mathcal{E}$. If S contains no occurrence of a sort symbol defined in $\mathcal{E}$, then the
procedure returns S. Otherwise, it begins by substituting a defined sort
occurring in S by its definition in $\mathcal{E}$ to yield a new feature term equivalent
to S. The process is now repeated for the new feature term. Because $\mathcal{E}$ is
noncyclic, this process must terminate eventually and will yield a feature
term S' equivalent to S which contains no occurrence of a defined sort.

Now consider the consistency of the feature term S'. If there is no feature
algebra $\mathcal{I}$ such that $[\![S']\!]^{\mathcal{I}} \neq \emptyset$, then clearly there is no model of $\mathcal{E}$ in which S'
has a non-empty denotation. Thus S' (and hence also S) is inconsistent with
respect to $\mathcal{E}$. Alternatively, suppose that there is some feature algebra $\mathcal{I}$ (not
necessarily a model for $\mathcal{E}$) such that $[\![S']\!]^{\mathcal{I}} \neq \emptyset$. Clearly, the denotation of
S' in the feature algebra $\mathcal{I}$ cannot depend on the interpretation of any sort
symbol defined in $\mathcal{E}$. But this means that S' has a non-empty denotation
in *any* feature algebra that is like $\mathcal{I}$, except possibly with respect to the
interpretation of defined sorts. It follows that S' (and hence S) has a non-
empty denotation in a model for $\mathcal{E}$ (assuming $\mathcal{E}$ has a model), whence S is
consistent with respect to $\mathcal{E}$.

More generally, determining the consistency of feature terms with respect to arbitrary sort systems is undecidable. This is not especially surprising when it is realized that cyclic sort systems allow for the statement of recursive relations such as 'member' and 'append'. For example, the following sort equation effectively defines the member relation on lists:

Member $\doteq$ (item $\downarrow$ list first $\sqcup$

(call list $\downarrow$ list rest $\sqcap$ call : Member $\sqcap$ item $\downarrow$ call item))

Höhfeld and Smolka (1988) have shown how feature structure description languages can be integrated with concepts from constraint logic programming. The approach to sorted feature terms introduced by Smolka has also been generalized by Dörre and Eisele (1991) to allow for the specification of parameterized sorts. They describe a *comprehensive unification-based formalism* (CUF) which provides for the recursive definition of relations over feature structures. The introduction of relational dependencies allows for a particularly elegant formulation of HPSG-style grammars, in which functions and relations over feature structures play an important role. Relational dependencies have also been incorporated into the unification-based formalism STUF (Dörre and Seifert 1991).

2.6   Summary

This chapter has surveyed and compared a number of logical approaches to feature structures and their descriptions. Each approach offers a definition of the notion 'feature structure' and provides an appropriate logical language for describing and reasoning about these structures. A broad distinction can be drawn between those approaches which take feature structures to be inherently partial representations of linguistic objects, and those which view feature structures as complete or totally instantiated objects.

The 'partial objects' view is exemplified by the logical framework introduced by Rounds and Kasper, which is motivated by problems in the specification and implementation of unification-based grammars. On this approach, feature structures are regarded as inherently partial representations of linguistic objects which may be ordered according to information content (subsumption) and combined by unification. In terms of information processing, the amount of information which is available about a linguistic object may grow as a computation proceeds. In order to ensure that this information can be processed efficiently, it is desirable that constraints on linguistic objects can be solved incrementally. Thus, if a feature structure satisfies some constraint, then the constraint should remain satisfied regardless of how much additional information is taken into account (monotonicity).

In the work of both Johnson and Smolka on the other hand, feature structures are taken to be complete or totally instantiated objects, while descriptions are partial in the sense that they pick out sets of admissible structures. One advantage in adopting this approach is that it leads to a somewhat simpler, classical account of the semantics of feature structure descriptions (particularly with regard to description negation). Furthermore, it appears that the computational problem of solving constraints on feature structures involving general description negation is no harder than solving constraints involving only conjunctions and disjunctions.

The approaches can also be differentiated according to whether the description language used is 'custom built' (as in the work of Rounds and Kasper) or whether it is viewed as a fragment of first order logic (as in the work of Johnson). Johnson (1990, 1991) argues that first-order logic provides a suitable basis for axiomatising a wide variety of feature structures and for expressing constraints on these structures. This has particular benefits, since many results concerning first order logic (e.g. completeness, compactness) are immediately applicable to work on feature structure descriptions. On the other hand, the distinction between the approaches may be more apparent than real. Both Reape (1991) and Blackburn (1991) have studied feature logics extensively from a modal perspective. They show that Rounds-Kasper logic and its extensions can be viewed as fragments of normal modal languages, for which many interesting results also exist. Blackburn (1992) argues that the 'custom built' approach to feature logics can be viewed as an appropriate strategy for striking the right balance between computational tractability and expressive power.

Current work on feature logics is concerned with extending these languages in linguistically motivated, yet computationally tractable ways. Thus, Smolka has considered the introduction of sort information while Carpenter has investigated an object-oriented type discipline for feature structures. The use of sort or type definitions to model recursion has been explored by Rounds and Manaster-Ramer, Smolka and Carpenter. A rather different approach to recursive descriptions is found in the work of Gazdar et al. On this approach, modal operators are used to express quantification over feature values within a feature structure. The following chapters investigate the properties of a feature logic which incorporates a related, but more powerful quantificational mechanism: the device of *functional uncertainty* introduced by Kaplan and Zaenen (1986) for the succinct description of unbounded dependency constructions.

Chapter 3

Regular Rounds-Kasper Logic

This chapter explores a rather natural extension of the language of Rounds-Kasper logic introduced in section 2.2 of the previous chapter. In *Regular Rounds-Kasper logic*, descriptions of paths in feature structures are generalized to regular expressions over the set of available feature labels. A linguistic motivation for investigating this language stems from the device of *functional uncertainty* — a novel approach to the description of unbounded dependency proposed by Kaplan and Zaenen (1986) within the framework of Lexical Functional Grammar. The phenomenon of unbounded dependency in natural languages is therefore briefly described in section 3.1. Next, section 3.2 provides an overview of Lexical Functional Grammar and the functional uncertainty mechanism. The language of Regular Rounds-Kasper logic is presented in section 3.3 together with a number of laws of logical equivalence for descriptions. It is observed that the language can be used to express certain kinds of infinite disjunction and that the problem of determining equivalence for descriptions is PSPACE-hard. The remainder of the chapter is concerned with the *satisfiability problem* for Regular Rounds-Kasper logic: given an arbitrary description, does it have a satisfying feature structure? Building on an algorithm due to Kaplan and Maxwell (1988), it is shown that this problem is decidable subject to an acyclicity condition on feature structures.

3.1 Unbounded Dependencies

One of the most challenging problems in the description of natural languages is the phenomenon of so-called *unbounded* (*non-local*, or *long-distance*) *dependencies*. It is characteristic of constructions exhibiting unbounded dependencies that a syntactic dependency or relation of some kind exists between two phrases, but this dependency is not restricted to a fixed, local domain (e.g. a simple verb phrase or clause). Unbounded dependency constructions (UDCs) are by no means exceptional in the world's languages and may well be universal. Examples of such constructions in English include topicalizations (13a), relative clauses (13b), constituent questions (13c), clefts (13d) and missing object constructions (13e).

(13) a. *Moira, Tom said that Bill saw.*

     b. *The woman who Tom said that Bill saw (laughed).*

     c. *Who did Tom say that Bill saw?*

     d. *It is Moira Tom said that Bill saw.*

     e. *Moira is easy for Bill to see.*

The important properties of UDCs may be illustrated with respect to the topicalization constructions given in (14) below. In each of these examples, a fronted (topicalized) element *Moira* can be understood as being related to an empty position or 'gap' (indicated by __) which is some distance away in the sentence. Intuitively, the gap marks the site of a 'dislocated' constituent for which the fronted element acts as a 'filler'.

(14) a. *Moira, Bill saw __ yesterday.*

     b. *Moira, Bill said __ saw Tom yesterday.*

     c. *Moira, Bill said that Anna believed Tom saw __ yesterday.*

In (14a) the topicalized element *Moira* bears the syntactic relation of object to the main verb *saw*. In (14b) on the other hand, *Moira* is the subject of a sentential complement to the main verb *said*. Finally, in (14c) *Moira* is the object of a sentential complement to *believed*, which in turn occurs in a sentential complement to the main verb *said*. It is not difficult to see that in constructions of this kind, a potentially unbounded amount of material may intervene between the topicalized element and the 'gap'.

It has often been observed that certain kinds of construction appear to block unbounded dependencies. A number of such constructions were pointed out and classified by Ross (1967, 1986), who referred to them as *islands*[1]. The notion of islandhood is illustrated by the ungrammatical 'topicalizations' presented in (15) below (where the constructions which function as islands are bracketed). As the examples show, constructions with island status include relative clauses (15a), noun complement clauses (15b), embedded questions (15c) and coordinate structures (15d).

(15)   a.   *Moira, Bill met the woman [who saw __]

       b.   *Moira, Tom believes the claim [that Bill saw __]

       c.   *Moira, Tom asked [where Bill saw __]

       d.   *Moira, Bill saw [Tom and __]

In view of the variety of construction types exhibiting unbounded dependencies commonly found in natural languages, it is clear that natural language grammar formalisms must provide appropriate machinery for handling the phenomenon. Two key technical issues arise in this respect. First, there is the problem of capturing the linkage between the 'filler' and the 'gap', which as noted above, may be indefinitely far apart; and second, there is the problem of expressing restrictions on unbounded dependencies in order to account for facts about islands, as exemplified in (15) above. A wide range of devices have been proposed in different grammar formalisms to handle UDCs. Examples include transformational rules, the HOLD register in Augmented Transition Networks, the 'slash categories' of Generalized Phrase Structure Grammar, and functional composition and type-raising in categorial grammars. In spite of this diversity however, a common view of the problem of unbounded dependencies emerges:

- the problem of capturing the linkage between filler and gap is generally resolved by reducing unbounded dependencies to sequences of local or bounded dependencies;

- restrictions on the distribution of fillers and gaps in UDCs are expressed in terms of the geometry of phrase structure representations: i.e. in terms of the configuration and labelling of phrase structure nodes.

---

[1]Much of the technical vocabulary which is often used to discuss unbounded dependencies (e.g. 'extraction', 'movement') derives from various proposals for their treatment within transformational grammar. The term 'island' is meant to suggest a constituent out of which no subpart can be moved (although the constituent may generally be moved as a single unit).

For example, since the early 1970s, transformational accounts of UDCs have assumed that such constructions may be described in terms of iterated movement. In *Conditions on Transformations* (Chomsky 1973) Chomsky argues that unbounded dependencies are in fact chains of local dependencies arising from the successive cyclic application of transformational rules such as 'wh-movement'. General conditions on the application of all transformational rules (for example, subjacency) are held to explain restrictions on unbounded dependencies such as the island phenomena illustrated in (15). The restrictions themselves are expressed in terms of configurations of phrase structure nodes.

Non-transformational approaches to UDCs have also adopted a phrasal orientation. Many of these approaches rely heavily on the use of complex non-terminal symbols (e.g. the derived categories of categorial grammar, first-order terms in logic grammars, features structures in unification-based formalisms) in order to record information about the presence or absence of gaps within a phrase. In this way it becomes possible to characterize unbounded dependencies by redeploying the apparatus used to describe phrase structure. A representative example of such an approach is the use of 'slash categories' originally developed within the framework of GPSG.

In GPSG, syntactic category information is represented in terms of features and values. A distinguished feature **slash** takes as its value a syntactic category encoding information about a missing constituent within a phrase. Three putatively universal feature instantiation principles — the *Head Feature Convention* (HFC), the *Foot Feature Principle* (FFP) and the *Control Agreement Principle* (CAP) — govern the distribution of this information in local trees (i.e. trees of depth one). In particular, the FFP ensures that a **slash** specification instantiated on the mother category is also instantiated on at least one of the daughters (and vice-versa). Unbounded dependencies then arise as a global consequence of such local feature correspondences: the linkage between filler and gap is realised as a chain of mother-daughter categories which carry identical **slash** values. This is illustrated in figure 3.1, which shows a typical GPSG analysis of the topicalized sentence *Moira, Tom says Bill saw.*

In the figure, the notation X/Y (read "X slash Y") is used to abbreviate that category like X but with **slash** value Y — a constituent X missing a Y. At the 'top' of the UDC, a constituent with an NP gap is introduced as a daughter of S. Intuitively, the **slash** value corresponds to the fronted NP constituent *Moira*. The 'middle' of the UDC consists of a chain of mothers and daughters, all of which bear identical **slash** specifications. In

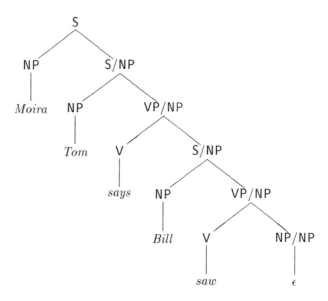

Figure 3.1: GPSG analysis of unbounded dependency

this way, syntactic information about the topicalised constituent is carried to the 'bottom' of the UDC where the chain is terminated in a gap: a constituent NP/NP which dominates the empty string. Restrictions on the distribution of fillers and gaps in UDCs arise from the interaction of the feature instantiation principles, and the use of additional meta-grammatical devices (e.g. the 'slash termination' metarules). All of the components of a generalized phrase structure grammar are ultimately conditions on the well-formedness of local trees. It follows that restrictions on UDCs are expressed in terms of local configurations of phrase structure nodes.

A rather different approach to the problem of unbounded dependencies has been proposed by Kaplan and Zaenen (1986) within the framework of Lexical Functional Grammar. They argue that facts about UDCs traditionally stated in phrasal terms are better expressed in terms of the predicate-argument structure of sentences. This claim is supported by certain properties of the phrase structure of Icelandic which rule out any purely phrasal account of island phenomena in that language. On the other hand, the linguistic data is amenable to an account of UDCs given in terms of underlying grammatical relations. In order to express the relevant generalisations, Kaplan and Zaenen introduce a new formal device of *functional uncertainty*

$$\begin{bmatrix} \text{subj} & \begin{bmatrix} \text{pred} & \text{`Moira'} \\ \text{person} & 3 \\ \text{num} & \text{sg} \end{bmatrix} \\ \text{tense} & \text{past} \\ \text{pred} & \text{`see}\langle(\uparrow \text{subj})(\uparrow \text{obj})\rangle\text{'} \\ \text{obj} & \begin{bmatrix} \text{pred} & \text{`Bill'} \\ \text{person} & 3 \\ \text{num} & \text{sg} \end{bmatrix} \end{bmatrix}$$

Figure 3.2: A typical LFG f-structure

which allows for the succinct description of the possible grammatical roles of dislocated elements in UDCs. The basic architecture of LFG, and the functional uncertainty mechanism are described in the following section.

3.2 LFG and Functional Uncertainty

A lexical-functional grammar characterizes two distinct levels of syntactic representation for sentences: *c-structure* (constituent-structure) and *f-structure* (functional-structure). A c-structure is just a parse tree with nodes labelled by atomic symbols such as S, NP, VP, etc., and provides a representation of the surface form of a sentence (i.e. the hierarchical grouping and linear order of constituents). In contrast to many other grammatical frameworks (but like say Relational Grammar), LFG takes grammatical relations such as 'subject' and 'object' to be basic notions. Information about grammatical relations (the predicate-argument structure of a sentence or phrase) is encoded at the level of f-structure. An f-structure is a feature structure, with feature labels such as subj, pred and obj.

An example of a simple f-structure for the sentence *Moira saw Bill* is shown in figure 3.2. The f-structure states that the subject of the sentence is *Moira* and the object *Bill*. The value of the feature label pred in the outermost f-structure is the 'semantic form' 'see$\langle(\uparrow$ subj$)(\uparrow$ obj$)\rangle$'. This indicates that the predicate *see* subcategorizes for (and governs) a subject and an object. In addition to representing underlying grammatical relations, the f-structure also encodes information about various agreement features such as number and person.

The c-structure and f-structure assigned to a particular sentence by a lexical functional grammar are not described independently, but are related by means of a 'structural correspondence'. This correspondence can be understood as a function which maps from c-structure nodes to elements of the f-structure. In this way, aspects of c-structure are used to constrain or determine aspects of f-structure. The required mapping is achieved by annotating c-structure nodes with schematic equations (*functional schemata*) from which an appropriate description of f-structure may be derived. In order to generate such annotated c-structures, a lexical functional grammar employs rules such as that shown in (16) below, together with lexical entries which associate terminal symbols with sets of functional schemata.

(16)   S →   NP   VP
               ($\uparrow$ subj) $= \downarrow$ $\uparrow = \downarrow$

In the above rule, the category symbols on the right of the rule are associated with functional schemata. These can be understood as expressing simple propositions about the f-structures corresponding to the c-structure nodes admitted by the rule. The up and down arrows ($\uparrow$ and $\downarrow$) are metavariables which may be conveniently read as 'my mother's f-structure' and 'my f-structure', respectively. For example, the equation ($\uparrow$ SUBJ) $= \downarrow$ associated with the NP states that the subj value of the f-structure associated with the S node is just the f-structure associated with the NP node. In order to determine f-structure, the functional schemata which annotate c-structure nodes are first instantiated by replacing the metavariables with actual variables denoting f-structure elements. The instantiated equations, or *function-application expressions* have the basic form $(f\, l) = g$, where f and g denote f-structures and l is a feature label. The interpretation of a function-application expression is as shown in (17).

(17) $(f\, l) = g$ holds $\Leftrightarrow$ $\langle l, g \rangle \in f$

In other words, the f-structure f is defined for the feature label l which has as its value the f-structure g. More generally, the notation for function-application expressions may be extended to paths in f-structure by noting the following equivalences: $(f\epsilon) \equiv f$ (where ϵ is the empty path), and $(f\, lp) \equiv ((f\, l)\, p)$ where l is a feature label and p a path. The set of all function-application expressions comprises a *functional description* for the sentence and the final step is to solve this description to determine the f-structure associated with the S node in c-structure (see Kaplan and Bresnan (1982, S4.4)).

In this way, LFG provides for the simultaneous description of two distinct yet correlated levels of syntactic representation. Information about predicate-argument structure is recovered from the surface form of a sentence in terms of the hierarchical grouping and linear order of constituents. In general, the grammatical role of a constituent can be determined purely locally, by inspecting the constraints on f-structure associated with the constituent's root node in c-structure. For example, any NP constituent introduced according to the rule given in (16) above is designated as the subject of the S by virtue of the equation ($\uparrow$ subj) $=\downarrow$. In the case of unbounded dependencies however, local properties of the surface structure are not sufficient to uniquely determine the underlying grammatical relations. The grammatical role of some phrase may depend on another constituent which is unpredictably distant in c-structure, and the wider context within which a phrase occurs must also be taken into account. Consider for example the topicalizations in (18).

(18)   a.   *Moira, Bill saw.*

      b.   *Moira, Tom said that Anna believed Bill saw.*

In (18a) the topicalized element *Moira* functions as the object of the (local) predicate *saw*. In principle, the required dependency could be specified by associating with this phrase a simple constraint ($\uparrow$ topic) $=$ ($\uparrow$ obj). Regarding (18b) however, *Moira* is the object of a non-local predicate which occurs as part of a sentential complement to the predicate *believed*, which in turn forms part of a sentential complement to the (local) predicate *said*. The required constraint in this case might be appropriately specified by the equation ($\uparrow$ topic) $=$ ($\uparrow$ comp comp obj). More generally, and in view of the unbounded nature of topicalization constructions, it appears that the grammatical role of the fronted element must be specified by some equation of the following form:

(19) ($\uparrow$ topic) $=$ ($\uparrow$ comp ...comp obj)

In (19) comp ...comp stands for a finite (possibly empty) sequence of comp features. As Kaplan and Zaenen observe, the problem now is that there is an infinite number of equations of this general type.

In order to express the relevant generalizations about unbounded dependencies in predicate-argument terms, Kaplan and Zaenen propose to extend the notion of a function-application expression. Specifically, *regular sets* of paths are now permitted to appear as arguments. Accordingly, the definition of a function-application expression is extended to include constraints of the form $(f\,\alpha) = g$, where α is a regular set of paths (the *uncertainty set*). The interpretation of a constraint of this form may be defined as follows:

(20) $(f\,\alpha) = g \Leftrightarrow \exists p \in \alpha$ such that $(f\,p) = g$.

If the uncertainty set α is finite, then clearly this just amounts to a finite disjunction of function-application expressions without uncertainty. If α is infinite on the other hand, the constraint corresponds to an infinite disjunction of more basic function-application expressions. Consider for example the functional schemata shown in (21) below, where **GF** denotes the set of all primitive grammatical relations (i.e. **subj**, **obj**, **comp**, etc.).

(21) $(\uparrow \text{topic}) = (\uparrow \text{comp}^*\text{GF})$

In this equation, the uncertainty set consists of an infinite set of paths, where each path is a (possibly empty) sequence of **comp** features followed by an element of the set **GF**. Consequently, (21) provides a succinct description of the potential grammatical roles of topicalized phrases. Language-specific restrictions on UDCs are accounted for by constraining either the uncertainty set, or the set of grammatical relations which are permitted to appear at the 'bottom' of a UDC (i.e. the set **GF** in (21) above). For example, a more accurate statement of the conditions on English topicalization constructions might be given by the following constraint:

(22) $(\uparrow \text{topic}) = (\uparrow \text{comp}^* (\text{GF} \setminus \text{comp}))$

In (22) $(\text{GF} \setminus \text{comp})$ denotes the set of all primitive grammatical relations minus **comp**. That is, in English a topicalized phrase cannot function as a complement.

The functional uncertainty mechanism has already proved useful in the analysis of various problems in natural languages. Saiki (1986) describes an application of functional uncertainty to the problem of island constraints in Japanese relative clauses, while Karttunen (1986) provides a treatment of unbounded dependencies in Finnish using the functional uncertainty mechanism within the framework of Categorial Unification Grammar (CUG). A number of researchers have also applied functional uncertainty to phenomena not usually thought of as involving unbounded dependencies. Thus, Johnson (1986) presents a treatment of Dutch infinitival constructions, and Netter (1986) shows that functional uncertainty can be applied to the treatment of extraposed infinitival constructions and the position of the finite verb in German. An account of word order in infinitival complements in Continental West Germanic is described by Kaplan and Zaenen (1988). Halvorsen and Kaplan (1988) have applied functional uncertainty to the treatment of quantifier scope ambiguities in semantic structures. Carlson (1988) has described a new grammar formalism *Regular Unification Grammar* which draws of the idea of functional uncertainty.

3.3   Regular Rounds-Kasper Logic

This section provides a formalisation of the linguistically useful device of functional uncertainty within the framework of Rounds-Kasper logic. In *Regular Rounds-Kasper logic* (**RRK**), descriptions of paths in feature structures are generalised to regular expressions over the set of available feature labels. In general, **RRK** descriptions may be *infinitary* in the sense that they have an infinite number of most general satisfiers. This contrasts with the situation in Rounds-Kasper logic, where the logical equivalence classes of **RK** descriptions are completely characterized by the finite sets of subsumption-incomparable feature structures. The syntax and semantics of the description language **RRK** are presented in the following section. Next, a number of laws of logical equivalence for descriptions are discussed and it is shown that the *equivalence problem* for descriptions is PSPACE-hard.

3.3.1   The Language of Regular Rounds-Kasper Logic

Let L and A be finite, non-empty sets of *feature labels* and *atoms* respectively. The set R of *regular path expressions* (or *path descriptors*) is defined as a set of regular expressions over L. More concretely, the set R is taken to be the smallest set which contains:

- λ (the null path descriptor);

- l for each $l \in L$;

- $(r + s)$ for $r, s \in R$ \hspace{2em} (Union)

- $(r \cdot s)$ for $r, s \in R$ (Concatenation)

- (r^*) for $r \in R$ (Closure)

A regular path expression $r \in R$ denotes a (possibly infinite) set of paths in L^*. The null path descriptor λ denotes the singleton set $\{\epsilon\}$ which contains only the empty path ϵ. A path descriptor l (for $l \in L$) denotes the singleton set $\{l\}$. If r and s are regular path expressions, then $(r + s)$ denotes the union of the path sets denoted by r and s separately, while $(r \cdot s)$ denotes the set of all paths obtained by concatenating each path in r with a path in s. Finally, a path descriptor r^* denotes the set of all paths obtained by concatenating together zero or more paths in r. The notation $p \in r$ is used to state that the path p belongs to the set of paths denoted by the regular path expression r.

Two regular path expressions r and s are said to be *equivalent* (written $r \sim s$) just in case they denote identical sets of feature paths: i.e. $p \in r \Leftrightarrow p \in s$. In general, there are many regular path expressions which denote a given set of paths. Some examples of equivalences for path descriptors are the following:

(23)   a. $(\lambda \cdot r) \sim r \sim (r \cdot \lambda)$

         b. $(r + (s + t)) \sim ((r + s) + t)$

         c. $(r \cdot (s \cdot t)) \sim ((r \cdot s) \cdot t)$

         d. $r^* \sim (\lambda + (r \cdot r^*))$

         e. $(r + s)^* \sim (r^* \cdot s^*)^*$

A regular path expression r will be called *finitary* if it denotes a finite set of paths, and otherwise it will be said to be *infinitary*. Furthermore, a regular path expression r will be called *unitary* if it picks out a unique feature path (i.e. r denotes a singleton set). Syntactically, a regular path expression is clearly unitary if it is either (i) the null path descriptor λ; or (ii) a feature label $l \in L$; or (iii) an expression of the form $(r \cdot s)$ where r and s are both unitary. However, it should be noted that a regular path expression of the form $(r + s)$ will also be unitary if r and s are unitary and $r \sim s$. A regular path expression (r^*) will only be unitary if $r \sim \lambda$. In the following, r, s, t will always be used to denote arbitrary regular path expressions, and u will be used as necessary to denote unitary path descriptors.

Example 3.1 Suppose that comp, subj, obj1 and obj2 are all feature labels in L, then the following is an example of a regular path expression:

$$((\text{comp} \cdot (\text{comp}^*)) \cdot ((\text{subj} + \text{obj1}) + \text{obj2}))$$

The regular path expression given above is infinitary. It denotes an infinite set of feature paths, where each member consists of a non-empty sequence of comp labels followed by one of either subj, obj1 or obj2.

When writing regular path expressions, it will be convenient to assume that the closure operator has higher precedence than either union or concatenation, and that the concatenation operator has higher precedence than union. This enables parentheses to be dropped in certain cases. In addition, the associativity of union (23b) and concatenation (23c) means that the parentheses used to group regular path expressions can often be omitted without introducing any ambiguity. Finally, the notation r^+ (*positive closure*) may be used as an abbreviation for $r \cdot r^*$, and r^n (for n a positive integer) will occasionally be employed to abbreviate the regular path expression $r \cdot r \cdot \ldots r$ (where r occurs n times). Given the operator precedences, the associativity of union and concatenation, and the positive closure abbreviation, the path expression of example 3.1 above can now be written unambiguously and more succinctly as follows:

$$(\text{comp}^+ \cdot (\text{subj} + \text{obj1} + \text{obj2}))$$

The language **RRK** is defined as the smallest set of descriptions which contains:

- $\top$

- $\bot$

- a for any $a \in A$

- $r : \phi$ for $r \in R$ and ϕ a description

- $(\phi \vee \psi)$ for ϕ, ψ descriptions

- $(\phi \wedge \psi)$ for ϕ, ψ descriptions

- $(r \doteq s)$ for $r, s \in R$.

The next two examples illustrate the syntax of descriptions and provide an informal account of their semantics.

Example 3.2 Suppose that cat, subj, obj and pred are feature labels in L and that S is an atom in A. The following expression is a well-formed **RRK** description:

$$(\text{cat} : S \wedge ((\text{subj} \cdot \text{agr}) \doteq (\text{pred} \cdot \text{agr})))$$

Example 3.2 is a particularly simple description which involves only unitary path descriptors. Informally, it can be understood as a partial description of a sentence (i.e. cat has the value S) in which the subject and predicate are constrained to carry identical agreement features (i.e. the value of the path subj agr is token-identical to the value of the path pred agr).

Example 3.3 Suppose that cat, topic, comp, subj and obj are feature labels in L, and that S is an atomic feature value in A. Then the following expression is a well-formed description:

$$(\text{cat} : S \wedge (\text{topic} \doteq (\text{comp}^* \cdot (\text{subj} + \text{obj}))))$$

Example 3.3 makes use of an infinitary path descriptor to describe the 'unbounded uncertainty' associated with topicalization constructions. It can be regarded as a description of a topicalized sentence, where the topic is either the subject or object of the whole clause, or else the subject or object of a (sentential) complement, or the complement's complement, or the complement's complement's complement, and so on. Examples of such sentences might include *Moira, Bill saw* (where the topic is the object of the main clause), *Moira, Bill said saw Tom* (where the topic is the subject of a sentential complement) or *Moira, Bill said that Tom believed Anna saw* (where the topic is the object of the complement's complement).

The conditions whereby a feature structure $\mathcal{A} = \langle Q, q_0, \delta, \pi \rangle$ satisfies a description ϕ (written $\mathcal{A} \models \phi$) are defined as follows:

- $\mathcal{A} \models \top$

- $\mathcal{A} \not\models \bot$

- $\mathcal{A} \models a \Leftrightarrow \pi(q_0) = a$

- $\mathcal{A} \models r : \phi \Leftrightarrow \exists p \in r$ such that $\mathcal{A}/p$ is defined and $\mathcal{A}/p \models \phi$

- $\mathcal{A} \models (\phi \vee \psi) \Leftrightarrow \mathcal{A} \models \phi$ or $\mathcal{A} \models \psi$

- $\mathcal{A} \models (\phi \wedge \psi) \Leftrightarrow \mathcal{A} \models \phi$ and $\mathcal{A} \models \psi$

- $\mathcal{A} \models (r \doteq s) \Leftrightarrow \exists p_r \in r, \exists p_s \in s$ such that $p_r \mathcal{N}_{\mathcal{A}} p_s$.

A formula ϕ of **RRK** is said to be *satisfiable* just in case there exists a feature structure $\mathcal{A}$ such that $\mathcal{A} \models \phi$. As a first result concerning the language **RRK** it can be observed that the satisfaction relation between feature structures and descriptions is monotonic with respect to subsumption.

Proposition 3.4 (*Monotonicity*) For any description ϕ and feature structure $\mathcal{A}$, if $\mathcal{A} \models \phi$ and $\mathcal{A} \sqsubseteq \mathcal{B}$, then $\mathcal{B} \models \phi$.

Proof: It is easy to see that the result holds when ϕ is either $\top$, $\bot$ or an atom a. Moreover, assuming that the result holds for arbitrary descriptions ψ and χ, then a simple inductive argument shows that the required result holds for $(\psi \vee \chi)$ and $(\psi \wedge \chi)$. It remains to consider the cases when ϕ is of the form $r : \psi$ or $(r \doteq s)$. Suppose then that $\mathcal{A} \models r : \psi$, and that the required result holds for ψ. In this case there is some path $p \in r$ such that $\mathcal{A}/p$ is defined and satisfies ψ. But clearly, for any feature structure $\mathcal{B} \sqsupseteq \mathcal{A}$ it must be that $\mathcal{B}/p$ is also defined and $\mathcal{A}/p \sqsubseteq \mathcal{B}/p$. It follows that $\mathcal{B}/p \models \psi$, whence $\mathcal{B} \models r : \phi$. The proof is similar for the case where ϕ is of the form $(r \doteq s)$. □

3.3.2   Logical Equivalences for Descriptions

This section presents a number of formal statements of logical equivalence for description in **RRK**. These equivalences can be of use in showing when two descriptions have precisely the same interpretation (i.e. are satisfied by the same class of feature structures). Many of the equivalences discussed below are obtained by suitably generalizing the laws of equivalence for **RK** given in section 2.3 of the previous chapter. The remaining laws are peculiar to **RRK** and are seen to derive from the properties of regular path expressions.

To begin with, it may be observed that the laws of equivalence for lattices with $\bot$ and $\top$ given in figure 2.3 of section 2.2.2 also hold for descriptions in **RRK**. None of these laws explicitly mentions path descriptors. The equivalences therefore hold solely in virtue of the interpretation of the boolean connectives $\wedge$ and $\vee$, and the two special descriptions $\bot$ and $\top$. Under certain circumstances, the remaining logical equivalences will also hold for **RRK** when descriptions of feature path are generalized to regular path expressions over feature labels. For example, the following laws of conjunction and disjunction of descriptions obtain:

(24)   a. $u : \phi \wedge u : \psi \simeq u : (\phi \wedge \psi)$

   b. $r : \phi \vee r : \psi \simeq r : (\phi \vee \psi)$

It is important to note that (24a) holds only for unitary path descriptors. It is not difficult to see that the equivalence does not hold for arbitrary regular path expressions. For example, the description $(\mathbf{f} + \mathbf{g}) : \mathbf{a} \wedge (\mathbf{f} + \mathbf{g}) : \mathbf{b}$ is clearly satisfiable, whereas the description $(\mathbf{f} + \mathbf{g}) : (\mathbf{a} \wedge \mathbf{b})$ is not. On the other hand, the equivalence in (24b) shows that arbitrary regular path expressions distribute over disjunctions.

Care must also be taken in generalizing the laws for path equality given previously in figure 2.3. In particular, the equivalences for transitivity and restricted substitutivity do not hold for arbitrary path descriptors. A suitably generalized statement of the transitivity law is the following:

(25) $(r \doteq u) \wedge (u \doteq s) \simeq (r \doteq u) \wedge (u \doteq s) \wedge (r \doteq s)$

Once again, it is easy to verify that this law holds only when the 'middle term' u is a unitary path descriptor. The left hand side of the equivalence states that there is some path in r which belongs to the same Nerode-equivalence class as the unique path picked out by u, and furthermore that there is some path in s which also belongs to this class. It follows that there is a path in r which is Nerode-equivalent to a path in s, whence $(r \doteq s)$.

Similarly, it is necessary to impose restrictions on the laws for substitutivity. The following versions of these laws hold for **RRK**:

(26)   a. $(r \doteq u) \wedge u : \phi \simeq (r \doteq u) \wedge u : \phi \wedge r : \phi$

   b. $(r \doteq u) \wedge (s \doteq (u \cdot t)) \simeq (r \doteq u) \wedge (s \doteq (u \cdot t)) \wedge (s \doteq (r \cdot t))$

On the other hand, the laws of (restricted) reflexivity and symmetry for path equations hold for arbitrary path descriptors.

Aside from those formal equivalences obtained by generalizing the laws for **RK**, there are many laws of equivalence which are special to **RRK** and which arise from the interpretation of the path expression operators. These additional equivalences may be classified as follows:

- equivalences which follow simply from the equivalence of regular path expressions;

- equivalences which depend on the relationship between the interpretation of the path expression operators and the interpretation of the logical connectives.

It was noted above that the same set of feature paths may be described by many different regular path expressions. For example, the regular path expressions r^* and $(\lambda + (r \cdot r^*))$ denote the same set of paths. Accordingly, for any description ϕ, the descriptions $r^* : \phi$ and $(\lambda + (r \cdot r^*)) : \phi$ have precisely the same interpretation. Similarly, $(r + s)^* : \phi \simeq (r^* \cdot s^*)^* : \phi$ from the equivalence $(r + s)^* \sim (r^* \cdot s^*)^*$. In general, replacing an occurrence of a regular path expression r in a description ϕ by an equivalent regular path expression s results in a logically equivalent description ϕ'. This observation is expressed formally by the following two laws.

(27)   a. $r : \phi \simeq s : \phi$ if $r \sim s$

      b. $(r \doteq t) \simeq (s \doteq t)$ if $r \sim s$.

The *equivalence problem* for **RRK** is the problem of determining for arbitrary descriptions ϕ and ψ whether $\phi \simeq \psi$. The following proposition provides a lower bound on the computational complexity of determining logical equivalence.

Proposition 3.5 The equivalence problem for **RRK** is PSPACE-hard.

Proof: It is clear from the laws given in (27) that the equivalence problem for descriptions contains the equivalence problem for regular expressions. The latter problem is known to be PSPACE-complete (Meyer and Stockmeyer (1973)) however, whence the equivalence problem for **RRK** is at least PSPACE-hard. □

Turning now to the second class of logical equivalences, it may be observed that the null path descriptor λ can be eliminated from descriptions in which it occurs. Accordingly:

(28) $\lambda : \phi \simeq \phi$

Next, it is noted that concatenation of regular path expressions is closely related to prefixing of descriptions. Stated formally, the following equivalences are obtained (note the restriction in (29b)):

(29)   a. $(r \cdot s) : \phi \simeq r : s : \phi$

      b. $((u \cdot r) \doteq (u \cdot s)) \simeq u : (r \doteq s)$

Of greater interest is the observation that the union operator '+' can often be eliminated in favour of logical disjunction. The following two equivalences hold for descriptions in **RRK**:

(30)   a. $(r + s) : \phi \simeq r : \phi \lor s : \phi$

       b. $((r + s) \doteq t) \simeq (r \doteq t) \lor (s \doteq t)$

To see (30a), note that a feature structure $\mathcal{A}$ satisfies $(r + s) : \phi$ just in case $\exists p \in (r + s)$ such that $\mathcal{A}/p$ is defined and satisfies ϕ. Equivalently, $\exists p \in r$ or $\exists p \in s$ such that $\mathcal{A}/p \models \phi$, whence $\mathcal{A} \models r : \phi$ or $\mathcal{A} \models s : \phi$. The equivalence in (30b) may be verified in a similar fashion.

The laws involving the concatenation and union given above show that occurrences of these operators can often be eliminated from descriptions. Consideration of the closure operator suggests that a similar elimination cannot be achieved. The following equivalence is noted as being of particular interest:

(31) $r^* : \phi \simeq \phi \lor r : r^* : \phi$

Actually, the equivalence in (31) says nothing new about the closure operator. It is easily derived from the equivalence $r^* : \phi \simeq (\lambda + (r \cdot r^*)) : \phi$ noted above, and the laws already given in (30a), (28) and (29a). The main interest in this law lies in the observation that it can be used, together with (24b), to 'unwind' a description $r^* : \phi$ into a longer and longer disjunction of descriptions. Regardless of how far the description is unwound however, the resulting disjunction will always contain an occurrence of the description $r^* : \phi$.

This suggests that the language **RRK** can be used to express certain kinds of infinite disjunction. More precisely, it can be shown that a description ϕ of **RRK** may be *infinitary* in the sense that the set of most general satisfiers for ϕ is of infinite size. A simple example of an infinitary description is shown in (32) below:

(32) $l^* : a$

One way of seeing that the set of most general satisfiers for (32) is of infinite size is as follows. Consider any path $p \in l^*$. Clearly, there is a subsumption-minimal feature structure $\mathcal{A}$ such that $\mathcal{A}/p$ is defined and $\mathcal{A}/p \models a$. Moreover, $\mathcal{A} \models l^* : a$, and it is not difficult to see that $\mathcal{A}$ is in fact minimal amongst those feature structures satisfying l^* : a (i.e. $\mathcal{A}$ is a most general satisfier). Now, for any two *distinct* paths in l^* the associated minimal feature structures are certainly subsumption-incomparable. But there are an infinite number of paths in l^* whence there are an infinite number of most general satisfiers for (32).

This result is to be contrasted with the situation in Rounds-Kasper logic. As noted in section 2.3 of the previous chapter, any description of **RK** has a finite set of most general satisfiers which are unique up to subsumption-equivalence. This means that the logical equivalence classes of **RK** formulas are completely characterized by the finite sets of subsumption-incomparable feature structures. The same is not true for **RRK**. Moreover, there is no simple disjunctive normal form result for **RRK** analogous to that obtained for the language **RK**. As a result, conversion to disjunctive normal form is not an option in determining the logical equivalence or consistency of descriptions, and an alternative method must be found.

A summary of the laws of logical equivalence discussed in this section (plus some additional laws) is presented in figure 3.3. This list does not include the laws for lattices with $\bot$ and $\top$ which are identical to those of figure 2.3 of the previous chapter. It is not known whether the laws of figure 3.3 are complete in the sense that they characterize all logical equivalences for **RRK**.

3.4   The Satisfiability Problem

This section considers the important *satisfiability problem* for **RRK** (i.e. the problem of determining whether a description has a satisfying feature structure). The main result presented in this section is a decision procedure for descriptions subject to an acyclicity condition on feature structures. That is, it is shown that it is decidable whether a description ϕ in **RRK** has an acyclic satisfying feature structure. An algorithm for determining the satisfiability of acyclic feature structure descriptions expressed in the language of function-application expressions with uncertainty sets has already been described by Kaplan and Maxwell (1988). It seems plausible that the ideas underlying their approach should also be applicable to **RRK**. Unfortunately, adapting the Kaplan-Maxwell algorithm to work directly with descriptions in **RRK** presents certain difficulties. In particular, problems arise with respect to the structure of **RRK** descriptions and the use of regular path expression equations to describe re-entrancy in feature structures.

1. Equivalences for Descriptions and Regular Path Expressions:

$$r : \bot \simeq \bot \qquad\qquad\qquad\qquad\qquad\qquad\qquad (\textit{Failure})$$
$$u : \phi \wedge u : \psi \simeq u : (\phi \wedge \psi) \qquad\qquad (\textit{Distribution of Path Expressions})$$
$$r : \phi \vee r : \psi \simeq r : (\phi \vee \psi)$$
$$((u \cdot r) \doteq (u \cdot s)) \simeq u : (r \doteq s)$$
$$a \wedge b \simeq \bot \text{ for } a, b \in A \text{ with } a \neq b \qquad\qquad\qquad (\textit{Clashes})$$
$$u^* : a \wedge u^* : b \simeq \bot \text{ for } a, b \in A \text{ with } a \neq b$$
$$a \wedge u : \phi \simeq \bot$$
$$\lambda : \phi \simeq \phi \qquad\qquad\qquad\qquad\qquad\qquad\qquad (\textit{Identity})$$
$$(r \cdot s) : \phi \simeq r : s : \phi \qquad\qquad\qquad\qquad (\textit{Concatenation})$$
$$(r + s) : \phi \simeq r : \phi \vee s : \phi \qquad\qquad\qquad (\textit{Union})$$
$$((r + s) \doteq t) \simeq (r \doteq t) \vee (s \doteq t)$$
$$r : \phi \simeq s : \phi \text{ if } r \sim s \qquad\qquad\qquad\qquad (\textit{Replacement})$$
$$(r \doteq t) \simeq (s \doteq t) \text{ if } r \sim s$$

2. Equivalences for Path Equations:

$$(r \doteq r) \simeq r : \top \qquad\qquad\qquad\qquad (\textit{Trivial Reflexivity})$$
$$((r \cdot s) \doteq t) \simeq ((r \cdot s) \doteq t) \wedge (r \doteq r) \qquad (\textit{Restricted Reflexivity})$$
$$r : \phi \simeq r : \phi \wedge (r \doteq r)$$
$$(r \doteq s) \simeq (s \doteq r) \qquad\qquad\qquad\qquad\qquad (\textit{Symmetry})$$
$$(r \doteq u) \wedge (u \doteq s) \simeq (r \doteq u) \wedge (u \doteq s) \wedge (r \doteq s) \qquad (\textit{Transitivity})$$
$$(r \doteq u) \wedge u : \phi \simeq (r \doteq u) \wedge u : \phi \wedge r : \phi \qquad (\textit{Restricted Substitutivity})$$
$$(r \doteq u) \wedge (s \doteq (u \cdot t)) \simeq (r \doteq u) \wedge (s \doteq (u \cdot t)) \wedge (s \doteq (r \cdot t))$$

Figure 3.3: Equivalences for descriptions in **RRK**

For these reasons an indirect approach is taken here. It is shown that any description of **RRK** may be translated into an 'equivalent' description of a simple language of equational constraints on feature structures. The simple constraint language is essentially just a restricted version of the language of function-application expressions with uncertainty sets. Accordingly, the Kaplan-Maxwell algorithm can be applied directly to constraints in this language in order to determine satisfiability.

The following section provides a brief overview of the ideas underlying the algorithm proposed by Kaplan and Maxwell. The problems of adapting this algorithm to work with **RRK** descriptions are then discussed, and section 3.4.3 introduces the equational constraint language. A mapping from description in **RRK** to constraints is defined, and it is shown that a description is satisfiable just in case it has a satisfiable translation.

3.4.1   The Kaplan-Maxwell Algorithm

It has been shown by Kaplan and Maxwell (1988) that there is an algorithm for determining the satisfiability of functional descriptions involving uncertainty expressions which is subject to an acyclicity condition on feature structures. They note that for trivial descriptions consisting of a single function-application expression $(f\alpha) = g$, determining satisfiability is easy. If α is the empty set then the description is clearly unsatisfiable. On the other hand, if α is non-empty, then the description is satisfied by any feature structure which meets the requirements for some path freely chosen from α. More generally however, functional descriptions do not have this desirable 'free choice' property. Given a conjunction of function-application expressions $(f\,\alpha) = g_\alpha \wedge (f\,\beta) = g_\beta$, the choice of paths $p \in \alpha$ and $p' \in \beta$ may be interdependent. For example, if $p' = pp''$ (i.e. the path chosen from α is a prefix of the path chosen from β) then this implies an additional constraint on the values g_α and g_β. More specifically, if $(f\,p) = g_\alpha$ and $((f\,p)\,p'') = g_\beta$ then $(g_\alpha\,p'') = g_\beta$.

The key to the Kaplan-Maxwell algorithm lies in the observation that for any conjunction of equations $(f\alpha) = g_\alpha$ and $(f\beta) = g_\beta$ there are only a finite number of ways in which paths chosen from α and β can interact. Moreover, it is possible to transform any conjunction of equations into a logically equivalent description in which paths may be freely chosen from uncertainty sets. Because the logically equivalent description is 'free' in this sense, satisfiability is not affected by a particular choice of paths. Accordingly, fairly standard techniques may be used in order to establish whether or not the description has a satisfying feature structure. For example, if each uncertainty set α is replaced by a member path (say a shortest one) then satisfiability can be determined using an algorithm such as that described by Kaplan and Bresnan (1982).

The way in which interactions between uncertainty sets are removed from formulas will now be described in more detail. The next two definitions follow those given by Kaplan and Maxwell (1988):

Definition 3.6 (*Canonical Form*) A functional description D is in *canonical form* if and only if $D = D_1 \vee D_2 \vee \ldots \vee D_n$ where each D_i is a conjunction of distinct function-application expressions such that:

- each function-application expression is of the form $(f\,\alpha) = g$ or $f = g$;

- no uncertainty set contains only the null path ϵ;

- for any equation $f = g$ (where f and g are distinct variables) one of the variables appears in no other conjoined equation.

There is a straightforward algorithm which converts any functional description into a logically equivalent description in canonical form. The next definition concerns the conditions under which a functional description in canonical form is said to be 'free':

Definition 3.7 (*Free descriptions*) Two function-application terms $(f\,\alpha)$ and $(g\,\beta)$ are *free* if and only if (i) the variables f and g are distinct; or (ii) there are no paths $p \in \alpha$, $p' \in \beta$ which share a non-empty prefix, and ϵ is in neither α nor β. Two function-application equations are *free* just in case their application expressions are free. Finally, a functional description is *free* just in case it is in canonical form, and all of its conjoined equations are pair-wise free.

The heart of the Kaplan-Maxwell algorithm is an operator *Free*, which isolates dependencies amongst paths in uncertainty sets. Applied to two function-application expressions, the *Free* operator produces a finite disjunction of conjoined equations which are pair-wise free. Each disjunct corresponds to one possible way in which paths chosen from the uncertainty sets in the original expressions may interact. The definition of the *Free* operator is motivated by two observations. Firstly, in a conjunction $(f\,\alpha) = g_\alpha \wedge (f\,\beta) = g_\beta$, all interactions between paths chosen from the uncertainty sets α and β are covered by the following three-way classification:

1. the path chosen from α is a prefix of the path chosen from β;

2. the path chosen from β is a prefix of the path chosen from α;

3. the chosen paths have a common prefix but then differ on some feature label.

Secondly, it may be observed that the paths in any uncertainty set α fall into a finite number of classes. This is trivially true if α contains only a finite number of feature paths. If α is infinite on the other hand, then consider a finite state automaton $M_\alpha = \langle Q_\alpha, q_0, \delta_\alpha, F_\alpha \rangle$ which accepts all and only the paths in α. For each state $q \in Q_\alpha$ let $Prefix(\alpha, q)$ denote the set of prefixes of paths in α which cause a transition to state q of M_α. Similarly let $Suffix(\alpha, q)$ denote the set of suffixes of paths in α whose prefixes lead to state q of M_α. The prefix and suffix languages defined in this way are clearly regular, and there are only a finite number of them (because there are only a finite number of states in Q_α). Moreover, every path in α belongs to a language $Prefix(\alpha, q)Suffix(\alpha, q)$ for some state q of M_α.

It follows that in considering the possible interactions between paths chosen from uncertainty sets it is sufficient to consider each of a finite number of interactions between classes of paths. For example, in a conjunction $(f\ \alpha) = g_\alpha \wedge (f\ \beta) = g_\beta$, the possibility that paths in α are prefixes of paths in β (case 1 in the three-way classification given above) is covered by the following disjunction (where $\alpha \cap Prefix(\beta, q)$ is the set of all paths in α which are also prefixes of paths in β passing through state q):

$$\bigvee_{q \in Q_\beta} [(f\ \alpha \cap Prefix(\beta, q)) = g_\alpha \wedge (g_\alpha\ Suffix(\beta, q)) = g_\beta]$$

Each disjunct consists of a pair of conjoined equations which are guaranteed to be free provided that the variables f and g_α are distinct. If f and g_α are not distinct, then the original description was cyclic. Cases where paths in β are prefixes of paths in α are analysed in an entirely similar fashion.

The final case in the classification given above covers the possibility that paths in α and β have a common prefix and then differ on some feature label. For each choice of states $q \in Q_\alpha$, $r \in Q_\beta$ and *distinct* feature labels l_α, l_β there will be a disjunct of the following form (where $g_{q,r}$ is a unique new variable):

$$(f\ Prefix(\alpha, q) \cap Prefix(\beta, r)) = g_{q,r}\ \wedge$$
$$(g_{q,r}\ l_\alpha Suffix(\alpha, \delta_\alpha(q, l_\alpha))) = g_\alpha \wedge (g_{q,r}\ l_\beta Suffix(\beta, \delta_\beta(r, l_\beta))) = g_\beta$$

Once again, the equations in the resulting conjunction are pair-wise free. The first conjunct cannot interact with either of the other conjuncts because the variables f and $g_{q,r}$ are distinct. The remaining two equations are free because of the stipulation that the feature labels l_α and l_β be distinct.

Bringing together all of the different ways in which paths may interact, the *Free* operator is defined as follows:

(33) $Free((f\,\alpha) = g_\alpha, (f\,\beta) = g_\beta) \equiv$

$$
\bigvee_{\substack{q \in Q_\alpha \\ r \in Q_\beta}}
\left[
\begin{array}{l}
[(f\,\alpha \cap Prefix(\beta, r)) = g_\alpha \wedge (g_\alpha\ Suffix(\beta, r)) = g_\beta] \\
\vee\ [(f\,\beta \cap Prefix(\alpha, q)) = g_\beta \wedge (g_\beta\ Suffix(\alpha, q)) = g_\alpha] \\
\vee\ \bigvee_{\substack{l_\alpha, l_\beta \in L \\ l_\alpha \neq l_\beta}}
\left[
\begin{array}{l}
(f\ Prefix(\alpha, q) \cap Prefix(\beta, r)) = g_{q,r} \wedge \\
\quad (g_{q,r}\ l_\alpha Suffix(\alpha, \delta_\alpha(q, l_\alpha))) = g_\alpha \\
\wedge\quad (g_{q,r}\ l_\beta Suffix(\beta, \delta_\beta(r, l_\beta))) = g_\beta
\end{array}
\right]
\end{array}
\right]
$$

It is shown by Kaplan and Maxwell that $Free((f\,\alpha) = g_\alpha, (f\,\beta) = g_\beta)$ is logically equivalent to the conjunction $(f\,\alpha) = g_\alpha \wedge (f\,\beta) = g_\beta$. The operator *Free* forms the basis of an iterative procedure which transforms a functional description D into a logically equivalent, but free description D'. The first step puts D into canonical form. If the result is free, then the transformation is complete. Otherwise there must be conjoined equations $(f\,\alpha) = g_\alpha$ and $(f\,\beta) = g_\beta$ in D which are not free. These equations are replaced by the logically equivalent but free description $Free((f\,\alpha) = g_\alpha, (f\,\beta) = g_\beta)$, and the procedure is then repeated. As long as the original functional description is not cyclic, this process will eventually terminate.

3.4.2   RRK and Free Descriptions

Determining satisfiability for description in **RRK** presents problems similar to those which arise in determining the satisfiability of functional descriptions with uncertainty sets. In particular, paths cannot always be freely chosen from the sets denoted by regular path expressions. If they could, then determining satisfiability would be relatively easy: simply replace each regular path expression by a freely chosen path and then apply an algorithm such as that proposed by Kasper (1987a). Indeed, for a large class of **RRK** descriptions determining satisfiability is not significantly more difficult than this. There is an effective procedure which transforms any description involving only *finitary* regular path expressions to an equivalent description in **RK**. This procedure makes use of the laws of equivalence given in the previous section and applies the following steps to a description ϕ:

1. replace each path description r occurring in ϕ with an equivalent path descriptor $(u_1+u_2+\ldots+u_k)$ where each u_i is a unitary path descriptor;

2. apply the path union laws from left to right to eliminate all occurrences of the path operator '+' in favour of logical disjunctions;

3. apply the appropriate path concatenation law from left to right to convert any description $(r \cdot s) : \psi$ to $r : s : \psi$;

4. apply the identity law to rewrite any description $\lambda : \psi$ as ψ;

5. replace each description $(u_1 \doteq u_2)$ by $(p_1 \doteq p_2)$ where $p_1 \in u_1$ and $p_2 \in u_2$.

Because all regular path expressions are assumed to be finitary, the first step is clearly possible. Moreover, it is easy to verify that following the second and third steps every description $r : \psi$ is such that r is either a feature label $l \in L$, or the null path descriptor λ. If not, then step 2 and/or step 3 should have applied. Also, in every description $(r \doteq s)$, both r and s must be unitary path descriptors. Again, if this is not the case then step 2 should have applied. Applying the identity law at step 4 eliminates all occurrences of the null path descriptor λ. The substitution of paths for unitary path descriptors at step 5 is technically necessary, given the syntax of path equations in **RK** (as presented in section 2.2 of chapter 2). The first 4 steps of the algorithm preserve logical equivalence and step 5 has an obvious semantic justification. The result is a logically equivalent description in **RK** to which Kasper's algorithm may be applied in order to determine satisfiability.

More generally of course, **RRK** descriptions may contain infinitary regular path expressions. It seems plausible to suppose that an analysis of the possible interactions between feature paths similar to that underlying the Kaplan-Maxwell algorithm may be applicable. Consider a conjunction $r : \phi \wedge s : \psi$. The possible interactions between paths chosen from r and s are covered by the three-way classification given previously. In principle these interactions could be removed in a manner analogous to the way in which the *Free* operator removes interactions amongst uncertainty sets. Suppose for example that every path in the set denoted by r is a prefix of a path in the set denoted by s. Ignoring the distinction between regular path expressions and the sets they denote[2], the conjunction $r : \phi \wedge s : \psi$ can be re-written as the following logically equivalent disjunction of descriptions:

$$\bigvee_{q \in Q_s} (r \cap \mathit{Prefix}(s, q)) : (\phi \wedge \mathit{Suffix}(s, q) : \psi)$$

In the new description, dependencies between paths from r and s have been effectively eliminated. This is not the end of the story however, as it may still be necessary to remove interactions from each of the conjunctions $(\phi \wedge \mathit{Suffix}(s, q) : \psi)$. In contrast to the simple iterative style of the Kaplan-Maxwell algorithm, any procedure for removing interactions between path sets must apply recursively.

Additional complications arise from the presence of path equations. In a description $(r \doteq s)$ dependencies may be present amongst the sets of paths denoted by r and s. It is easy to see that these interactions can be eliminated in much the same way as before. However, a problem remains concerning the interaction of path equations involving infinitary path descriptors with other **RRK** descriptions. As a simple illustration of the problem, consider the following conjunction of descriptions:

(34) $\mathbf{f}^+ : a \wedge \mathbf{g}^+ : b \wedge (\mathbf{f}^+ \doteq \mathbf{g}^+)$

The description given in (34) above is clearly satisfiable. In fact, it is satisfied by any feature structure of the following form (where each $\mathbf{f} \cdots$ represents an arbitrary, non-empty path of $\mathbf{f}$s, and similarly for each $\mathbf{g} \cdots$):

$$\begin{bmatrix} \mathbf{f} \cdots & \begin{bmatrix} \mathbf{f} \cdots & a \end{bmatrix} \boxed{1} \\ \mathbf{g} \cdots & \begin{bmatrix} \mathbf{g} \cdots & b \end{bmatrix} \boxed{1} \end{bmatrix}$$

In (34), the regular path expressions $\mathbf{f}^+$ and $\mathbf{g}^+$ do not interact. There are no paths $p \in \mathbf{f}^+$ and $p' \in \mathbf{g}^+$ which share a common prefix, and neither expression denotes a set of paths containing the null path ϵ. It follows that the first two conjuncts of (34) are pair-wise free. Moreover, the path equation $(\mathbf{f}^+ \doteq \mathbf{g}^+)$ is also free when considered in isolation. It is clear however, that certain choices of paths can still affect satisfiability. For example, choosing

---

[2]From a computational perspective this step cannot be taken so lightly. Further comments on the distinction between regular path expressions and the path sets they denote are made in the following subsection.

the path $\mathbf{f}$ for *each* occurrence of $\mathbf{f}^+$ in (34) and choosing $\mathbf{g}$ for each occurrence of $\mathbf{g}^+$ implies that $\mathbf{f} : (\mathbf{a} \wedge \mathbf{b})$, which is not satisfiable. In other words, the description in (34) is not free. The problem now it that there is simply no way of transforming (34) into a logically equivalent, but free description of **RRK**. The dependencies which exist between the first two conjuncts and the path equation $(\mathbf{f}^+ \doteq \mathbf{g}^+)$ cannot be 'factored out' of the description by isolating them in different disjuncts. In other words, the Kaplan-Maxwell algorithm cannot be modified to work directly with descriptions in **RRK**.

3.4.3   An Indirect Approach to the Satisfiability Problem

In this section it is shown that any description in **RRK** may be expressed as a formula of a language of equational constraints on feature structures. The constraint language is essentially a restricted version of the language of function-application expressions with uncertainty introduced by Kaplan and Zaenen (1986). The Kaplan-Maxwell algorithm can therefore be applied directly to formulas of this language to determine satisfiability. It follows that the satisfiability of **RRK** descriptions is decidable subject to an acyclicity condition on feature structures. As a corollary of the proof given below, the language of function-application expressions with uncertainty is at least as expressive as the language **RRK**.

The syntax of the equational language is defined with respect to three non-empty, pair-wise disjoint, denumerable sets of symbols: a set V of *variables*, a set A of *atoms* and a set L of *feature labels*. For reasons which will become apparent later, it is assumed that the set of variable symbols is given by $V = \{x_\sigma | \sigma \in \{0, 1\}^*\}$. That is, variables in V are of the form x_σ where σ is a (possibly empty) string of ones and zeros. Formulas of the language are strings over the alphabet $V \cup A \cup R \cup \{\approx, \wedge, \vee, (,)\}$, where R is the set of regular path expressions over L. In the following, the symbols v and w (possibly with subscripts) belong to the meta-language used to talk about formulas of the constraint language and denote variables in V. Similarly, the symbols a and b are used to denote atoms in A, while r, s, u, etc. refer to path descriptors in R. The constraint language is defined as the smallest set of constraints which contains:

- $(v \approx w)$ for $v, w \in V$;

- $(v \approx a)$ for $v \in V$ and $a \in A$.

- $((v\, r) \approx w)$ for $v, w \in V$, and $r \in R$.

- $(C \wedge C')$ for C, C' constraints.

- $(C \vee C')$. for C, C' constraints.

Constraints are interpreted in the set of feature structures defined over atoms in A and labels in L. Because constraints contain occurrences of free variables, it is necessary to introduce the notion of a *variable assignment*. Accordingly, a *model* is defined as a pair $\langle \mathcal{A}, \alpha \rangle$, where $\mathcal{A} = \langle Q, q_0, \delta, \pi \rangle$ is a feature structure, and $\alpha : V \to Q$ is a total function from variables to states of $\mathcal{A}$ (an $\mathcal{A}$-*assignment*). It should be noted that an $\mathcal{A}$-assignment α is not necessarily onto. That is, there may be states in Q which are not equal to $\alpha(v)$ for any variable v. The satisfaction relation $\models$ between models and constraints is defined as follows:

- $\langle \mathcal{A}, \alpha \rangle \models (v \approx w) \Leftrightarrow \alpha(v) = \alpha(w)$

- $\langle \mathcal{A}, \alpha \rangle \models (v \approx a) \Leftrightarrow \pi(\alpha(v)) = a$

- $\langle \mathcal{A}, \alpha \rangle \models ((v\, r) \approx w) \Leftrightarrow \exists p \in r$ such that $\delta^*(\alpha(v), p) = \alpha(w)$

- $\langle \mathcal{A}, \alpha \rangle \models (C \wedge C') \Leftrightarrow \langle \mathcal{A}, \alpha \rangle \models C$ and $\langle \mathcal{A}, \alpha \rangle \models C'$

- $\langle \mathcal{A}, \alpha \rangle \models (C \vee C') \Leftrightarrow \langle \mathcal{A}, \alpha \rangle \models C$ or $\langle \mathcal{A}, \alpha \rangle \models C'$

A constraint C is *satisfiable* just in case there is a feature structure $\mathcal{A}$ and $\mathcal{A}$-assignment α such that $\langle \mathcal{A}, \alpha \rangle \models C$.

Proposition 3.8 The satisfiability problem for constraints involving only unitary path descriptors of the form $(l_1 \cdot l_2 \cdot \ldots l_k)$ for $k \geq 1$ is decidable.

Proof: There are various ways to establish the proposition. For example, it is possible to provide a reduction to the quantifier-free first order theory of equality similar to that described by Johnson (1988) for the attribute-value languages.   □

Proposition 3.9 Let C be an arbitrary constraint. If C is non-cyclic, then it is possible to construct a constraint C' involving only unitary path descriptors of the kind required by proposition 3.8, and such that C is satisfiable if and only if C' is satisfiable.

Proof: It can be shown that the Kaplan-Maxwell algorithm may be applied to the constraint C to remove any interactions between path descriptors. An apparent problem here concerns the distinction between regular path expressions and the sets of paths they denote. In particular, the *Free* operator manipulates sets of paths and not path descriptors. To overcome this problem, it is necessary to find an alternative representation for path sets such that:

- representations may be manipulated in exactly the same way as path sets; and

- the representations can be computed from regular path expressions (and *vice-versa*).

An obvious candidate for such a representation is the finite state automaton. For any regular path expression r it is possible to construct an automaton M_r which recognises the set of paths denoted by r (Hopcroft and Ullman 1979). In addition, appropriate prefix and suffix automata may be constructed corresponding to the prefix and suffix sets used in the definition of *Free*. Finally, given automata M_r and M_s it is possible to build a product automaton $M_r \times M_s$ which recognizes the intersection of the sets of paths accepted by M_r and M_s separately. Thus, it is possible to regard the *Free* operator as removing dependencies between path sets represented in terms of finite state automata. Once all possible interactions between feature paths have been removed from a constraint C, the constraint C' is obtained by replacing each 'path set automaton' by some unitary path descriptor $(l_1 \cdot l_2 \cdot \ldots l_n)$ where $l_1 l_2 \ldots l_n$ is accepted by that automaton[3].   □

It is now shown that any **RRK** description may be expressed in the language of equational constraints. A mapping from descriptions to constraints is defined, with the property that a description is satisfiable if and only if it has a satisfiable translation. Before defining this mapping, some complications arising from the use of variables in the constraint language will be noted.

---

[3] This isn't yet quite correct, as it overlooks the possibility that the set of paths recognized by some automaton M is empty. However, if the path set recognized by M is empty, then any equation $((v\,M) \approx w)$ in which it appears must be unsatisfiable. In this case, the equation can be replaced by some other 'obviously unsatisfiable' constraint of an appropriate form; e.g. $(v \approx a) \wedge (v \approx b)$ for $a, b \in A$ with $a \neq b$.

First, according to the interpretation of constraints given above, variables pick out states in a feature structure $\mathcal{A}$, and may be regarded as denoting or referring to certain feature values. Precisely what feature value in $\mathcal{A}$ a particular variable denotes depends on the choice of the $\mathcal{A}$-assignment α. However, the same variable always refers to the same value wherever it appears in a constraint. For example, the conjunction $((vl) \approx g_f) \wedge ((vl') \approx g_g)$ states that the (complex) value referred to by v is defined for the feature labels l and l'. In the absence of any further information about the values g_f and g_g, such a constraint might be expressed in **RRK** as $l : \top \wedge l' : \top$. In this case, the fact that the descriptions $l : \top$ and $l' : \top$ constrain the same feature value is indicated simply by conjoining them. In translating from **RRK** to the simple constraint language then, variables must be introduced which 'tie together' equational constraints in an appropriate fashion.

Second, it is necessary to keep track of variables as they are introduced during the translation process. Consider a conjunction $l : \phi \wedge l' : \phi$. In translating each occurrence of the description ϕ a *different* set of variables must be used. Otherwise, additional and unwarranted constraints may be placed on the values of the feature labels l and l'. This shows that the mapping from **RRK** to the constraint language should be sensitive to the structure of **RRK** descriptions: 'identical' sub-expressions need to be given different translations depending on where they occur in a description.

Accordingly, a whole family of translation functions $\{\tau_\sigma\}_{\sigma \in \Sigma}$ is defined. The members of this family are indexed by elements of the set $\Sigma = \{0, 1\}^*$. The idea is that $\tau_\sigma(\phi)$ represents the translation of the **RRK** description ϕ viewed as a constraint on the feature value denoted by the variable x_σ. Let ϕ be a description. For each $\sigma \in \Sigma$ the mapping τ_σ is defined as follows:

1. ϕ is $\perp \Rightarrow \tau_\sigma(\phi) = (x_\sigma \approx a) \wedge (x_\sigma \approx b)$ for $a, b \in A$ with $a \neq b$.

2. ϕ is $\top \Rightarrow \tau_\sigma(\phi) = (x_\sigma \approx x_\sigma)$

3. ϕ is $a \in A \Rightarrow \tau_\sigma(\phi) = (x_\sigma \approx a)$

4. ϕ is $r : \psi \Rightarrow \tau_\sigma(\phi) = ((x_\sigma \, r) \approx x_{\sigma 0}) \wedge \tau_{\sigma 0}(\psi)$

5. ϕ is $(\psi \wedge \chi) \Rightarrow \tau_\sigma(\phi) = (x_\sigma \approx x_{\sigma 0}) \wedge (x_\sigma \approx x_{\sigma 1}) \wedge \tau_{\sigma 0}(\psi) \wedge \tau_{\sigma 1}(\chi)$

6. ϕ is $(\psi \vee \chi) \Rightarrow \tau_\sigma(\phi) = \tau_\sigma(\psi) \vee \tau_\sigma(\chi)$

7. ϕ is $(r \doteq s) \Rightarrow \tau_\sigma(\phi) = ((x_\sigma \, r) \approx x_{\sigma 0}) \wedge ((x_\sigma \, s) \approx x_{\sigma 0})$

The following example illustrates the way in which a description in **RRK** is translated into the equational constraint language.

Example 3.10 Consider the following **RRK** description:

$$\mathsf{cat} : \mathsf{S} \land (\mathsf{topic} \doteq (\mathsf{comp}^* \cdot (\mathsf{subj} + \mathsf{obj})))$$

The translation of this description viewed as a constraint on the value referred to by the variable x_ϵ is given by:

$$
\begin{aligned}
&\tau_\epsilon(\mathsf{cat} : \mathsf{S} \land (\mathsf{topic} \doteq (\mathsf{comp}^* \cdot (\mathsf{subj} + \mathsf{obj})))) \\
&= (x_\epsilon \approx x_0) \land (x_\epsilon \approx x_1) \land \tau_0(\mathsf{cat} : \mathsf{S}) \\
&\qquad \land\ \tau_1((\mathsf{topic} \doteq (\mathsf{comp}^* \cdot (\mathsf{subj} + \mathsf{obj})))) \\
&= (x_\epsilon \approx x_0) \land (x_\epsilon \approx x_1) \land ((x_0\, \mathsf{cat}) \approx x_{00}) \land \tau_{00}(\mathsf{S}) \\
&\qquad \land\ \tau_1((\mathsf{topic} \doteq (\mathsf{comp}^* \cdot (\mathsf{subj} + \mathsf{obj})))) \\
&= (x_\epsilon \approx x_0) \land (x_\epsilon \approx x_1) \land ((x_0\, \mathsf{cat}) \approx x_{00}) \land (x_{00} \approx \mathsf{S}) \\
&\qquad \land\ \tau_1((\mathsf{topic} \doteq (\mathsf{comp}^* \cdot (\mathsf{subj} + \mathsf{obj})))) \\
&= (x_\epsilon \approx x_0) \land (x_\epsilon \approx x_1) \land ((x_0\, \mathsf{cat}) \approx x_{00}) \land (x_{00} \approx \mathsf{S}) \\
&\qquad \land\ ((x_1\, \mathsf{topic}) \approx x_{10}) \land ((x_1\, (\mathsf{comp}^* \cdot (\mathsf{subj} + \mathsf{obj}))) \approx x_{10})
\end{aligned}
$$

It is shown below that a description ϕ in **RRK** is satisfiable just in case it has a satisfiable translation. More precisely, is is shown that ϕ is satisfied by a feature structure $\mathcal{A}$ if and only if the constraint $\tau_\sigma(\phi)$ has a model $\langle \mathcal{A}, \alpha \rangle$. The significance of this result is that any algorithm for computing the model $\langle \mathcal{A}, \alpha \rangle$ can also be considered as an algorithm for computing a satisfying feature structure for ϕ. Before presenting the proof, some additional notions and lemmas are required.

For any constraint C, let $Vars(C) \subseteq V$ denote the set of all variables which occur in C. For example, $Vars(((x_\sigma r) \approx x_{\sigma 1})) = \{x_\sigma, x_{\sigma 1}\}$. Note that $Vars((C \land C'))$ is given by $Vars(C) \cup Vars(C')$ (and similarly for a disjunctive constraint). Two constraints C and C' are called *independent* just in case $Vars(C) \cap Vars(C') = \emptyset$. Also, for α an $\mathcal{A}$-assignment and $X \subseteq V$ a set of variables, let $\alpha | X$ be that *partial* function from variables to states of $\mathcal{A}$ such that $\alpha | X(v) = \alpha(v)$ if $v \in X$; and $\alpha | X(v)$ is undefined otherwise. The following lemma shows that in considering whether a model satisfies some constraint C, assignments to variables which do not actually appear in C are irrelevant and can therefore be ignored:

Lemma 3.11 *Let $\mathcal{A}$ be a feature structure and α and β $\mathcal{A}$-assignments. For any constraint C, if $\alpha|\text{Vars}(C) = \beta|\text{Vars}(C)$ then $\langle \mathcal{A}, \alpha \rangle \models C$ iff $\langle \mathcal{A}, \beta \rangle \models C$.*

Proof: The proof is by straightforward induction on the structure of constraints. Let $\mathcal{A}$, α and β be as in the lemma. It must be shown that: (1) the required result holds for any constraint consisting of a single equation; and (2) assuming that the required result holds for constraints C' and C'', then it also holds for $(C' \wedge C'')$ and $(C' \vee C'')$.

1. It is shown that the result holds when C is of the form $((v\ r) \approx w)$, the other cases being similar. By definition, $\langle \mathcal{A}, \alpha \rangle \models C$ iff $\exists p \in r$ such that $\delta^*(\alpha(v), p) = \alpha(w)$. If $\alpha|\text{Vars}(C) = \beta|\text{Vars}(C)$, then this is equivalent to $\delta^*(\beta(v), p) = \beta(w)$, whence $\langle \mathcal{A}, \alpha \rangle \models C$ iff $\langle \mathcal{A}, \beta \rangle \models C$.

2. Suppose C is of the form $(C' \wedge C'')$. If $\alpha|\text{Vars}(C) = \beta|\text{Vars}(C)$, then since $\text{Vars}(C) = \text{Vars}(C') \cup \text{Vars}(C'')$ it follows that $\alpha|\text{Vars}(C') = \beta|\text{Vars}(C')$ and $\alpha|\text{Vars}(C'') = \beta|\text{Vars}(C'')$. By hypothesis, $\langle \mathcal{A}, \alpha \rangle \models C'$ iff $\langle \mathcal{A}, \beta \rangle \models C'$ and $\langle \mathcal{A}, \alpha \rangle \models C''$ iff $\langle \mathcal{A}, \beta \rangle \models C''$. But then $\langle \mathcal{A}, \alpha \rangle \models C$ iff $\langle \mathcal{A}, \beta \rangle \models C$. The case where C is of the form $(C' \vee C'')$ is entirely similar.

□

The next lemma states that a constraint C has a model $\langle \mathcal{B}, \alpha \rangle$ just in case it has a model $\langle \mathcal{A}, \alpha \rangle$ which is 'larger' in the sense that $\mathcal{B}$ is the value of some path p in A.

Lemma 3.12 *Let $\mathcal{A}$ be a feature structure, $p \in \text{Paths}(\mathcal{A})$ and α an $\mathcal{A}/p$-assignment. For any constraint C, $\langle \mathcal{A}/p, \alpha \rangle \models C$ iff $\langle \mathcal{A}, \alpha \rangle \models C$.*

Proof: The proof is again by induction on the structure of constraints. Since it proceeds in almost exactly the same way as the proof of lemma 3.11, the details are omitted here.

□

The final lemma given here proves useful in reasoning about models of constraints obtained 'by translation' from descriptions in **RRK**.

Lemma 3.13 *For any description ϕ in* **RRK** *$\text{Vars}(\tau_\sigma(\phi)) \subset \{x_{\sigma\sigma'}|\sigma' \in \Sigma\}$*

Proof: Inspecting the definition of τ_σ, it is obvious that the result holds when ϕ is of the form $\bot$, $\top$, a or $(r \doteq s)$. Moreover, assuming that the result holds for descriptions ψ and χ, it is easy to verify that it holds when ϕ is $r : \psi$, $(\psi \wedge \chi)$ or $(\psi \vee \chi)$. For example, if ϕ is $r : \psi$ then

$$
\begin{aligned}
Vars(\tau_\sigma(\phi)) \;&=\; Vars(((x_\sigma\, r) \approx x_{\sigma 0})) \cup Vars(\tau_{\sigma 0}(\psi)) \\
&\subset\; \{x_\sigma, x_{\sigma 0}\} \cup \{x_{\sigma 0 \sigma'} | \sigma' \in \Sigma\} \\
&\subset\; \{x_{\sigma \sigma'} | \sigma' \in \Sigma\}
\end{aligned}
$$

$\square$

A straightforward and useful corollary of lemma 3.13 stated here without proof is that for any descriptions ϕ and ψ, the constraints $\tau_{\sigma 0}(\phi)$ and $\tau_{\sigma 1}(\psi)$ are independent. The main result can now be stated:

Theorem 3.14 *Let ϕ be a description in* **RRK** *and $\mathcal{A} = \langle Q, q_0, \delta, \phi \rangle$ a feature structure. $\mathcal{A} \models \phi$ if and only if there exists an $\mathcal{A}$-assignment α such that $\langle \mathcal{A}, \alpha \rangle \models \tau_\sigma(\phi)$ and $\alpha(x_\sigma) = q_0$.*

Proof: The proof proceeds by induction on the structure of a description ϕ in **RRK**. If ϕ is either $\bot$, $\top$ or an atom a, then the required result follows almost immediately from the definition of τ_σ. If ϕ is a path equation $(r \doteq s)$, then note that $\mathcal{A} \models \phi$ iff $\exists p \in r$ and $\exists p' \in s$ such that $\delta^*(q_0, p)$ and $\delta^*(q_0, p')$ are defined and denote the same state in $\mathcal{A}$. Let α be an $\mathcal{A}$-assignment such that $\alpha(x_\sigma) = q_0$ and $\alpha(x_{\sigma 0}) = \delta^*(q_0, p) = \delta^*(q_0, p')$. Then $\mathcal{A} \models \phi$ iff $\langle \mathcal{A}, \alpha \rangle \models ((x_\sigma\, r) \approx x_{\sigma 0})$ and $\langle \mathcal{A}, \alpha \rangle \models ((x_\sigma\, s) \approx x_{\sigma 0})$, which in turn is just equivalent to $\langle \mathcal{A}, \alpha \rangle \models \tau_\sigma(r \doteq s)$.

Now suppose that the required result holds for descriptions ψ and χ. It is shown that the result holds when ϕ is of the form $r : \psi$, $(\psi \wedge \chi)$ or $(\psi \vee \chi)$. If ϕ is $r : \psi$, then $\mathcal{A} \models \phi$ iff $\exists p \in r$ such that $\delta^*(q_0, p)$ is defined and $\mathcal{A}/p \models \psi$. Note that $\delta^*(q_0, p)$ is the start state of $\mathcal{A}/p$. By hypothesis, $\mathcal{A}/p \models \psi$ iff there is some $\mathcal{A}/p$-assignment β such that $\langle \mathcal{A}/p, \beta \rangle \models \tau_{\sigma 0}(\psi)$, where $\beta(x_{\sigma 0}) = \delta^*(q_0, p)$. But by lemma 3.12, $\langle \mathcal{A}/p, \beta \rangle \models \tau_{\sigma 0}(\psi)$ iff $\langle \mathcal{A}, \beta \rangle \models \tau_{\sigma 0}(\psi)$, and by lemma 3.11, for any $\mathcal{A}$-assignment α if $\alpha | Vars(\tau_{\sigma 0}(\psi)) = \beta | Vars(\tau_{\sigma 0}(\psi))$, then $\langle \mathcal{A}, \alpha \rangle \models \tau_{\sigma 0}(\psi)$ iff $\langle \mathcal{A}, \beta \rangle \models \tau_{\sigma 0}(\psi)$. From lemma 3.13, $x_\sigma \notin Vars(\tau_{\sigma 0})$, so it is possible to choose α such that $\alpha(x_\sigma) = q_0$. But then $\delta^*(\alpha(x_\sigma), p) = \alpha(x_{\sigma 0})$ and also $\langle \mathcal{A}, \alpha \rangle \models \tau_{\sigma 0}(\psi)$, which is just equivalent to $\langle \mathcal{A}, \alpha \rangle \models ((x_\sigma\, r) \approx x_{\sigma 0})$ and $\langle \mathcal{A}, \alpha \rangle \models \tau_{\sigma 0}(\psi)$, and in turn to $\langle \mathcal{A}, \alpha \rangle \models \tau_\sigma(\phi)$

If ϕ is $(\psi \wedge \chi)$, then by hypothesis there are $\mathcal{A}$-assignments β and β' such that $\mathcal{A} \models \psi$ iff $\langle \mathcal{A}, \beta \rangle \models \tau_{\sigma 0}(\psi)$, and $\mathcal{A} \models \chi$ iff $\langle \mathcal{A}, \beta' \rangle \models \tau_{\sigma 1}(\chi)$, where $\beta(x_{\sigma 0}) = \beta'(x_{\sigma 1}) = q_0$. Now from lemma 3.13 the constraints $\tau_{\sigma 0}(\psi)$ and

$\tau_{\sigma 1}(\chi)$ are independent. Furthermore, the variable x_σ occurs in neither constraint. It follows that there is some $\mathcal{A}$-assignment α such that:

(i) $\alpha| \operatorname{Vars}(\tau_{\sigma 0}(\psi)) = \beta| \operatorname{Vars}(\tau_{\sigma 0}(\psi))$;

(ii) $\alpha| \operatorname{Vars}(\tau_{\sigma 1}(\chi)) = \beta'| \operatorname{Vars}(\tau_{\sigma 1}(\chi))$; and

(iii) $\alpha(x_\sigma) = q_0$.

By lemma 3.11, $\langle \mathcal{A}, \alpha \rangle \models \tau_{\sigma 0}(\psi)$ iff $\langle \mathcal{A}, \beta \rangle \models \tau_{\sigma 0}(\psi)$. Similarly $\langle \mathcal{A}, \beta \rangle \models \tau_{\sigma 1}(\chi)$ iff $\langle \mathcal{A}, \beta' \rangle \models \tau_{\sigma 1}(\chi)$. It follows that $\mathcal{A} \models \phi$ iff $\langle \mathcal{A}, \alpha \rangle \models \tau_{\sigma 0}(\psi) \wedge \tau_{\sigma 1}(\chi)$. Moreover, $\alpha(x_{\sigma 0}) = \alpha(x_\sigma) = \alpha(x_{\sigma 1})$ so $\langle \mathcal{A}, \alpha \rangle \models (x_\sigma \approx x_{\sigma 0}) \wedge (x_\sigma \approx x_{\sigma 1})$ whence $\langle \mathcal{A}, \alpha \rangle \models (x_\sigma \approx x_{\sigma 0}) \wedge (x_\sigma \approx x_{\sigma 1}) \wedge \tau_{\sigma 0}(\psi) \wedge \tau_{\sigma 1}(\chi)$ if and only if $\langle \mathcal{A}, \alpha \rangle \models \tau_\sigma(\phi)$.

The case where ϕ is of the form $(\psi \vee \chi)$ is similar. □

3.5   Conclusions

The feature logic described in this chapter can be viewed as an extension of Rounds-Kasper logic which incorporates the linguistically useful device of functional uncertainty due to Kaplan and Zaenen. The language of Regular Rounds-Kasper logic can be used to express certain kinds of infinite disjunction, and has applications to the analysis of unbounded dependencies in natural languages. The properties of this logic have been investigated and the principal results of this investigation are as follows.

- The logical equivalence classes of **RRK** formulas cannot be characterized in terms of finite sets of subsumption-incomparable feature structures. Thus, **RRK** is strictly more expressive than **RK**: there are statements about feature structures expressible in the former language which are ineffable in the latter (but not *vice-versa*)

- The logical equivalence problem for **RRK** descriptions contains the equivalence problem for regular expressions as a subproblem, and is thus PSPACE-hard. It is not yet known whether or not the problem of determining equivalence for descriptions is PSPACE-complete.

- It has been shown that the satisfiability problem for **RRK** is decidable subject to an acyclicity condition on feature structures. Designing a procedure for determining satisfiability which works directly with **RRK** is complicated by the structure of descriptions and the use of path equations to express re-entrancy in feature structures. In particular, it is not possible in general to transform a description ϕ into a logically equivalent description ϕ' in which paths may be freely chosen from the sets denoted by path descriptors. For this reason, the proof is stated in terms of a translation from **RRK** to a simpler language of equational constraints on feature structures.

In the next chapter the language **RRK** is further extended to incorporate description negation. It is shown that the resulting language is strong enough to capture generalizations about features and their values, and allows for the possibility of expressing 'recursive' definitions of particular classes of feature structures.

Chapter 4

Regular Rounds-Kasper Logic with Negation

In this chapter, the domain of descriptions of Regular Rounds-Kasper logic is extended to incorporate negative constraints on feature structures. The primary motivation for investigating this extension stems from the observation that regular path expressions express existential quantification over particular feature values within a feature structure. With the introduction of negation, it becomes possible to express universal quantification over feature values, allowing for the statement of powerful constraints which apply to successively embedded levels of structure. The language of *Regular Rounds-Kasper logic with Negation* (**NRRK**) introduced in this chapter is strong enough to express generalizations about features and their values.

The ability to express generalizations in **NRRK** recalls the constraint language L_C (Category Logic) introduced by Gazdar et al. (1988). Category Logic includes two modal operators $\Box$ and $\Diamond$ which allow for the formulation of generalized constraints on features and their values. Section 4.3 explores the relationship between the languages **NRRK** and L_C, and it is shown that the modal operators of L_C can be simulated in terms of regular path expressions and negation. In fact, Category Logic can be viewed as just a restricted version of **NRRK**.

Section 4.4 provides a demonstration that the satisfiability problem for **NRRK** is undecidable. This result is obtained by a reduction from the halting problem for Turing machines to **NRRK** satisfiability. Given a Turing machine M and input string x, it is possible to construct a description ϕ in **NRRK** with the property that ϕ is satisfiable just in case M halts

94

on x. It is also noted that the undecidability result is due to the possibility of expressing generalizations involving constraints on re-entrancy in feature structures. More precisely, the fragment of **NRRK** without path equations is shown to be a variant of the language of *Deterministic Propositional Dynamic Logic* (**DPDL**), which is known to be decidable (Ben-Ari et al. (1982), Harel (1984)).

4.1   Syntax and Semantics

The language of *Regular Rounds-Kasper logic with Negation* is defined as the language **RRK** with the addition of a unary negation operator $\neg$ (read 'not'). More precisely, the language **NRRK** is taken as the smallest set of descriptions formed according to all of the rules for **RRK** given in the previous chapter, together with the following:

- $\neg\phi$ for ϕ a description

The following abbreviations will also be adopted: $(\phi \to \psi)$ for $(\neg\phi \vee \psi)$, and $(\phi \leftrightarrow \psi)$ for $((\phi \to \psi) \wedge (\psi \to \phi))$.

The interpretation of description negation considered here is entirely classical: a feature structure $\mathcal{A}$ satisfies a negative description $\neg\phi$ just in case it fails to satisfy ϕ. Thus, the appropriate clause in the definition of the satisfaction relation $\models$ is as shown below:

$$\mathcal{A} \models \neg\phi \text{ iff } \mathcal{A} \not\models \phi$$

A description ϕ in **NRRK** is said to be *satisfiable* if there exists a feature structure $\mathcal{A}$ such that $\mathcal{A} \models \phi$, and otherwise ϕ is said to be *unsatisfiable*. The description ϕ is said to be *valid* if $\mathcal{A} \models \phi$ for every feature structure $\mathcal{A}$. Some examples of descriptions in **NRRK** which are valid under the intended semantics are presented next.

(35) $r : (\phi \vee \psi) \leftrightarrow r : \phi \vee r : \psi$

$(r \cdot s) : \phi \leftrightarrow r : s : \phi$

$(r + s) : \phi \leftrightarrow r : \phi \vee s : \phi$

$r^* : \phi \leftrightarrow \phi \vee r : r^* : \phi$

The valid descriptions (more correctly, description schemas) in (35) are derived from the laws of logical equivalence for **RRK** discussed in section 3.3.2

of the previous chapter. In general, for any equivalence $\phi \simeq \psi$ of **RRK** it can be shown that the description $\phi \leftrightarrow \psi$ is valid in **NRRK**. In addition, if $\phi \simeq \phi \wedge \psi$ is an equivalence of **RRK**, then $\phi \rightarrow \psi$ is valid in **NRRK**. Consequently, the following conditional descriptions (amongst others) are also valid:

$$(36) \qquad ((r \cdot s) \doteq t) \rightarrow (r \doteq r)$$
$$(r \doteq u) \wedge (u \doteq s) \rightarrow (r \doteq s)$$
$$(r \doteq u) \wedge u : \phi \rightarrow r : \phi$$

The next validity asserts that if a particular path has some value, then it cannot have some other (incompatible) value. This can be viewed as one of the defining properties of feature structures, and amounts to a formal statement of the *functional uniqueness* condition on f-structures in Lexical Functional Grammar:

$$(37) \quad u : \phi \rightarrow \neg u : \neg \phi$$

It is notable that the validities given in (35) above bear a striking resemblance to the axioms of *Propositional Dynamic Logic* (**PDL**) (Fischer and Ladner (1977, 1979), Segerberg (1977), Harel (1984)). Dynamic logic is an outgrowth of modal logic which has proved useful in the field of computer science for reasoning about properties of programs. In **PDL**, programs are interpreted as relations on computational states and may be regarded as modal operators on formulas. Furthermore, programs may be composed in various ways. For example, if π and π' are programs, then $\pi ; \pi'$ means "do π and then do π'", $\pi \cup \pi'$ means "nondeterministically do either π or π'" and π^* means "repeat π a finite, nondeterministic number of times". If π is a program (possibly non-deterministic) and p a proposition, then it is possible to construct a new proposition $\langle \pi \rangle p$ meaning that on some termination of the program π, the proposition p is true. Similarly, an assertion $[\pi]p$ means that on every termination of π the proposition p holds. The second validity given in (35) above is expressed in **PDL** by a proposition of the form $\langle \pi ; \pi' \rangle p \leftrightarrow \langle \pi \rangle \langle \pi' \rangle p$. In words, p holds on termination of "do π and then do π'" just in case on termination of π, the statement that p holds on termination of π' is true.

The conditional validities in (36) have no counterpart in **PDL**, which lacks any means of expressing identity between computational states. However, the **NRRK** validity in (37) is essentially equivalent to the characteristic axiom of *Deterministic Propositional Dynamic Logic* (**DPDL**).

In **DPDL** the elementary programs are deterministic, and are interpreted as functions (rather than more general relations) on computational states. Later on, the correspondence between **NRRK** and **DPDL** will prove useful in studying the computational properties of **NRRK**. First however, it will be shown that the language is strong enough to express generalizations about features and their values.

4.2   Expressing Generalizations in NRRK

In the language **NRRK**, the combination of regular path expressions and negation provides the power necessary to state generalizations about feature structures. In the previous chapter it was seen that regular path expressions can be used to express existential quantification over feature values within a feature structure. That is to say, a description $r : \phi$ is satisfied by a feature structure $\mathcal{A}$ just in case there is *some* path $p \in r$ such that $\mathcal{A}/p$ is defined and satisfies ϕ. If the path descriptor r is infinitary, then a description of this kind may represent an infinite disjunction of descriptions, where each disjunct corresponds to a particular choice of path from the set denoted by r. With the introduction of description negation, it becomes possible to convert existential quantification over feature values to universal quantification according to the familiar equivalence: $\forall x \phi(x) \Leftrightarrow \neg \exists x \neg \phi(x)$.

Proposition 4.1 Let r be a path descriptor and ϕ a description.

$$\mathcal{A} \models \neg r : \neg \phi \Leftrightarrow \forall p \in r, p \in Paths(\mathcal{A}) \Rightarrow \mathcal{A}/p \models \phi$$

Proof: $\mathcal{A} \models \neg r : \neg \phi$ just in case $\neg \exists p \in r$ where $p \in Paths(\mathcal{A})$ and $\mathcal{A}/p \not\models \phi$. Equivalently, $\forall p \in r$, if $p \in Paths(\mathcal{A})$ then $\mathcal{A}/p \models \phi$.   □

There is a clear connection between the ability to express universal quantification over feature values, and the ability to state generalizations about feature structures. This is the content of the following proposition.

Proposition 4.2 Let r be a path descriptor and ϕ a description.

$$\mathcal{A} \models \neg r^* : \neg \phi \Leftrightarrow \mathcal{A} \models \phi \text{ and } \forall p \in r, p \in Paths(\mathcal{A}) \Rightarrow \mathcal{A}/p \models \neg r^* : \neg \phi$$

Proof: From proposition 4.1:

$$
\begin{aligned}
\mathcal{A} \models \neg r^* : \neg\phi \;\;\Leftrightarrow\;\; & \forall p \in r^*, p \in Paths(\mathcal{A}) \Rightarrow \mathcal{A}/p \models \phi \\
\Leftrightarrow\;\; & \forall p \in (\lambda + r \cdot r^*), p \in Paths(\mathcal{A}) \Rightarrow \mathcal{A}/p \models \phi \\
\Leftrightarrow\;\; & \mathcal{A} \models \phi \text{ and } \forall p \in r \cdot r^*, p \in Paths(\mathcal{A}) \Rightarrow \mathcal{A}/p \models \phi \\
\Leftrightarrow\;\; & \mathcal{A} \models \phi \text{ and } \mathcal{A} \models \neg(r \cdot r^*) : \neg\phi \\
& \text{(again from proposition 4.1)} \\
\Leftrightarrow\;\; & \mathcal{A} \models \phi \text{ and } \mathcal{A} \models \neg r : r^* : \neg\phi \\
\Leftrightarrow\;\; & \mathcal{A} \models \phi \text{ and } \mathcal{A} \models \neg r : \neg\neg r^* : \neg\phi \\
\Leftrightarrow\;\; & \mathcal{A} \models \phi \text{ and } \forall p \in r, p \in Paths(\mathcal{A}) \Rightarrow \mathcal{A}/p \models \neg r^* : \neg\phi \\
& \text{(from proposition 4.1)}
\end{aligned}
$$

$\square$

In **NRRK**, a description of the form $\neg r^* : \neg\phi$ expresses a generalization about the values of paths in r^* which are defined within a feature structure. Such generalizations can be used to characterize particular classes of feature structures, as illustrated by the following example.

Example 4.3 There is a widely used scheme for representing lists or sequences of elements in feature structures (see for example Shieber (1986a) and Johnson (1988)). This scheme depends on the following inductive definition of list structures: a list is either empty, or it consists of a first element followed by the rest of the list. In order to encode a list in a feature structure, the empty list is represented by some distinguished atomic value such as nil. A non-empty list can then be encoded in a feature structure with the attributes **first** and **rest**, where the value of **first** represents the first element of the list and the value of **rest** represents the list of remaining elements. For example, a feature structure representing the three element list $[a, b, c]$ is given in matrix form in figure 4.1.

Note that under the suggested scheme, any feature structure $\mathcal{A}$ which represents a list satisfies the following description:

(38) $((\mathsf{first} : \top \wedge \mathsf{rest} : \top) \vee \mathsf{nil})$

If $\mathcal{A}$ represents the empty list, then $\mathcal{A}$ satisfies nil; otherwise $\mathcal{A}$ represents a non-empty list and accordingly is defined for the feature labels **first** and **rest**. In the latter case of course, the feature structure $\mathcal{A}/\mathsf{rest}$ represents the list of remaining elements and therefore must also satisfy (38).

$$\left[\begin{array}{ll} \text{first} & \text{a} \\ \text{rest} & \left[\begin{array}{ll} \text{first} & \text{b} \\ \text{rest} & \left[\begin{array}{ll} \text{first} & \text{c} \\ \text{rest} & \text{nil} \end{array}\right] \end{array}\right] \end{array}\right]$$

Figure 4.1: Feature structure representation of a list

Consider now the following description, which expresses a generalization about the values of paths in rest^*:

(39) $\neg\text{rest}^* : \neg((\text{first} : \top \wedge \text{rest} : \top) \vee \text{nil})$

It can be shown that the description in (39) amounts to a definition of the class of list structures (as represented in feature structures). That is, a feature structure $\mathcal{A}$ satisfies (39) just in case $\mathcal{A}$ is a representation of a list. Suppose first that $\mathcal{A}$ is a feature structure which represents some list of items. In this case it is clear that the following holds:

(40) $\forall p \in \text{rest}^*$, if $p \in Paths(\mathcal{A})$ then $\mathcal{A}/p$ satisfies (38)

For example, the feature structure of figure 4.1 meets this condition. But then from proposition 4.1 it must be that $\mathcal{A}$ satisfies (39).

Now consider a feature structure $\mathcal{A}$ which satisfies (39). A simple inductive argument suffices to show that $\mathcal{A}$ represents a list. Let $|\mathcal{A}|_{\text{rest}}$ denote the largest integer n such that $\exists p \in \text{rest}^n$ where $\mathcal{A}/p$ is defined. Suppose that $|\mathcal{A}|_{\text{rest}} = 0$. By proposition 4.2 it must be that $\mathcal{A}$ satisfies (38). Furthermore, because $\mathcal{A}/\text{rest}$ is undefined, it can only be that $\mathcal{A} \models \text{nil}$, whence $\mathcal{A}$ is a representation of the empty list.

Now suppose that the required result holds for any feature structure $\mathcal{B}$ such that $|\mathcal{B}|_{\text{rest}} < k$ for some $k > 0$. Suppose that $\mathcal{A}$ is a feature structure such that $|\mathcal{A}|_{\text{rest}} = k$. In this case, $\mathcal{A}/\text{rest}$ is defined and clearly $|\mathcal{A}/\text{rest}|_{\text{rest}} < k$. By proposition 4.2, $\mathcal{A}$ satisfies (38), and since $\mathcal{A}/\text{rest}$ is defined, it cannot be that $\mathcal{A} \models \text{nil}$, whence $\mathcal{A}$ is defined for both first and rest. Moreover, $\mathcal{A}/\text{rest}$ satisfies (39) and so by hypothesis $\mathcal{A}/\text{rest}$ represents a list. It follows that $\mathcal{A}$ also represents a list.

4.3   NRRK and Category Logic

It is interesting to compare the language **NRRK** introduced in this chapter with the constraint language L_C due to Gazdar et al. (1988). In this section it is shown that L_C can be regarded as a restricted version of the language **NRRK**. The syntax and semantics of L_C have already been described in section 2.3 of chapter 2. The language L_C resembles the logic of Rounds and Kasper, but incorporates (classical) negation, and two modal operators on descriptions, $\diamond$ and $\square$. The modal operators allow for the formulation of 'recursive' descriptions, which apply to successively embedded feature values within a feature structure. Consider for example the following L_C constraint:

(41) $\square((n : 1 \wedge v : 0) \rightarrow \text{case})$

The description in (41) requires that any feature structure specified for the feature labels n and v, with values 1 and 0 respectively, is also specified for **case**. Moreover, this constraint applies to *all* (complex) feature values within a given feature structure. In effect, the modal operator $\square$ introduces universal quantification over embedded feature values. As usual, the modal operator $\diamond$ is the dual of $\square$ and is used to express existential quantification over embedded feature values.

Given certain reasonable assumptions about the interpretation of the modal operators $\square$ and $\diamond$, it turns out that any formula of L_C can be expressed as an 'equivalent' description in **NRRK**. In the following, it is shown that there is a mapping from formulas of L_C to descriptions in **NRRK**, such that a formula of L_C and its translation into **NRRK** are equisatisfiable.

4.3.1   A Translation From L_C to NRRK

Before presenting the translation from L_C to **NRRK**, some remarks on the notion of satisfiability for the language L_C are in order. It is important to observe that the interpretation of a formula of L_C is given with respect to some category structure Σ. Consequently, two possible definitions of the notion of satisfiability for formulas are available:

1. A formula ϕ is *satisfiable* (*simpliciter*) just in case there is some category structure Σ, and some category α in Σ such that $\alpha \models_\Sigma \phi$.

2. Given a category structure Σ, a formula ϕ is *satisfiable* (*in* or *with respect to* Σ), just in case there is some category α in Σ such that $\alpha \models_\Sigma \phi$.

To see the difference between these two notions of satisfiability, consider the following simple L_C constraint:

(42) f : a

According to the first definition given above, this formula of L_C is certainly satisfiable. For example, the set of categories induced by the category structure

$$\Sigma = \langle \{f\}, \{a\}, \{\langle f, 0 \rangle\}, \{\langle f, \{a\} \rangle\} \rangle$$

contains the category $\{\langle f, a \rangle\}$ which clearly satisfies (42). Thus, there is a category structure Σ and a category α in Σ such that $\alpha \models_\Sigma$ f : a.

Under the second definition however, whether or not f : a is satisfiable depends on the given category structure. For example, suppose that the category structure Σ is given by:

$$\Sigma = \langle \{f, g\}, \{a, b\}, \{\langle f, 0 \rangle, \langle g, 0 \rangle\}, \{\langle f, \{b\} \rangle, \langle g, \{a\} \rangle\} \rangle$$

In this case there is no category α in the set induced by Σ such that $\alpha(f) = a$, whence f : a is *not* satisfiable with respect to Σ.

It is the second notion of satisfiability which is of interest here. In view of the overall objectives of the framework introduced by Gazdar et al., considering satisfiability with respect to a given category structure seems more appropriate. Formulas of L_C are intended to be used to pick out a subset of 'legal' categories within the set of 'possible' categories induced by a given category structure Σ. In this case however, the important question is whether a particular category in Σ satisfies a given L_C constraint ϕ. The question of whether ϕ is satisfied by a category in some hitherto unspecified category structure is of less interest.

The satisfiability of a formula ϕ of L_C will therefore be taken relative to a given category structure Σ. It follows that the translation of ϕ into **NRRK** should also be dependent on the particular choice of category structure. There are two reasons for this. First, a category structure $\Sigma = \langle F, A, \tau, \rho \rangle$ imposes certain constraints on feature labels and their values. Specifically, the type function τ partitions the set of features label F into a set F^0 of type

0 or atom-valued feature labels and a set F^1 of type 1 or category-valued feature labels. In addition, the function ρ associates with each type 0 feature label a set of possible values in A. Presumably, the **NRRK** translation of a formula ϕ of L_C should reflect these constraints. Second, the translation of the modal operators $\Box$ and $\Diamond$ depends on the set of type 1 feature labels F^1. If $F^1 = \{f_1, f_2, \ldots f_n\}$, then it turns out that the modality $\Diamond$ may be expressed in **NRRK** by the regular path expression $(f_1 + f_2 + \cdots + f_n)^*$.

The mapping from L_C to **NRRK** is defined as follows. First, let $\Sigma = \langle F, A, \tau, \rho \rangle$ be a given category structure, with F^0 the set of atom-valued feature labels and $F^1 = \{f_1, f_2, \ldots, f_n\}$ the set of category-valued feature labels. Let M_Σ abbreviate the regular path expression $(f_1 + f_2 + \cdots + f_n)^*$. Now, for ϕ a formula of L_C, the **NRRK** translation of ϕ with respect to the category structure Σ is given by $t_\Sigma(\phi)$ where:

$$t_\Sigma(\phi) = \left(\neg M_\Sigma : \bigvee_{a \in A} a \right) \wedge \left(\neg M_\Sigma : \bigvee_{f \in F^0} (f : \neg \bigvee_{a \in \rho(f)} a) \right) \wedge t'_\Sigma(\phi)$$

and where $t'_\Sigma(\phi)$ is defined as follows:

- If ϕ is f then $t'_\Sigma(\phi) = f : \top$

- If ϕ is $f : a$ then $t'_\Sigma(f : a) = f : a$

- If ϕ is $f : \psi$ then $t'_\Sigma(\phi) = f : t'_\Sigma(\psi)$

- If ϕ is $\neg \psi$ then $t'_\Sigma(\phi) = \neg t'_\Sigma(\psi)$

- If ϕ is $(\psi \wedge \chi)$ then $t'_\Sigma(\phi) = (t'_\Sigma(\psi) \wedge t'_\Sigma(\chi))$

- If ϕ is $\Diamond \psi$ then $t'_\Sigma(\phi) = M_\Sigma : t'_\Sigma(\psi)$

Remark: The definition of the mapping t'_Σ does not explicitly provide for the translation of L_C constraints involving the connectives '$\vee$', '$\rightarrow$' or '$\leftrightarrow$'. It may be noted however, that these connectives can always be expressed in terms of the connectives '$\wedge$' and '$\neg$', for which translations are given. Similarly, any L_C constraint of the form $\Box \phi$ can be expressed as a description $\neg \Diamond \neg \phi$. This means that there is no need to provide an explicit translation for L_C constraints with the general form $\Box \phi$.

The translation into **NRRK** of an L_C constraint ϕ consists of three conjoined descriptions and may be explained informally as follows. The final conjunct $t'_\Sigma(\phi)$ provides a translation of an L_C constraint ϕ which is 'liberal' in the sense that it ignores the restrictions on features and their values imposed by the type function τ and range function ρ of Σ. These restrictions are captured by the first and second conjuncts respectively. Intuitively, the first conjunct ensures that there is no type 1 feature label which has as its value an atom in A, while the second conjunct ensures that any type 0 feature label must have as its value an atom in the specified range $\rho(f)$.

It is shown below that for any category structure Σ and constraint ϕ of L_C, ϕ is satisfiable in Σ just in case the **NRRK** description $t_\Sigma(\phi)$ has a satisfying feature structure. Before proceeding, it will be convenient to prove a lemma which provides some justification for the claim that the modal operator $\Diamond$ of L_C can always be simulated in terms of regular path expressions. In the following, if α is a syntactic category and p a path, then the notation $\alpha(p)$ is used to denote the value of the path p in α (when this is defined). The following lemma shows that the modal operator $\Diamond$ of L_C expresses existential quantification over the values of type 1 feature paths within a syntactic category. Intuitively, this means that, for any given category structure Σ, the operator $\Diamond$ may be simulated by the regular path expression $\mathbf{M}_\Sigma$ (where this is as defined above).

Lemma 4.4 *Let $\Sigma = \langle F, A, \tau, \rho \rangle$ be a category structure and α a syntactic category in Σ.*

$$\alpha \models_\Sigma \Diamond\phi \Leftrightarrow \exists p \in (F^1)^*, \alpha(p) \text{ is defined and } \alpha(p) \models_\Sigma \phi.$$

Proof: Let the *depth* of a category α be given by $|p|$, where $p \in F^*$ is a longest path such that $\alpha(p)$ is defined. The proof of the lemma proceeds by induction on the depth of the category α.

Suppose that α is of depth 0. In this case $\alpha(f)$ is undefined for all $f \in F^1$, whence $\alpha \models_\Sigma \Diamond\phi$ just in case $\alpha \models_\Sigma \phi$. Trivially, $\alpha \models_\Sigma \phi$ just in case $\alpha(\epsilon) \models_\Sigma \phi$, and since $\epsilon \in (F^1)^*$ the lemma holds.

Now suppose that the lemma holds for all categories of depth less than k (for some $k > 0$). Let α be a category of depth k. By definition, $\alpha \models_\Sigma \Diamond\phi$ just in case $\alpha \models_\Sigma \phi$ or $\exists f \in F^1$ such that $\alpha(f)$ is defined and $\alpha(f) \models_\Sigma \Diamond\phi$. Now $\alpha(f)$ is a category of depth less than k and so by hypothesis this is just equivalent to the following: $\alpha \models_\Sigma \phi$ or $\exists f \in F^1 \exists p \in (F^1)^*$ such that $(\alpha(f))(p) = \alpha(fp)$ is defined and $\alpha(fp) \models_\Sigma \phi$. Equivalently:

$$\alpha \models_\Sigma \phi \text{ or } \exists p \in (F^1)^+ \text{ such that } \alpha(p) \text{ is defined and } \alpha(p) \models_\Sigma \phi$$

if and only if

$$\exists p \in (F^1)^* \text{ such that } \alpha(p) \text{ is defined and } \alpha(p) \models_\Sigma \phi$$

□

The main result can now be stated. The following theorem shows that a description ϕ of L_C and its translation $t_\Sigma(\phi)$ are equisatisfiable.

Theorem 4.5 *A formula ϕ of L_C is satisfiable with respect to a given category structure Σ if and only if its translation $t_\Sigma(\phi)$ into the language* **NRRK** *is satisfiable.*

Proof: Let ϕ be a formula of L_C and let $\Sigma = \langle F, A, \tau, \rho \rangle$ be the given feature structure. It must be shown that:

1. if ϕ is satisfiable in Σ, then there is a feature structure $\mathcal{A}$ such that $\mathcal{A} \models t_\Sigma(\phi)$; and

2. if $t_\Sigma(\phi)$ is satisfiable, then there is a category in Σ which satisfies ϕ.

Suppose that there is a category α in Σ such that $\alpha \models_\Sigma \phi$. Let $\mathcal{A}_\alpha = \langle Q, q_0, \delta, \pi \rangle$ be defined as follows:

1. Q is the smallest set such that $\alpha \in Q$, and for any $\beta \in Q$ and $f \in F$, if $\beta(f)$ is defined, then $\beta(f) \in Q$.

2. $q_0 = \alpha$.

3. $\delta : Q \times F \to Q$ is that partial function given by $\delta(\beta, f) = \beta(f)$ when this is defined; and is undefined otherwise;

4. $\pi : Q \to A$ is that partial function given by $\pi(a) = a$ for $a \in Q \cap A$; and is undefined otherwise.

It is easy to check that $\mathcal{A}_\alpha$ is a feature structure. First, the partial transition function δ is clearly deterministic. Moreover, $\mathcal{A}_\alpha$ is connected: for any $\beta \in Q$, there exists a path $p \in F^*$ such that $\alpha(p) = \beta$ and thus $\delta^*(\alpha, p) = \beta$. Finally, whenever $\pi(a)$ is defined then $\delta(a, f)$ is undefined for all feature labels $f \in F$ (atomic values do not have labels). An observation which proves useful later is the following: for any feature label $f \in F$, if $\alpha(f)$ is defined then the feature structure $\mathcal{A}_\alpha/f$ is defined and is given by $\mathcal{A}_{\alpha(f)}$. More generally, for any path $p \in F^*$, if $\mathcal{A}_\alpha/p$ is defined then it is just $\mathcal{A}_{\alpha(p)}$.

It is claimed that $\mathcal{A}_\alpha \models t_\Sigma(\phi)$. Equivalently:

S1: $\mathcal{A}_\alpha \models \neg\mathsf{M}_\Sigma : \bigvee_{a \in A} a$

S2: $\mathcal{A}_\alpha \models \neg\mathsf{M}_\Sigma : \bigvee_{f \in F^0} (f : \neg \bigvee_{a \in \rho(f)} a)$

S3: $\mathcal{A}_\alpha \models t'_\Sigma(\phi)$

Suppose that S1 does not hold. In this case there must be a path $p \in \mathsf{M}_\Sigma$ such that $\mathcal{A}_\alpha/p$ is defined and satisfies a, for some atomic value $a \in A$. But then $\alpha(p)$ is defined and $\alpha(p) = a$, whence α is not a well-formed category in Σ, for either p is the empty path and $\alpha \in A$ (i.e. α is an atomic value and hence not a category at all); or p is non-empty and α contains a type 1 feature label with an atomic value. It may be concluded that S1 does hold.

It is shown by similar reasoning that S2 holds. For if not, then there must be some path $p \in \mathsf{M}_\Sigma$ and some $f \in F^0$ such that $\mathcal{A}_\alpha/pf$ is defined and satisfies $\neg a$ for all atomic values $a \in \rho(f)$. It follows that $\alpha(pf)$ is defined and $\alpha(pf) \notin \rho(f)$. This is not possible and so it may be concluded that S2 holds.

Finally, it is shown by induction on the structure of ϕ that if $\alpha \models_\Sigma \phi$, then $\mathcal{A}_\alpha \models t'_\Sigma(\phi)$. If ϕ is of the form f or $f : a$ then the required result is immediate from the definition of $\mathcal{A}_\alpha$. Moreover, assuming that the result holds for descriptions ψ and χ, it is straightforward to establish that it holds for $f : \psi$, $\neg\psi$ and $(\psi \wedge \chi)$. The case where ϕ is of the form $\Diamond\psi$ requires a little more work, most of which is contained in lemma 4.4. From the lemma, if $\alpha \models_\Sigma \Diamond\psi$, then there is some path $p \in (F^1)^*$ such that $\alpha(p)$ is defined and $\alpha(p) \models_\Sigma \psi$. By hypothesis, $\mathcal{A}_{\alpha(p)} \models t'_\Sigma(\psi)$ whence $\mathcal{A}_\alpha/p \models t'_\Sigma(\psi)$. Finally, since $p \in (F^1)^*$ just in case $p \in \mathsf{M}_\Sigma$, it follows that $\mathcal{A}_\alpha \models \mathsf{M}_\Sigma : t'_\Sigma(\psi)$, whence $\mathcal{A}_\alpha \models t'_\Sigma(\Diamond\psi)$.

For the second half of the proof, suppose that there exists a feature structure $\mathcal{A} = \langle Q, q_0, \delta, \pi \rangle$ which satisfies $t_\Sigma(\phi)$. Let $val : Q \to V$ to be that total function from the states of $\mathcal{A}$ to values in $V \cong [F \to V] + A$ given by[1]:

1. $val(q) = \pi(q)$ if $\pi(q)$ is defined;

2. $val(q) = \{\langle f, val(\delta(q, f))\rangle \mid f \in F$ and $\delta(q, f)$ is defined$\}$ if $\pi(q)$ is undefined.

---

[1]The domain $[F \to V] + A$ comprises atomic values in A and partial functions (both finite and infinite) from feature labels in F to values in V.

Let $\alpha = val(q_0)$. It can be shown that α is a finite partial function from feature labels to values (i.e. a finite element of $F \to V$). Furthermore, α is consistent with the type function τ, and range function ρ of Σ. In other words, α is a possible syntactic category in the space of categories induced by the category structure Σ. To see this, note first that if $\alpha = val(q_0) \in A$, then $\mathcal{A}$ must be the the one-state feature structure with $\pi(q_0) \in A$. But $\mathcal{A} \models t_\Sigma(\phi)$ so

$$\mathcal{A} \models \neg \mathsf{M}_\Sigma : \bigvee_{a \in A} a$$

and

$$\mathcal{A} \not\models \bigvee_{a \in A} a$$

whence $\pi(q_0) \notin A$ — a contradiction. It may be concluded that α is a partial function in the domain $F \to V$. Moreover, by definition of val and the fact that feature structures are finite objects, α is clearly a finite partial function in this domain.

To check that α is consistent with the type function τ of Σ, it suffices to note that since

$$\mathcal{A} \models \neg \mathsf{M}_\Sigma : \bigvee_{a \in A} a$$

there can be no path $p \in (F^1)^*$ such that $\mathcal{A}/p$ is defined and $\mathcal{A}/p \models a$, for some atom $a \in A$. But then it is easy to show that there can be no type 1 feature label in α which has as its value an atom in A. Similarly, consistency with the range function ρ of Σ follows from the fact that

$$\mathcal{A} \models \neg \mathsf{M}_\Sigma : \bigvee_{f \in F^0} (f : \neg \bigvee_{a \in \rho(f)} a)$$

This ensures that any type 0 feature label f occurring in $\mathcal{A}$ takes as its value an atom in the appropriate range $\rho(f)$. It follows from the definition of val that the category α also obeys this constraint.

Finally, it may be shown that $\alpha \models_\Sigma \phi$. The proof again proceeds by a straightforward induction on the structure of ϕ. Here it is simply shown that the required result holds when ϕ is of the form $\Diamond \psi$ (this again being the most difficult case). In this case, $\mathcal{A} \models t'_\Sigma(\Diamond \psi)$ and by definition of t'_Σ

it follows that $\mathcal{A} \models \mathsf{M}_\Sigma : t'_\Sigma(\psi)$, which in turn implies that there exists a path $p \in \mathsf{M}_\Sigma$ such that $\mathcal{A}/p$ is defined and $\mathcal{A}/p \models t'_\Sigma(\psi)$. By hypothesis $val(\delta^*(q_0, p)) \models_\Sigma \psi$. But it is easy to show that $val(\delta^*(q_0, p))$ is just $\alpha(p)$ (the proof is by induction on the length of the path p) whence $\alpha(p) \models_\Sigma \psi$ and so by lemma 4.4, $\alpha \models \Diamond\psi$. $\square$

Theorem 4.5 shows that any L_C constraint ϕ can be expressed as a description $t_\Sigma(\phi)$ of **NRRK**. Gazdar et al. propose that a theory of syntactic categories be specified as a pair $\langle \Sigma, C \rangle$, where Σ is a category structure and C a set of L_C constraints. The idea is that the set of 'legal' or 'permissible' categories characterized by the theory is given as the set of those possible syntactic categories induced by Σ which also satisfy each of the constraints in C. Given the translation from L_C to **NRRK** described in this section, a theory of syntactic categories $\langle \Sigma, C \rangle$ may now be expressed as a description $t_\Sigma(\hat{C})$ of **NRRK** (where $\hat{C}$ denotes the conjunction of all of the descriptions in the set C). Intuitively, for each feature structure $\mathcal{A}$ such that $\mathcal{A} \models t_\Sigma(\hat{C})$ there is an associated syntactic category α which belongs to the space of syntactic categories defined by the theory $\langle \Sigma, C \rangle$. In fact, it is not difficult to show that the set of all categories associated with feature structures in this way is just the set of syntactic categories defined by the theory[2].

In conclusion, it has been shown that the language **NRRK** subsumes the constraint language L_C. The modal operator $\Diamond$ of L_C can be simulated in **NRRK** in terms of an infinitary path descriptor which quantifies over category-valued feature labels within a feature structure. In other words, $\Diamond$ corresponds to a restricted form of functional uncertainty. The modal operator $\square$ can be simulated using both regular path expressions and negation, according to the equivalence $\square\phi$ iff $\neg\Diamond\neg\phi$. This provides a link between L_C and the logical model of feature structures and descriptions due to Rounds and Kasper.

4.4   NRRK and the Satisfiability Problem

In this section it is shown that the satisfiability problem for the language **NRRK** is undecidable. That is, there is no algorithm for deciding in general whether a given description in **NRRK** has a satisfying feature structure.

---

[2]Strictly speaking, it is necessary to consider the interpretation of $t_\Sigma(\phi)$ with respect to a suitably large domain of feature structures. More specifically, this domain should contain all those feature structures which can be defined over the set of feature labels F and atomic values A of the category structure Σ.

This result is obtained by showing that the language **NRRK** can be used to encode the computations of an arbitrary Turing machine. More specifically, given a Turing machine M and input string x, it is possible to construct a description which characterizes the configurations which M may go through when presented with x. Deciding whether M halts on x can then be reduced to the problem of determining whether a particular formula has a satisfying feature structure. As is well known, the problem of determining whether a given Turing machine halts on a given input is undecidable in general. The expressivity of feature logics with negation and functional uncertainty has also be studied by Baader et al. (1991), who provide an alternative proof of undecidability.

4.4.1   Encoding a Turing Machine in NRRK

The following definition of a Turing machine is adapted from that presented by Hopcroft and Ullman (1979, Ch.7).

Definition 4.6 A Turing machine is a structure $M = \langle Q, T, I, \delta, B, q_0, q_f \rangle$ where:

- Q is a finite set of *states*

- T is a set of *tape symbols* (Q and T are disjoint sets)

- $I \subset T$ is a set of *input symbols*

- $\delta : Q \times T \to Q \times T \times \{L, R\}$ is a (partial) *next move function*

- $B \in (T - I)$ is a distinguished *blank symbol*

- $q_0 \in Q$ is a distinguished *start state*;

- $q_f \in Q$ is a distinguished *final state*;

The operation of a Turing machine (TM) can be described in terms of *configurations* of the form xqy, where $xy \in T^*$ is the string of symbols on the tape (ignoring all trailing blanks) and $q \in Q$ is the current state. It will be assumed that the tape head is scanning the first symbol of the string y (unless y is the empty string, in which case the tape head is taken to be scanning the blank symbol B). An initial configuration q_0x has the TM in state q_0 with the tape head scanning the first symbol of the input string $x \in I^*$.

The partial function δ determines the way in which the TM can move from one configuration to the next. Let $X_1X_2 \ldots X_{i-1}qX_iX_{1+1} \ldots X_n$ be the current configuration and suppose that $\delta(q, X_i) = (p, Y, L)$. In this case, the TM is in state q and scanning the ith symbol on the tape (or the blank symbol B if $i - 1 = n$). If $i = 1$, then the string of symbols to the left of the tape head is empty, and no move is allowed (the tape head is not allowed to fall off the left end of the tape). Otherwise, the TM enters state p, writes the symbol Y and moves the tape head one symbol to the left. The resulting configuration is $X_1X_2 \ldots X_{i-2}pX_{i-1}YX_{i+1} \ldots X_n$. If $\delta(q, X_i) = (p, Y, R)$, on the other hand, then the TM enters state p, writes the symbol Y and moves one symbol to the right. In this case, the configuration which results is $X_1X_2 \ldots X_{i-1}YpX_{i+1} \ldots X_n$.

A TM computation consists of a sequence $C_0, C_1, \ldots C_k \ldots$ of configurations, where C_0 is the initial configuration and each C_i $(i \geq 1)$ is derived from C_{i-1} by the next move function δ. A transition from C_{i-1} to C_i licenced by δ is called a *move*. An input string x in I^* is *recognized* by a TM M just in case M enters a final configuration yq_fz (q_f is the final state) when started in the initial configuration q_0x. The language $L(M)$ accepted by M consists of all those input strings which it recognizes. Without loss of generality, it can be assumed that the TM *halts* (i.e. has no next move) whenever it recognizes an input string. On the other hand, it is possible that the TM may continue computing indefinitely if the input is not recognized.

It is now shown that given a Turing machine $M = \langle Q, T, I, \delta, B, q_0, q_f \rangle$ and input string $x \in I^*$, it is possible to construct a description $\mathsf{RUN}_{M,x}$ of **NRRK**, which correctly simulates the effect of running M on x. First it is necessary to provide an appropriate representation for the configurations of a TM. A configuration xqy may be represented by a feature structure defined for the labels **state**, **scanning**, **left** and **right**, where:

1. the value of **state** is an atom representing the current state q;

2. the value of **scanning** is an atom representing the symbol X currently being read by the tape head;

3. the value of **right** is a list representing the string of symbols y to the right of the tape head.

4. the value of **left** is a list representing the string of symbols x to the left of the tape head, starting with the symbol closest to the head (i.e. the string x is actually encoded 'in reverse').

$$
\left[
\begin{array}{ll}
\text{left} & \left[\begin{array}{ll} \text{first} & 1 \\ \text{rest} & \left[\begin{array}{ll} \text{first} & 0 \\ \text{rest} & \text{nil} \end{array} \right] \end{array} \right] \\
\text{state} & q_1 \\
\text{scanning} & 1 \\
\text{right} & \left[\begin{array}{ll} \text{first} & 1 \\ \text{rest} & \left[\begin{array}{ll} \text{first} & 0 \\ \text{rest} & \text{nil} \end{array} \right] \end{array} \right]
\end{array}
\right]
$$

Figure 4.2: Representing a configuration of a Turing Machine

For example, the configuration $01q_110$ may be represented by the feature structure of figure 4.2. In this case, the string to the right of the tape head is not empty, and the value of **scanning** is the first symbol in this string as required. The value of **left** is a representation of the list $[1, 0]$, which encodes the string of symbols to the left of the tape head, in order from the right.

A (finite) sequence of TM configurations may now be represented as follows. Suppose that the feature structure $\mathcal{A}$ represents the configuration C_i. The next configuration in the sequence, C_{i+1} if this exists, will be represented by the feature structure $\mathcal{A}/\text{next}$. If C_i is a final configuration xq_fy on the other hand, then the value of **next** will be taken to be the atom **halt**.

Having provided a suitable representation for TM configurations, a number of descriptions are now defined which guarantee the correct behaviour of M during a computation. To begin with, the following constraint on (representations of) TM configurations ensures that the symbol being scanned is either the first symbol in the **right** string (in case this string in non-empty), or the special blank symbol B (in case the **right** string is empty).

SCAN: $((\text{scanning} \doteq (\text{right} \cdot \text{first})) \vee (\text{right} : \text{nil} \wedge \text{scanning} : B))$

The constraint on TM configurations given below ensures that M can halt on reaching a final state (there is no next configuration, the value of **next** is **halt**):

HALT: $(\text{state} : q_f \wedge \text{next} : \text{halt})$

Next, it is necessary to construct descriptions characterizing the possible moves of M. The partial function δ consists of a set of tuples of the form $\langle q, X, p, Y, D \rangle$, where p, q are states, X, Y are tape symbols and D (the direction) is in $\{L, R\}$. A particular tuple $\langle q, X, p, Y, D \rangle$ corresponds to one possible way in which M can move from the 'current' configuration to the next and is encoded as a description $\mathsf{MOVE}_{\langle q, X, p, Y, D \rangle}$ defined as shown below. There are two cases to consider:

- Change state, write a symbol and move left:

$$
\begin{aligned}
\mathsf{MOVE}_{\langle q, X, p, Y, L \rangle} : \quad & \mathsf{state} : q \wedge \mathsf{scanning} : X \\
\wedge \quad & \mathsf{next} : (\mathsf{state} : p \wedge \mathsf{right} : \mathsf{rest} : \mathsf{first} : Y) \\
\wedge \quad & ((\mathsf{next} \cdot \mathsf{left}) \doteq (\mathsf{left} \cdot \mathsf{rest})) \\
\wedge \quad & ((\mathsf{next} \cdot \mathsf{right} \cdot \mathsf{first}) \doteq (\mathsf{left} \cdot \mathsf{first})) \\
\wedge \quad & \left[\begin{array}{l} ((\mathsf{next} \cdot \mathsf{right} \cdot \mathsf{rest} \cdot \mathsf{rest}) \doteq (\mathsf{right} \cdot \mathsf{rest})) \\ \vee\ (\mathsf{right} : \mathsf{nil} \wedge \mathsf{next} : \mathsf{right} : \mathsf{rest} : \mathsf{rest} : \mathsf{nil}) \end{array} \right]
\end{aligned}
$$

- Change state, write a symbol and move right:

$$
\begin{aligned}
\mathsf{MOVE}_{\langle q, X, p, Y, R \rangle} : \quad & \mathsf{state} : q \wedge \mathsf{scanning} : X \\
\wedge \quad & \mathsf{next} : (\mathsf{state} : p \wedge \mathsf{left} : \mathsf{first} : Y) \\
\wedge \quad & ((\mathsf{next} \cdot \mathsf{left} \cdot \mathsf{rest}) \doteq \mathsf{left}) \\
\wedge \quad & \left[\begin{array}{l} ((\mathsf{next} \cdot \mathsf{right}) \doteq (\mathsf{right} \cdot \mathsf{rest})) \\ \vee\ (\mathsf{right} : \mathsf{nil} \wedge \mathsf{next} : \mathsf{right} : \mathsf{nil}) \end{array} \right]
\end{aligned}
$$

Taking all of the different ways in which the TM can move, it is easy to see that the partial function δ can be expressed as a single disjunctive description as shown below:

$$
\mathsf{MOVE}_{\delta} : \qquad \bigvee_{\langle q, X, p, Y, D \rangle \in \delta} \mathsf{MOVE}_{\langle q, X, p, Y, D \rangle}
$$

Now suppose that the input string $x \in I^*$ is given by $x = a_1 a_2 \ldots a_n$. Define the description INIT_x representing an initial configuration with x on the leftmost portion of the tape as follows:

$$
\begin{aligned}
\mathsf{INIT}_x : \quad & (\mathsf{state} : q_0 \wedge \mathsf{left} : \mathsf{nil} \\
\wedge \quad & \mathsf{right} : (\mathsf{first} : a_1 \wedge \mathsf{rest} : (\ldots (\mathsf{first} : a_n \wedge \mathsf{rest} : \mathsf{nil}) \ldots))
\end{aligned}
$$

Finally, the effect of running the Turing machine M on the input string x is simulated by the description $\mathsf{RUN}_{M,x}$ defined by:

$$\mathsf{RUN}_{M,x}: \quad \mathsf{INIT}_x \wedge \neg\mathsf{next}^*: \neg(\mathsf{SCAN} \wedge (\mathsf{MOVE}_\delta \vee \mathsf{HALT}))$$

It is claimed that the description $\mathsf{RUN}_{M,x}$ correctly simulates the operation of the machine M when presented with the input x. Intuitively, INIT_x guarantees that M starts out from an initial configuration $q_0 x$ as required. The rest of the description expresses a generalisation about the values of paths in next^* (i.e. about configurations in any computation). It states that $(\mathsf{SCAN} \wedge (\mathsf{MOVE}_\delta \vee \mathsf{HALT}))$ is true in every configuration in a sequence. The description SCAN just ensures that in each configuration, M is scanning the correct symbol on the tape. The description $(\mathsf{MOVE}_\delta \vee \mathsf{HALT})$ guarantees that the next configuration in the sequence is either derived from the current configuration according to the next move function δ (if this is defined for the current configuration) or alternatively, that there is no next configuration and M has halted on reaching a final state. In this way, $\mathsf{RUN}_{M,x}$ guarantees the correct behaviour of M during a computation. Moreover, it characterizes all legal sequences of configurations for M.

Theorem 4.7 *There is no algorithm for deciding for an arbitrary description ϕ in* **NRRK** *whether ϕ has a satisfying feature structure.*

Proof: It is not difficult to see that the problem of determining whether M halts on x is equivalent to determining the satisfiability of the following description, which just requires that there be some reachable configuration which has no next configuration:

$$\mathsf{next}^*: \mathsf{halt} \wedge \mathsf{RUN}_{M,x}$$

Given that the halting problem for Turing machines is known to be undecidable, it follows that there can be no algorithm for determining the satisfiability of arbitrary descriptions in **NRRK**.   □

It is interesting to note that the description $\mathsf{RUN}_{M,x}$ does not involve path equations of the form $(r \doteq s)$ where either r or s is an *infinitary* path descriptor. In other words, the undecidability result still holds for a restricted version of the language in which infinitary path descriptors are not allowed to appear in path equations. On the other hand, it can be shown that the undecidability result does crucially depend on the ability of **NRRK** to express generalizations involving re-entrancy in feature structure. In particular, the fragment of **NRRK** without path equations is closely related to the language of *Deterministic Propositional Dynamic Logic* (**DPDL**) (Ben-Ari et al. (1982), Harel (1984)) which is known to be decidable. To conclude this section, a translation from this fragment of **NRRK** to **DPDL** is sketched below.

First, a basic translation of a description ϕ in **NRRK** (without path equations) into **DPDL** can be achieved by performing a simple syntactical transformation. For each subformula $r : \psi$ of ϕ, the regular path expression r is replaced by the modality $\langle \pi_r \rangle$, where the program π_r is given by:

- if r is a feature label l, then π_r is the atomic program l;

- if r is $(s + t)$, then π_r is $(\pi_s \cup \pi_t)$;

- if r is $(s \cdot t)$, then π_r is $(\pi_s ; \pi_t)$;

- if r is s^*, then π_r is π_s^*.

The main difference between the two languages lies in the interpretation of atomic propositions. In particular, the following descriptions are not satisfiable in **NRRK**: $a \wedge b$ (for a and b distinct atoms) and $a \wedge l : \phi$ (for a an atom and l a feature label). That is, in **NRRK** distinct atomic feature values do not unify and furthermore, atoms do not unify with complex values. The problem is that the basic translations of these descriptions *are* consistent in **DPDL**. This is easily remedied by conjoining a number of additional constraints to a basic translation in order to ensure that atomic values behave 'correctly'.

Let Λ denote that program $(l_1 \cup l_2 \cup \ldots \cup l_n)$ which 'contains' all of the atomic program symbols occurring in the basic translation (i.e. all of the feature labels which occur in the original **NRRK** description). Also, let P denote the set of all atomic propositions introduced into the basic translation (i.e. the set of all atoms occurring in the original **NRRK** description). Now, for each atomic proposition $a \in P$ it is necessary to conjoin a **DPDL** formula of the following kind:

$$\neg \langle \Lambda^* \rangle (a \wedge \bigvee_{\substack{b \in P \\ b \neq a}} b)$$

This ensures that in any state in which the proposition a holds, no proposition b holds for $b \neq a$. Conjoining each formula of this kind to the basic translation guarantees that at most one atomic proposition in P holds in any state.

Finally, it is necessary to ensure that if an atomic proposition holds in any state, then there are no outgoing transitions. This is achieved by conjoining the following formula to the basic translation:

$$\neg\langle \Lambda^* \rangle (\bigvee_{a \in P} a \wedge \langle \Lambda \rangle \textsf{true})$$

(where **true** is some formula which is true in any state).

A practical decision procedure for **DPDL** which runs in deterministic time 2^{cn} (for some constant $c \geq 1$) has been given by Ben-Ari, Halpern and Pnueli (1982). As Harel (1984) has pointed out, this means that as far as is currently known, it is no easier to decide the propositional calculus (for which satisfiability is NP-complete) than it is to decide **DPDL**. For the case of **NRRK** without path equations, it may be noted at least that there is an exponential polynomial time bound on decidability. This is worse than the situation for **DPDL**, the additional complexity arising from the treatment of atomic propositions. The **DPDL** formulas which are conjoined to the basic translation to ensure that at most one atomic proposition holds in any state are of size $O(n)$ (where n is the size of the **NRRK** formula). In the worst case, this means that the size of the resulting **DPDL** translation will be $O(n^2)$. Of course, there may be more efficient ways of representing formulas of the **NRRK** fragment in **DPDL**.

4.5   Conclusions

In this chapter, the language of Regular Rounds-Kasper logic with Negation (**NRRK**) has been defined as **RRK** with (classical) negation. The combination of general negation and regular path expressions results in a language with considerable expressive power. It has been shown that **NRRK** can be used to write descriptions which express generalizations about feature values within feature structures. In addition, the constraint language L_C introduced by Gazdar et al. can be viewed as a restricted version of **NRRK**. A translation from L_C to **NRRK** has been given in which the modal operators $\Diamond$ and $\Box$ of L_C are simulated in terms of regular path expressions and negation. Finally, it has been shown that the language **NRRK** can be used to encode the computations of an arbitrary Turing machine, and that the satisfiability problem for the language **NRRK** is undecidable. The undecidability result stems from the ability of **NRRK** to express generalizations about re-entrancy in feature structures.

Chapter 5

Infinitary Descriptions and Grammars

In the preceding chapter, it was observed that the language **NRRK** is powerful enough to express generalizations about features and their values. Building on this observation, it is now shown that **NRRK** can be viewed as a 'stand alone' formalism for representing grammars. More specifically, a grammar can be expressed by a description which captures a generalization about linguistic objects (e.g. constituent-structure trees). Within such a description, the traditional grammar components (i.e. 'rules', 'lexical entries', and so on) are represented in a uniform way as constraints on the local well-formedness of structures. The language **NRRK** thus provides a general, logical framework for representing linguistic information or knowledge.

The present approach to the logical representation of grammar differs in two key respects from previous work. First, the relationship between a grammar and the objects it characterizes is viewed as essentially the same as the relationship between a logical formula and its models. Thus, a feature structure represents a well-formed linguistic object just in case it *satisfies* the grammar in a model-theoretic sense. By comparison, work in the tradition of logic grammar (e.g. DCGs) has tended to emphasize a conception of grammar as a branch of proof theory, and syntactic structure as proof structure. Second, the present approach makes no use of sort or type definitions of the kind proposed by Rounds and Manaster-Ramer (1987), Smolka (1988, 1989), or Carpenter (1991, 1992) in order to model recursion in a grammar. Rather, the power to express generalizations about linguistic objects arises from the ability of regular path expressions to 'quantify' over feature values within a feature structure. A grammar is expressed as a single logical description and has a direct, model-theoretic semantics.

Because the language **NRRK** employs no special devices for describing constituent-structure, the next section introduces a simple scheme for representing constituent-structure trees in terms of feature structures. This scheme provides a basis for the logical encoding of a number of rather different grammar formalisms described in section 5.2. There it is shown that the language **NRRK** can be used to capture the descriptive devices employed in simple Context-Free Grammar, ID/LP grammar, the unification-based formalism PATR, classical Categorial Grammar and Tree Adjoining Grammar. The chapter concludes with a discussion of the encodings employed, and their relationship to the known formal properties of these systems.

5.1   Constituent Structure

The representation of constituent-structure described below is based on the generalized list encoding for trees commonly used in computer science. This has been chosen on the grounds of its simplicity and generality rather than for any particular linguistic merit, although very similar techniques are employed in unification-based grammar formalisms in order to encode information about subcategorization and grammatical relations (Shieber (1986a), Pollard and Sag (1987), Johnson (1988)). Given a suitable representation for trees, the language **NRRK** can be used to 'talk about' various aspects of constituent structure. In particular, it is possible to construct regular path expressions which capture relations between nodes such as *immediate dominance* and *dominance*. Universal quantification over nodes then yields a natural definition of well-formedness for representations of constituent-structure trees: a tree is globally well-formed just in case every one of its nodes is locally well-formed.

5.1.1   A Representation for Constituent-Structure Trees

Tree structures are widely used in linguistics to represent information about the syntactic structure of natural language expressions. An example of a typical constituent-structure tree is shown in figure 5.1[1]. In order to

---

[1]In the following, some familiarity with the notion of a constituent-structure tree and the terminology used to discuss these objects (e.g. *nodes*, *dominance*, etc.) is assumed. Suitable definitions can be found in Wall (1972) and Partee et al. (1990).

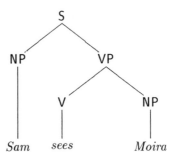

Figure 5.1: A simple constituent-structure tree

represent constituent-structure trees in feature structures, it is necessary to find some way of encoding information about the nodes of a tree. For present purposes, a constituent-structure tree can be regarded as being composed of just two kinds of node.

- *Terminal nodes*: these represent the 'basic' or unanalyzed constituents of a phrase (i.e. words or phonemes). A terminal node is labelled with a grammatical formative and has no daughter nodes (i.e. no constituent parts). The nodes labelled *Sam*, *knows* and *Moira* in figure 5.1 are terminals.

- *Non-terminal nodes*: these represent the 'complex' constituents of a phrase (e.g. sentences, noun phrases, etc.). A non-terminal node is labelled with a category symbol and has a number of daughter nodes. For example, the node labelled S in figure 5.1 is a non-terminal node with two daughters (both of which are non-terminal nodes).

A tree such as that shown in figure 5.1 will be represented in the following way. Each terminal node is represented simply by an atomic feature value corresponding to the grammatical formative which labels the node. For example, the terminal node with label *knows* in figure 5.1 is represented by a feature structure $\mathcal{A} = \langle \{q_0\}, q_0, \delta, \pi \rangle$ where $\pi(q_0) = knows$. Each non-terminal node is represented by a feature structure with two attributes **cat** and **dtrs**. The value of the feature label **cat** is a feature structure representing the node's category label. In the simplest case this will just be an atomic symbol, but more generally may be some object with internal structure. The value of the feature label **dtrs** is a feature structure representing the node's daughters as a list.

$$\left[\begin{array}{l} \text{cat} \quad \text{S} \\ \text{dtrs} \quad \left\langle \left[\begin{array}{l} \text{cat} \quad \text{NP} \\ \text{dtrs} \quad \langle Sam \rangle \end{array} \right], \left[\begin{array}{l} \text{cat} \quad \text{VP} \\ \text{dtrs} \quad \left\langle \left[\begin{array}{l} \text{cat} \quad \text{V} \\ \text{dtrs} \quad \langle knows \rangle \end{array} \right], \left[\begin{array}{l} \text{cat} \quad \text{NP} \\ \text{dtrs} \quad \langle Moira \rangle \end{array} \right] \right\rangle \end{array} \right] \right\rangle \end{array} \right]$$

Figure 5.2: Representation of a constituent-structure tree

Figure 5.2 shows a feature structure representing the tree of figure 5.1. For convenience, the value of the feature label **dtrs** is written as a sequence of feature structures enclosed in angle brackets ('$\langle$' and '$\rangle$'). However, it is assumed that the **dtrs** list is actually encoded in the manner described in section 4.2 of the previous chapter. Thus, the first element of the list (which represents the **NP** daughter) is the value of the feature path **dtrs first**, while the second element (which represents the **VP** daughter) is the value of the feature path **dtrs rest first**, and so on. It may be noted that proposed representation scheme actually conflates the notions 'tree' and 'node': a feature structure which represents (complete) information about a node of a tree is just a representation of the subtree rooted at that node.

5.1.2   Describing Constituent Structure

Suppose that $\mathcal{A}$ is a feature structure which represents a non-terminal node of a tree. The node's nth daughter (if such a daughter exists) is represented as the nth element of $\mathcal{A}$'s **dtrs** list. That is, the nth daughter is represented by a feature structure which appears as the value of the path **dtrs rest**$^{n-1}$ **first**. Consider a description of the following kind:

(43) $(\text{dtrs} \cdot \text{rest}^{n-1} \cdot \text{first}) : \phi$

The description in (43) states that the value of the path **dtrs rest**$^{n-1}$ **first** satisfies the description ϕ. Consequently, it can be understood as a partial description of a non-terminal node which has at least n daughters, where the nth daughter satisfies the given description[2]. Some illustrative examples are presented below:

(44)   a. $(\text{dtrs} \cdot \text{first}) : \text{cat} : \text{NP}$

---

[2] For the purposes of exposition it will often be convenient to speak of *nodes* satisfying descriptions of **NRRK** rather than *representations of nodes*.

    b.   (dtrs · rest · first) : cat : VP

    c.   ¬(dtrs · rest · rest · first) : ⊤

The description in (44a) is satisfied by any node whose first daughter is a non-terminal node with category label NP, while (44b) describes a node whose second daughter is labelled VP. It is easy to check that both of these descriptions are satisfied by the feature structure of figure 5.2. On the other hand, neither description is satisfied by the feature structures which represent the NP and VP daughters of the S node. The description in (44c) states that the feature path dtrs rest rest first is undefined (i.e. there is no third daughter). This description is also satisfied by the feature structure of figure 5.2.

A description of the kind shown in (43) above can be used to pick out a particular daughter of a given non-terminal node (assuming that the node in question has such a daughter). In contrast, the next schema simply states that there must be *some* daughter of the given node which satisfies the description ϕ.

(45) (dtrs · rest* · first) : ϕ

Consider a feature structure $\mathcal{A}$ which represents some node of a constituent-structure tree, and suppose that $\mathcal{A}$ satisfies (45). In this case, there must be some path $p \in$ (dtrs · rest* · first) such that $\mathcal{A}/p$ is defined and satisfies ϕ. But then it is clear that $\mathcal{A}$ represents a non-terminal node with at least one daughter which satisfies ϕ. It will be convenient to introduce the abbreviation ID for the path descriptor (dtrs · rest* · first). Intuitively, ID : ϕ is a partial description of a node which *immediately dominates* some node satisfying the description ϕ. For example, the following description is satisfied by any node which immediately dominates nodes labelled NP and VP.

(46) (ID : cat : NP) ∧ (ID : cat : VP)

Once again it is easy to see that the description in (46) is satisfied by the feature structure of figure 5.2. On the other hand, it should be noted that the description itself does not require that the node have *only* two daughters. The description is quite compatible with (representations of) nodes which have more than two daughters, provided that there is at least one daughter labelled NP and one labelled VP.

Given the path descriptor ID it is not difficult to find a regular path expression which can be used for talking about the *dominance* relation between nodes. The dominance relation is just the transitive and reflexive closure of immediate dominance, which suggests that the following schema may be of interest:

(47) $\text{ID}^* : \phi$

It is not difficult to show that $\mathcal{A} \models \text{ID}^* : \phi$ if and only if there is some integer $k \geq 0$ such that $\mathcal{A} \models \text{ID}^k : \phi$. Now if $\mathcal{A}$ represents some node n_0 of a parse tree, then $\mathcal{A} \models \text{ID}^k : \phi$ just in case n_0 is the first in a chain of $k + 1$ nodes $n_0, n_1, \ldots, n_k$ where each n_i immediately dominates n_{i+1}, and the node n_k satisfies the description ϕ. Consequently, (47) can be understood as a partial description of a node which *dominates* a node satisfying the description ϕ. The path descriptor ID^* will be abbreviated by DOM. Note that the description in (48) is satisfied by non-terminal nodes which dominate nodes labelled NP, VP, and *knows*.

(48) $(\text{DOM} : \text{cat} : \text{NP}) \wedge (\text{DOM} : \text{cat} : \text{VP}) \wedge (\text{DOM} : knows)$

The regular path expression DOM can be used to express existential quantification over the nodes of a constituent-structure tree. That is, a description $\text{DOM} : \phi$ states that there exists at least one node in the tree which satisfies the description ϕ. Using negation, it is possible to write descriptions which apply to every node in a tree:

(49) $\neg\text{DOM} : \neg\phi$

The schema in (49) can be glossed "there is no node which does not satisfy the description ϕ", or equivalently "every node does satisfy ϕ". By careful choice of ϕ, a description of the kind shown in (49) can serve as a definition of global well-formedness for representations of constituent-structure trees. In practice, ϕ must be chosen so as to provide an appropriate definition of *local* well-formedness for representations of nodes. This is illustrated by the following example.

Example 5.1 Consider the set of all constituent-structure trees in which non-terminal nodes are labelled by elements of a finite set $N = \{A_1, \ldots, A_m\}$ and terminal nodes are labelled by elements of a finite set $T = \{a_1, \ldots, a_n\}$. For example, if $\{\text{S}, \text{NP}, \text{VP}, \text{V}\} \subseteq N$ and $\{Sam, Moira, sees\} \subseteq T$ then the constituent-structure tree shown in figure 5.1 of the previous section belongs to this set. Consider the following descriptions:

TNode : $(a_1 \vee \cdots \vee a_n)$

NNode :   cat : $(A_1 \vee \cdots \vee A_m) \wedge$ dtrs : $\neg$rest* : $\neg((\text{first} : \top \wedge \text{rest} : \top) \vee$ nil$)$

The descriptions TNode and NNode provide definitions of (local) well-formedness for representations of terminal and non-terminal nodes respectively. For example, a feature structure $\mathcal{A}$ is a well-formed representation of a terminal node just in case $\mathcal{A} \models a$ for some terminal symbol $a \in T$. Similarly, a feature structure is a locally well-formed representation of a non-terminal node just in case it is defined for the feature labels cat and dtrs, where the value of cat is a category label $A \in N$, and the value of dtrs is (a representation of) a list. Now consider the following description:

Tree : $\neg$DOM : $\neg($NNode $\vee$ TNode$)$

The description Tree expresses a generalization about the values of paths in DOM. It is not difficult to show that Tree provides a definition of *global* well-formedness for representations of constituent-structure of the required kind.

Suppose first that $\mathcal{A}$ is a feature structure which represents a tree. In this case it it can be shown that $\mathcal{A} \models$ Tree. Clearly, $\forall p \in$ DOM, if $\mathcal{A}/p$ is defined then it represents a node (either terminal or non-terminal). If $\mathcal{A}/p$ represents a terminal node then $\mathcal{A}/p \models$ TNode. If $\mathcal{A}/p$ represents a non-terminal node then it is defined for the feature label cat (with value some category label $A \in N$) and the feature label dtrs (with value a feature structure representing a list of nodes). But then it is clear that $\mathcal{A}/p \models$ NNode. Either way, $\mathcal{A}/p \models ($NNode $\vee$ TNode$)$ and because this holds for every such path $p \in$ DOM it follows that $\mathcal{A} \models$ Tree.

Now suppose that $\mathcal{A} \models$ Tree. It can be shown that $\mathcal{A}$ represents a constituent-structure tree with non-terminal nodes labelled by elements of N and terminal nodes labelled by elements of T. Let $|\mathcal{A}|_{\text{ID}}$ denote the largest integer n such that $\mathcal{A}/p$ is defined for some $p \in$ ID^n. If $|\mathcal{A}|_{\text{ID}} = 0$, then it is not difficult to see that $\mathcal{A}$ represents either a tree consisting of a single terminal node, or a well-formed non-terminal node with no daughters (in other words, a tree consisting of a single non-terminal node). Now suppose that the required result holds for any feature structure $\mathcal{B}$ with $|\mathcal{B}|_{\text{ID}} < k$ for some integer $k \geq 0$, and furthermore that $|\mathcal{A}|_{\text{ID}} = k$. In this case, the feature structure $\mathcal{A}$ must be of the following form:

$$\left[\begin{array}{ll} \text{cat} & A \\ \text{dtrs} & \langle \mathcal{A}_1, \mathcal{A}_2, \ldots, \mathcal{A}_m \rangle \end{array} \right]$$

Consider the ith element $\mathcal{A}_i$ of the **dtrs** list of $\mathcal{A}$. There must be some (non-empty) path $p \in$ **ID** such that $\mathcal{A}/p = \mathcal{A}_i$, whence $|\mathcal{A}_i|_{\text{ID}} < k$. But from proposition 4.2, $\mathcal{A}_i \models$ **Tree** and by assumption, $\mathcal{A}_i$ is a well-formed representation of a constituent-structure tree. Since this holds for every feature structure in the **dtrs** list, it follows that $\mathcal{A}$ also represents a tree.

In the preceding example, the description **Tree** provided a definition of a set of trees in terms of local constraints on the structure of nodes. The following section extends this idea to the sets of parse trees characterized by particular grammars.

5.2 Representing Grammars in NRRK

In this section it is shown that grammars written in a number of rather different formalisms developed in theoretical and computational linguistics can be expressed in the language **NRRK**. The approach builds on the feature structure based representation for constituent-structure trees described in the previous section. A grammar is represented as a single description which characterizes a class of feature structures representing the parse trees of the grammar.

As a first illustration of the approach, the section begins with a treatment of simple Context-Free Grammar (CFG). It is shown that CFG rules may be expressed as logical constraints which furnish an appropriate definition of local well-formedness for representations of non-terminal nodes. Next, it is shown that a similar encoding can be obtained for context-free grammars written in the *Immediate Dominance/Linear Precedence* (ID/LP) format introduced by Pullum and Gazdar (Pullum 1982, Gazdar and Pullum 1981, Gazdar and Pullum 1982). In the ID/LP formalism, information about the hierarchical and linear ordering of constituents is factored into separate rule systems. It is shown that the same reorganization of syntactic information can be achieved in **NRRK**. In this way, the logical representation of ID/LP grammar captures the linguistic intuitions underlying the original formalism. Section 5.2.3 considers the unification-based formalism PATR. The logical treatment of PATR builds on the representation for CFGs and provides an alternative to the denotational model of the formalism proposed by Pereira and Shieber.

Classical Categorial grammars are considered in section 5.2.4. A basic assumption underlying this formalism is that syntactic structures may be characterized in terms of functors and arguments which are combined under the operation of function application. In **NRRK**, function application is expressed as a local constraint on constituent-structure trees having nodes labelled by complex categories. It is shown that the approach can be extended to account for more complex combinatory operations such as functional composition and type raising. Finally, section 5.2.5 presents a novel, logical treatment of Tree Adjoining Grammar (TAG). In the TAG formalism a grammar is specified by a set of elementary trees which may be composed under a single operation of adjoining. The logical account of the formalism presented below treats elementary trees as constraints on the eventual structure of a parse tree, and shows how the adjoining operation can be reformulated in terms of feature structure unification.

5.2.1   Simple Context-Free Grammar

Simple context-free grammars (CFGs) and the context-free languages (CFLs) which they characterize were first described by Chomsky (1956). The CFGs have been intensively studied by both linguists and computer scientists and are well-understood from the point of view of both parsing and compilation. Although the formalism is generally regarded as inadequate for the description of natural languages, the CFGs continue to be of interest for a number of reasons.

First, while the simple CFG formalism lacks the necessary expressivity to provide particularly revealing or intuitive analyses of syntactic phenomena, clear-cut examples of natural languages with non-CFL string sets are notoriously difficult to find. Pullum and Gazdar (1982) have shown that many arguments purporting to show that certain natural languages are non-CFL have been either formally or empirically flawed. Second, there are rather natural extensions of the CFGs which yield formalisms with greater expressivity (though not necessarily greater generative power). For example, the GPSG formalism employs a finite feature system and meta-grammatical devices, yet remains weakly equivalent to the simple CFG formalism. On the other hand, many grammar formalisms make use of a context-free 'skeleton' grammar augmented by additional 'structure building' operations (e.g. Indexed Grammar (1968), Definite Clause Grammar (1980), LFG, PATR, etc.). Such 'augmented' rule systems retain many of the advantages of simple phrase-structure grammars, whilst their mathematical power transcends that of the CFGs. Finally, computational linguists have not missed the fact that the recognition problem for the CFLs is efficiently decidable. Algorithms exist which can perform context-free recognition in time proportional to n^3 (where n is the length of the input string) (Earley (1970), Kasami (1965), Younger (1967)). Efficient algorithms for parsing with CFGs can also yield practical procedures for processing 'augmented' formalisms such as those mentioned above (Shieber (1985), Kay (1985), Tomita (1986)).

The following definition of the simple context-free grammar formalism provides a basis for the logical treatment set out below.

Definition 5.2 A *context-free grammar* G is a structure $\langle N, T, P, S \rangle$ where:

- N is a finite, non-empty set (the *non-terminals*);

- T is a finite, non-empty set disjoint from N (the *terminals*);

- P is a finite set of *productions* or *rules* of the form $A \rightarrow \alpha$, where $A \in N$ is a non-terminal symbol and $\alpha \in (N \cup T)^*$ is a string of terminals and non-terminals;

- $S \in N$ is a distinguished non-terminal (the *start symbol*).

The productions of a context-free grammar are often formulated as 'string re-writing' rules (i.e. relations on strings). A rather different interpretation of the formalism is adopted here however. Following McCawley (1968), each production will be regarded as a *node-admissibility condition* — a local constraint on the well-formedness of configurations of nodes in a constituent-structure tree. For example, the rule given in (50) below states that a node is *admissible* if it is labelled with a non-terminal A and immediately dominates three nodes, the first (i.e. leftmost) with label B, the second with label C and the third with label D:

(50) A → B C D

Given a context-free grammar $G = \langle N, T, P, S \rangle$ a node will be said to be *admissible* (*for* G) just in case it is admissible for at least one of the productions in P. A constituent-structure tree is a *parse tree* (*for* G) if and only if:

1. the root node of the tree is labelled with the start symbol S; and

2. every node of the tree is either

   (a) a non-terminal node which is admissible for G; or

   (b) a terminal node labelled with a terminal symbol in T

Under the node-admissibility interpretation of grammar productions, the (string) language $L(G)$ described by a CFG G is taken to be the set of all strings which are the yield of some parse tree for G.

Example 5.3 The following set of rules is an example of a simple CFG. The constituent-structure tree of figure 5.1 is a parse tree for the grammar, and the string *Sam knows Moira* therefore belongs to the language it describes.

$$
\begin{array}{ll}
\text{S} \rightarrow \text{NP VP} & \text{NP} \rightarrow Sam \\
\text{VP} \rightarrow \text{V NP} & \text{NP} \rightarrow Moira \\
\text{VP} \rightarrow \text{V S} & \text{V} \rightarrow knows
\end{array}
$$

It is now shown that a context-free grammar G may be expressed as a description $\tau(G)$ of **NRRK**. The description $\tau(G)$ captures the meaning of G in the sense that a feature structure $\mathcal{A}$ satisfies $\tau(G)$ just in case it represents a parse tree for the grammar. Let $G = \langle N, T, P, S \rangle$ be a context-free grammar. The mapping τ is defined as follows:

1. for $a \in T$, $\tau(a) = a$

2. for $A \in N$, $\tau(A) = (\text{cat} : A)$

3. for $\rho \in P$ a production of the form $A \rightarrow \alpha$, $\tau(\rho) = (\tau(A) \wedge \text{dtrs} : \sigma(\alpha))$ where $\sigma(\alpha)$ is given by:

   (a) if $\alpha = \epsilon$ then $\sigma(\alpha) = \text{nil}$;

   (b) if $\alpha = X\alpha'$ then $\sigma(\alpha) = (\text{first} : \tau(X) \wedge \text{rest} : \sigma(\alpha'))$.

4. $\tau(T) = \displaystyle\bigvee_{a \in T} \tau(a)$

5. $\tau(P) = \displaystyle\bigvee_{\rho \in P} \tau(\rho)$.

6. $\tau(G) = \tau(S) \wedge \neg\text{DOM} : \neg(\tau(P) \vee \tau(T))$

Remark: Because the set of productions P, and the set of terminal symbols T of a context-free grammar are both finite, the expressions $\tau(T)$, $\tau(P)$ and $\tau(G)$ are all well-defined descriptions in **NRRK**.

Example 5.4 Let G be the context-free grammar specified in example 5.3. The description $\tau(G)$ is given by:

$$(\text{cat} : \text{S}) \wedge \neg\text{DOM} : \neg(\tau(P) \vee (\textit{Sam} \vee \textit{Moira} \vee \textit{knows}))$$

where $\tau(P)$ is the disjunction:

$\quad ((\text{cat} : \text{S}) \wedge \text{dtrs} : (\text{first} : (\text{cat} : \text{NP}) \wedge \text{rest} : (\text{first} : (\text{cat} : \text{VP}) \wedge \text{rest} : \text{nil})))$
$\vee\ ((\text{cat} : \text{VP}) \wedge \text{dtrs} : (\text{first} : (\text{cat} : \text{V}) \wedge \text{rest} : (\text{first} : (\text{cat} : \text{NP}) \wedge \text{rest} : \text{nil})))$
$\vee\ ((\text{cat} : \text{VP}) \wedge \text{dtrs} : (\text{first} : (\text{cat} : \text{V}) \wedge \text{rest} : (\text{first} : (\text{cat} : \text{S}) \wedge \text{rest} : \text{nil})))$
$\vee\ ((\text{cat} : \text{NP}) \wedge \text{dtrs} : (\text{first} : \textit{Sam} \wedge \text{rest} : \text{nil}))$
$\vee\ ((\text{cat} : \text{NP}) \wedge \text{dtrs} : (\text{first} : \textit{Moira} \wedge \text{rest} : \text{nil}))$
$\vee\ ((\text{cat} : \text{V}) \wedge \text{dtrs} : (\text{first} : \textit{knows} \wedge \text{rest} : \text{nil}))$

It is not difficult to see that $\tau(G)$ describes a class of feature structures which represent constituent-structure trees. This follows from the fact that the descriptions $\tau(P)$ and $\tau(T)$ provide appropriate definitions of local well-formedness for non-terminal and terminal nodes respectively. To see that a feature structure $\mathcal{A}$ represents a parse tree for G if $\mathcal{A} \models \tau(G)$, it suffices to note that:

1. $\mathcal{A} \models \tau(S)$; and

2. $\forall p \in \text{DOM}$ if $\mathcal{A}/p$ is defined then:

    (a) $\exists \rho \in P$ such that $\mathcal{A} \models \tau(\rho)$; or

    (b) $\exists a \in T$ such that $\mathcal{A} \models \tau(a)$

These two conditions may be compared with the definition of a parse tree given previously. Intuitively, condition (1) means that $\mathcal{A}$ represents a tree with root node labelled by S. Condition (2) shows that every node of the tree represented by $\mathcal{A}$ is either (a) a non-terminal node which is admissible by one of the productions in P; or (b) a terminal node labelled by some element of T. It may be concluded that $\mathcal{A}$ represents a parse tree for G.

5.2.2   ID/LP Grammar

Immediate Dominance/Linear Precedence (ID/LP) grammar was originally proposed by Pullum and Gazdar (Pullum (1982), Gazdar and Pullum (1981), Gazdar and Pullum (1982)) and subsequently adopted within the framework of Generalized Phrase Structure Grammar. The linguistic motivation for the formalism arises in part from the need to account for constituent order in languages where dominance and precedence are independent (an example is the Bantu language Makua). Standard CFG rules embody information about both of these aspects of constituent structure. For example, a rule A→B C D states not only that a constituent of category A may consist of constituents of categories B, C and D, but also that the B constituent precedes the C constituent which in turn precedes the D constituent. For languages with relatively free constituent order, such a strict correlation between immediate dominance and linear precedence can result in highly redundant and unintuitive analyses. More importantly, the standard CFG formalism is not expressive enough to capture generalizations about the order of constituents within a given language. The ID/LP formalism overcomes this problem by factoring information about immediate dominance and linear precedence into separate rule systems: immediate dominance (ID) rules and linear precedence (LP) rules, respectively.

The definition of ID/LP grammar presented below follows that of Shieber (1984b)[3]:

Definition 5.5 An *ID/LP grammar* G is a structure $\langle N, T, ID, LP, S \rangle$ where

- N is a finite, non-empty set (the *non-terminals*);

- T is a finite, non-empty set disjoint from N (the *terminals*);

- *ID* is a finite set of *ID-rules* of the form $A \rightarrow \alpha$ where $A \in N$ is a non-terminal symbol and $\alpha \subseteq (N \cup T)$ is a set of terminal and non-terminal symbols.

- *LP* is a relation in $(N \cup T) \times (N \cup T)$ which is transitive, irreflexive and asymmetric (a strict partial order).

- $S \in N$ is a distinguished non-terminal (the *start symbol*).

---

[3]This definition is more restrictive than the original formalism (see for example (Gazdar et al. 1985)) in that the right-hand side of an ID-rule is required to be a *set* of symbols rather than a *multiset*. The extension to multisets is considered later.

An ID-rule of the form $A{\rightarrow}\alpha$ where $\alpha = \{X_1, X_2, \ldots X_n\}$ will be written as $A{\rightarrow}X_1, X_2, \ldots, X_n$. A pair $(X, X') \in LP$ is written $X < X'$, and referred to as an *LP-rule*. In practice, the transitivity of the *LP* relation means that there is no need to list every single LP-rule.

The rules of an ID/LP grammar G will again be interpreted as node admissibility conditions. For example, the following ID-rule states that a node is admissible if it is labelled with the non-terminal A and immediately and exhaustively dominates three nodes labelled B, C and D:

(51) A → B, C, D

It should be noted that the rule in (51) places no restrictions on the left-to-right order of the daughter nodes. It is compatible with any one of six different node configurations corresponding to the six permutations of B,C and D. A node will be said to be *ID-admissible (for G)* just in case it admissible by at least one of the ID-rules of G.

The *LP* relation constrains the linear order of nodes which occur as sisters in a constituent-structure tree. For example, the LP-rule in (52) states that whenever a node labelled B occurs as sister to a node labelled C, then the B node must be ordered to the left of the C node.

(52) B < C

In conjunction with the ID-rule in (51) the above LP-rule eliminates three of the six possible node configurations permitted by the ID-rule alone. A node of a constituent-structure tree is said to be *LP-admissible (for G)* just in case its daughters obey the ordering constraints imposed by the *LP* relation of G (i.e. by *all* of the LP-rules).

Finally, a node is *admissible (for G)* just in case it is both ID-admissible for G and LP-admissible for G. With this new definition of node admissibility, the conditions under which a constituent-structure tree is said to be a parse tree for a grammar G are just as given in the previous section.

Example 5.6 The following ID/LP grammar characterizes the same language as the context-free grammar of example 5.3. In contrast to the CFG however, the ID/LP grammar provides explicit information about the linear order of constituents.

S → NP, VP	NP → *Bill*	NP < VP
VP → V, NP	NP → *Moira*	V < VP
VP → V, S	V → *knows*	V < S

The **NRRK** translation of an ID/LP grammar is defined in much the same way as the translation of context-free grammars given previously. A grammar $G = \langle N, T, ID, LP, S \rangle$ is expressed as a description

$$\tau(G) = \tau(S) \wedge \neg \mathsf{DOM} : \neg((\tau(ID) \wedge \tau(LP)) \vee \tau(T))$$

where the translations of the ID- and LP-rules are given as follows. Consider first the case of an individual ID-rule ρ of the general form $A \rightarrow X_1, X_2, \ldots X_n$ (for $n \geq 0$). The translation $\tau(\rho)$ is defined as:

$$\tau(\rho) \;=\; (\tau(A) \wedge (\bigwedge_{i \in \{1,\ldots,n\}} \mathsf{ID} : \tau(X_i)) \wedge (\mathsf{dtrs} \cdot \mathsf{rest}^n) : \mathsf{nil})$$

For example, the ID-rule $\mathsf{S} \rightarrow \mathsf{NP}, \mathsf{VP}$ is expressed as the following description:

(53) $(\mathsf{cat} : \mathsf{S} \wedge (\mathsf{ID} : (\mathsf{cat} : \mathsf{NP}) \wedge \mathsf{ID} : (\mathsf{cat} : \mathsf{VP})) \wedge (\mathsf{dtrs} \cdot \mathsf{rest} \cdot \mathsf{rest}) : \mathsf{nil})$

This describes a locally well-formed representation of a non-terminal node. The node has the category label S and immediately dominates nodes labelled NP and VP. The description $(\mathsf{dtrs} \cdot \mathsf{rest} \cdot \mathsf{rest}) : \mathsf{nil}$ ensures that these nodes are the only daughters of the S node. It may be noted that the order of the two daughter nodes is not fixed. That is, the description in (53) is quite compatible with representations of nodes where either the NP node precedes the VP node, or *vice versa*. The entire set of ID-rules of a grammar G is expressed as a disjunction $\tau(ID) = \bigvee_{\rho \in ID} \tau(\rho)$.

The **NRRK** translation of the set of LP rules must capture the appropriate notion of LP-admissibility for nodes. An LP-rule of the form $X_1 < X_2$ is expressed as a description of the following kind:

$$\neg \mathsf{dtrs} : \mathsf{rest}^* : (\mathsf{first} : \tau(X_2) \wedge \mathsf{rest}^* : \mathsf{first} : \tau(X_1))$$

For example, the translation of the LP-rule $\mathsf{NP} < \mathsf{VP}$ is given by:

(54) $\neg \mathsf{dtrs} : \mathsf{rest}^* : (\mathsf{first} : (\mathsf{cat} : \mathsf{VP}) \wedge \mathsf{rest}^* : \mathsf{first} : (\mathsf{cat} : \mathsf{NP}))$

The above description is most easily understood by considering the kind of feature structures which it rules out as ill-formed. For example, suppose that $\mathcal{A}$ represents a node of a constituent-structure tree, but that $\mathcal{A}$ does *not* satisfy (54). In that case:

$$\mathcal{A} \;\models\; \mathsf{dtrs} : \mathsf{rest}^* : (\mathsf{first} : (\mathsf{cat} : \mathsf{VP}) \wedge \mathsf{rest}^* : \mathsf{first} : (\mathsf{cat} : \mathsf{NP}))$$

Equivalently, there are integers $i, j \geq 0$ such that:

$$\mathcal{A} \models \mathsf{dtrs} : \mathsf{rest}^i : (\mathsf{first} : (\mathsf{cat} : \mathsf{VP}) \wedge \mathsf{rest}^j : \mathsf{first} : (\mathsf{cat} : \mathsf{NP}))$$

But then $\mathcal{A}$ represents a non-terminal node with daughters labelled VP and NP, where the VP node precedes the NP node. Clearly, such a node is not admissible with respect to the LP-rule NP<VP. Because a node is LP-admissible for G if it satisfies the ordering constraints imposed by all of the LP-rules, the translation $\tau(LP)$ of the set of LP-rules of G is given as the *conjunction* of the translations of the individual rules.

Example 5.7 Let G be the ID/LP grammar of example 5.6. The **NRRK** translation $\tau(G)$ of G is given by the following description:

$$(\mathsf{cat} : \mathsf{S}) \wedge \neg\mathsf{DOM} : \neg((\tau(ID) \wedge \tau(LP)) \vee (Bill \vee Moira \vee knows))$$

where $\tau(ID)$ is given by the disjunction:

$$
\begin{aligned}
&\quad\ ((\mathsf{cat} : \mathsf{S}) \wedge (\mathsf{ID} : (\mathsf{cat} : \mathsf{NP}) \wedge \mathsf{ID} : (\mathsf{cat} : \mathsf{VP})) \wedge (\mathsf{dtrs} \cdot \mathsf{rest} \cdot \mathsf{rest}) : \mathsf{nil}) \\
\vee\ &\quad ((\mathsf{cat} : \mathsf{VP}) \wedge (\mathsf{ID} : (\mathsf{cat} : \mathsf{V}) \wedge \mathsf{ID} : (\mathsf{cat} : \mathsf{NP})) \wedge (\mathsf{dtrs} \cdot \mathsf{rest} \cdot \mathsf{rest}) : \mathsf{nil}) \\
\vee\ &\quad ((\mathsf{cat} : \mathsf{VP}) \wedge (\mathsf{ID} : (\mathsf{cat} : \mathsf{V}) \wedge \mathsf{ID} : (\mathsf{cat} : \mathsf{S})) \wedge (\mathsf{dtrs} \cdot \mathsf{rest} \cdot \mathsf{rest}) : \mathsf{nil}) \\
\vee\ &\quad ((\mathsf{cat} : \mathsf{NP}) \wedge (\mathsf{ID} : Bill) \wedge (\mathsf{dtrs} \cdot \mathsf{rest}) : \mathsf{nil}) \\
\vee\ &\quad ((\mathsf{cat} : \mathsf{NP}) \wedge (\mathsf{ID} : Moira) \wedge (\mathsf{dtrs} \cdot \mathsf{rest}) : \mathsf{nil}) \\
\vee\ &\quad ((\mathsf{cat} : \mathsf{V}) \wedge (\mathsf{ID} : knows) \wedge (\mathsf{dtrs} \cdot \mathsf{rest}) : \mathsf{nil})
\end{aligned}
$$

and $\tau(LP)$ is given by the conjunction:

$$
\begin{aligned}
&\quad\ \neg\mathsf{dtrs} : \mathsf{rest}^* : (\mathsf{first} : (\mathsf{cat} : \mathsf{VP}) \wedge \mathsf{rest}^* : \mathsf{first} : (\mathsf{cat} : \mathsf{NP})) \\
\wedge\ &\quad \neg\mathsf{dtrs} : \mathsf{rest}^* : (\mathsf{first} : (\mathsf{cat} : \mathsf{NP}) \wedge \mathsf{rest}^* : \mathsf{first} : (\mathsf{cat} : \mathsf{V})) \\
\wedge\ &\quad \neg\mathsf{dtrs} : \mathsf{rest}^* : (\mathsf{first} : (\mathsf{cat} : \mathsf{S}) \wedge \mathsf{rest}^* : \mathsf{first} : (\mathsf{cat} : \mathsf{V}))
\end{aligned}
$$

The formulation of ID/LP grammar given by definition 5.5 differs in one respect from the formalism originally introduced by Pullum and Gazdar. Specifically, in their formalism the right-hand side of an ID-rule is allowed to contain repeated symbols. A typical example of such a rule is shown below:

(55) **VP → V, NP, NP**

The rule in (55) states that a constituent of category VP can be made up of three sub-constituents: one of category V, and the other two of category NP. Technically, this means that the definition of an ID-rule should allow for rules of the form $A \rightarrow \alpha$, where α is a *multiset*, rather than simply a set of symbols. In order to accommodate ID-rules of this kind, the translation function τ must be modified. Note that the rule in (55) cannot be adequately expressed as the following description:

$$(\mathsf{cat} : \mathsf{VP}) \quad \wedge \quad (\mathsf{ID} : (\mathsf{cat} : \mathsf{V}) \wedge \mathsf{ID} : (\mathsf{cat} : \mathsf{NP}) \wedge \mathsf{ID} : (\mathsf{cat} : \mathsf{NP}))$$
$$\wedge \quad (\mathsf{dtrs} \cdot \mathsf{rest} \cdot \mathsf{rest} \cdot \mathsf{rest}) : \mathsf{nil}$$

The problem here is that the description fails to capture the fact that the two NPs introduced by the rule in (55) must label *distinct* nodes. To overcome this problem, each occurrence of a non-terminal on the right-hand side of an ID-rule such as that shown in (55) will be associated with a unique numerical index. The index serves to distinguish a given non-terminal from all the other symbols introduced by the rule. For example, the ID-rule given in (55) above may now be translated as follows:

$$(\mathsf{cat} : \mathsf{VP})$$
$$\wedge \quad (\mathsf{ID} : (\mathsf{cat} : \mathsf{V} \wedge \mathsf{ind} : 1) \wedge \mathsf{ID} : (\mathsf{cat} : \mathsf{NP} \wedge \mathsf{ind} : 2) \wedge \mathsf{ID} : (\mathsf{cat} : \mathsf{NP} \wedge \mathsf{ind} : 3))$$
$$\wedge \quad (\mathsf{dtrs} \cdot \mathsf{rest} \cdot \mathsf{rest} \cdot \mathsf{rest}) : \mathsf{nil}$$

The presence of the indices ensures that the two NP constituents introduced by the rule are distinct, but otherwise has no effect on the class of structures defined by a grammar[4].

The logical treatment of ID/LP grammar presented above remains faithful to the linguistic insights underlying the original formalism in the following sense. Local constraints on the hierarchical and linear ordering of constituents are expressed as separate components of a definition of syntactic structure. (One alternative, though less faithful treatment would involve first converting the sets of ID- and LP-rules to an equivalent set of simple phrase structure rules.) The present approach shows that the language **NRRK** is sufficiently expressive to capture the notational devices employed in the ID/LP grammar formalism.

---

[4]Given the representation for trees adopted in this chapter, terminal nodes correspond to simple atomic values and thus cannot be distinguished by conjoining 'indices' in the proposed manner. However, it is not difficult to show that any ID/LP grammar has an 'almost strongly equivalent' grammar in which each terminal symbol $a \in T$ is introduced by a 'lexical' ID-rule of the form $A \rightarrow a$. The proposed solution will work for any grammar in this form.

5.2.3   PATR

The PATR formalism was originally developed by Stuart Shieber and his colleagues (Shieber et al. 1983, Shieber 1984a, Shieber 1986a) and is perhaps
the simplest of the unification-based grammars. PATR was designed primarily as a powerful computational tool for representing and processing natural
language. The formalism is entirely declarative and does not embody any
(non-trivial) restrictions on the kinds of grammar that can be written down.
A PATR grammar can be regarded as consisting of two components: a finite
set of lexical entries L, and a finite set of syntactic rules R. Each lexical
entry in L is a pair $a : D$, where a is an element of a finite set of terminal
symbols T, and D is a feature structure description (a set of path equations
of the kind described in section 2.1 of chapter 2). A typical lexical entry is
shown below. The entry states that the terminal symbol *Uther* is a third
person singular **NP**.

(56)   *Uther:*
       $\langle$cat$\rangle$ = **NP**
       $\langle$head agr number$\rangle$ = singular
       $\langle$head agr person$\rangle$ = third

As noted in section 2.1 of chapter 2, a PATR rule has two parts: a simple
context-free rule and a set of equational constraints amongst features and
values. An example of a typical syntactic rule is given next:

(57)   S   →   NP VP
               $\langle$S head$\rangle$ = $\langle$VP head$\rangle$
               $\langle$S head subj$\rangle$ = $\langle$NP head$\rangle$
               $\langle$NP case$\rangle$ = nom

In this rule the context-free part stipulates that a sentence may consist of a
noun phrase followed by a verb phrase. The equational constraints specify
equivalences which must hold amongst the feature structures associated with
the constituents introduced by the rule. Thus, the first constraint in (57)
states that the value of the **head** feature of (the feature structure associated
with) the **S** constituent is the same as that of the **head** feature of (the feature
structure associated with) the **VP** constituent.

The translation from PATR grammars to **NRRK** is illustrated here by
example. Consider first the lexical entry given in (56) above. This may be

expressed in **NRRK** as the following description:

$$\text{dtrs} : (\text{first} : \textit{Uther} \land \text{rest} : \text{nil})$$
$$\land \quad \text{cat} : \text{NP}$$
$$\land \quad (\text{head} \cdot \text{agr} \cdot \text{number}) : \text{singular}$$
$$\land \quad (\text{head} \cdot \text{agr} \cdot \text{person}) : \text{third}$$

It may be noted that the lexical entry is actually translated as a condition on *preterminal* nodes. The first line of the description states that the node has a single daughter labelled by the terminal symbol *Uther*. It should be reasonably clear how the rest of the translation relates to the PATR lexical entry given in (56). For example, the path equation ⟨head agr number⟩ = singular is simply translated as the description (head · agr · number) : singular. Given a translation $\tau(\ell)$ of each lexical entry $\ell \in L$, the entire lexicon is expressed in **NRRK** as a disjunction $\tau(L) = \bigvee_{\ell \in L} \tau(\ell)$.

Consider now the translation of the PATR rule given above in (57). The context-free part of this rule may be translated in exactly the same fashion as a context-free grammar production. The translation of the constraint equations is also quite straightforward. In general, each constraint is an equation $u = v$, where u is a term of the form ⟨A, p⟩ (for A a nonterminal and p a path) and v is either a term of the same kind or a constant. A term ⟨A, p⟩ denotes the value of the path p in the feature structure associated with the constituent labelled A introduced by the context-free rule. For example, the term ⟨S head⟩ in the above rule denotes the value of the feature head in the feature structure associated with the whole phrase. Similarly, ⟨NP head⟩ denotes the value of head in the feature structure associated with the second (i.e. NP) daughter. The constraint ⟨S head⟩ = ⟨NP head⟩ can therefore be expressed as the following description:

$$(\text{head} \doteq (\text{dtrs} \cdot \text{rest} \cdot \text{first} \cdot \text{head}))$$

The constraint ⟨NP case⟩ = nom in (57) specifies that the value of case for the first constituent is the constant nom. This path equation is expressed as a description (dtrs · first · case) : nom.

To obtain a translation for the whole rule, the translation of the context-free part is simply conjoined with the translations of each of the path equations. For the rule given in (57) the resulting translation is as shown below:

$$((\text{cat} : \text{S}) \quad \land \quad \text{dtrs} : (\text{first} : (\text{cat} : \text{NP}) \land \text{rest} : (\text{first} : (\text{cat} : \text{VP}) \land \text{rest} : \text{nil})))$$

$\wedge \quad (\text{head} \doteq (\text{dtrs} \cdot \text{rest} \cdot \text{first} \cdot \text{head})))$

$\wedge \quad ((\text{head} \cdot \text{subj}) \doteq (\text{dtrs} \cdot \text{first} \cdot \text{head}))$

$\wedge \quad (\text{dtrs} \cdot \text{first} \cdot \text{case}) : \text{nom}$

Given a suitable translation $\tau(\rho)$ of each syntactic rule $\rho \in R$, the set of rules is translated as a disjunction $\tau(R) = \bigvee_{\rho \in R} \tau(\rho)$. Finally, if T is the set of all terminal symbols which appear in the lexicon L, then $\tau(T) = \bigvee_{a \in T} a$. The translation of a PATR grammar G is then given by:

$$\tau(G) = (\text{cat} : \tau(S)) \wedge \neg\textbf{DOM} : \neg(\tau(R) \vee \tau(L) \vee \tau(T))$$

(where S is the start symbol of the grammar).

The translation from PATR to **NRRK** described above provides a model-theoretic semantics for the formalism which is simpler in some respects than the denotational semantics proposed by Pereira and Shieber (1984). It would be a trivial matter to extend the present treatment to account for disjunctive constraints amongst features and values (as suggested by Karttunen (1984) for example). The problem of dealing with disjunctive descriptions of feature structures within the denotational model has already been discussed in chapter 2. Shieber (1986b, 1988) has claimed that a number of grammar formalisms which employ feature structures to represent linguistic objects (e.g. FUG, LFG and GPSG) can be reconstructed using the descriptive apparatus of PATR. This suggests that these formalisms might also be represented in the language **NRRK**, and thereby furnished with a precise, model-theoretic semantics. Of course, this does not imply that **NRRK** is sufficiently expressive to capture, in a straightforward manner, all of the descriptive devices employed in these formalisms. In particular, FUG, LFG and GPSG make use of a variety of non-monotonic constructs for specifying or constraining the values of features. These include the ANY values of FUG, the constraints equations of LFG, and the Feature Specification Defaults of GPSG. Given that the language **NRRK** is Turing machine equivalent, it is clear that some way of simulating the behaviour of such constructs could always be found. However, the resulting grammar encodings would be neither intuitive nor particularly revealing.

The next example shows that the descriptive apparatus of Categorial Grammar can also be reconstructed in **NRRK**. In view of the logical formulation of PATR presented above, an essentially equivalent, model-theoretic treatment could be achieved 'indirectly', by embedding Categorial Grammar in PATR. For the sake of consistency, and to emphasize the model-theoretic aspects of the reformulation, this route will not be taken here.

5.2.4   Categorial Grammar

Categorial Grammar (CG) has its origins in the work of Ajdukiewicz (1935) (following Leśniewski (1929)) during the 1930s, and was later developed by Bar-Hillel (1953), Lambek (1958, 1961) and others. The last decade has seen a marked growth of interest in categorial systems for the description of natural languages. Recent developments include *Combinatory Grammar* (Ades and Steedman (1982), Steedman (1985, 1987)) and *Generalized Categorial Grammar* (Moortgat (1987)). A representative selection of contemporary work in this area can be found in the collection of papers edited by Oehrle, Bach and Wheeler (1988). In computational linguistics a number of researchers have investigated the integration of categorial systems of grammar with unification-based formalisms. Examples include *Categorial Unification Grammar* (CUG) (Uszkoreit (1986)) and *Unification Categorial Grammar* (UCG) (Calder et al. (1988), Zeevat et al. (1987)).

A categorial grammar consists of a *categorial lexicon*, and a set of *combinatory rules*. The categorial lexicon associates with each word of a language one or more syntactic categories, where a category is either *basic* or *derived*. Basic categories are elements of some finite, and usually small set of simple symbols (typically S, NP and N). Derived categories are complex symbols of the general form $(A\omega B)$, where A and B are categories (either basic or derived) and ω is a category formation operator. A derived category $(A\omega B)$ is understood as a function with domain (argument) B and range (result) A. The idea is that $(A\omega B)$ may be applied as a function to a category B as argument, to produce a category A as result.

The classical, *bidirectional* categorial grammars introduced by Bar-Hillel (1953) employ two category formation operators / and \. A derived category of the form A/B specifies that the argument must be taken from the right, whilst a category $A\backslash B$ specifies that the argument must be taken from the left. More formally, given a finite set of symbols N (the basic categories) a *bidirectional category system* $\mathcal{C}(N)$ is defined as the smallest set such that:

(a) if $A \in N$, then $A \in \mathcal{C}(N)$

(b) if $A, B \in \mathcal{C}(N)$, then $(A/B) \in \mathcal{C}(N)$

(c) if $A, B \in \mathcal{C}(N)$, then $(A\backslash B) \in \mathcal{C}(N)$

A set $\mathcal{C}(N)$ is a *unidirectional* category system if it satisfies (a) together with just one of either (b) or (c).

The precise manner in which categories may be combined is determined by the set of combinatory rules. In a classical bidirectional categorial grammar there are just two such rules: *Forward Function Application* (FA) and *Backward Function Application* (BA):

$$\text{FA:} \quad A/B \ B \ \Rightarrow \ A$$
$$\text{BA:} \quad B \ A\backslash B \ \Rightarrow \ A$$

Considered as node-admissibility conditions, the rules may be interpreted as follows. The rule FA admits as well-formed any binary-branching node with category label A, where the daughters are labelled (A/B) and B (in that order). Similarly, BA admits any binary-branching node with category label A where the daughters are labelled B and $(A\backslash B)$ respectively.

As may be clear, in a categorial grammar a great deal of syntactic information is encoded in the structure of categories. Specifying a categorial grammar amounts to little more than listing the categories assigned to words in the categorial lexicon:

Definition 5.8 A *bidirectional (unidirectional) categorial grammar* G is a structure $\langle N, T, F, S \rangle$ where:

- N is a finite set of symbols (the *basic categories*);

- T is a finite set of symbols (the *terminals*);

- F is a function from elements of T to finite, non-empty subsets of a bidirectional (unidirectional) category system $\mathcal{C}(N)$ (the *categorial lexicon*); and

- $S \in N$ is a distinguished basic category (the *start symbol*).

The categorial lexicon F can be regarded as admitting a class of pre-terminal nodes which can appear in the parse trees of G. Specifically, if $a \in T$ is a terminal symbol, then a node is admissible just in case it is labelled by some category in $F(a)$ and immediately dominates a single terminal node labelled by a. A constituent structure tree will be said to be a parse tree for a categorial grammar $G = \langle N, T, F, S \rangle$ just in case the root node is labelled by the start symbol S, and each non-terminal node is either admitted by one of the combinatory rules (i.e. FA or BA) or by the categorial lexicon. As usual, the language $L(G)$ of G is given as the set of

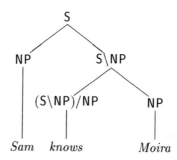

Figure 5.3: A categorial derivation

all strings of terminal symbols which are the yield of some parse tree for
G. It can be shown that the bidirectional categorial grammars with just
the two combinatory rules FA and BA are weakly equivalent to the context-
free grammars (Bar-Hillel et al. 1964). An example of a simple bidirectional
categorial grammar is presented next.

Example 5.9 Let $G = \langle N, T, F, S \rangle$ be a bidirectional categorial grammar
where:

1. N is the set $\{S, NP\}$

2. T is the set $\{Sam, Moira, knows\}$

3. $F(Sam) = \{NP\}$
   $F(Moira) = \{NP\}$
   $F(knows) = \{(S\backslash NP)/NP, (S\backslash NP)/S\}$

4. The start symbol of the grammar is S

A parse tree admitted by the grammar of example 5.9 is shown in figure 5.3. It is easy to see that each preterminal node is admissible according to the categorial lexicon F. For example, the terminal node labelled by *knows* is immediately dominated by a node with category label
$(S\backslash NP)/NP \in F(knows)$. Further, the non-terminal node labelled by $S\backslash NP$
is admissible according to the rule FA, and the node labelled S is admissible
according to the rule BA. It follows that *Sam knows Moira* belongs to the
language described by the grammar of example 5.9.

In order to express a categorial grammar as a description in **NRRK**, it is first necessary to choose a suitable representation for categories (both basic and derived). The representation employed here is a slightly modified version of that described by Gazdar et al. (1988). Each basic category A is simply represented by a feature structure $\mathcal{A} = \langle \{q_0\}, q_0, \delta, \pi \rangle$, where $\pi(q_0) = A$. A derived category can then be represented by a feature structure which is defined for the feature labels **domain**, **range** and **side**, where the values of **domain** and **range** represent the domain and range of the category respectively, and **side** takes a value in **left** or **right**, depending on whether the category takes its argument from the left- or right-hand side.

Consider first the translation of the combinatory rules. The rule FA may be interpreted as a node-admissibility condition which states that a node is (locally) well-formed if it has two daughters, and the following conditions hold:

- the first daughter is labelled by a derived category taking its argument from the right;

- the node's category label is the same as the range of the first daughter's category label;

- the second daughter's category label is the same as the domain of the first daughter's category label.

This may be expressed in **NRRK** as the following description:

FA :   dtrs : (first : (cat : (side : right)) $\wedge$ rest : (first : $\top$ $\wedge$ rest : nil))

$\wedge$ (cat $\doteq$ (dtrs $\cdot$ first $\cdot$ cat $\cdot$ range))

$\wedge$ ((dtrs $\cdot$ rest $\cdot$ first $\cdot$ cat) $\doteq$ (dtrs $\cdot$ first $\cdot$ cat $\cdot$ domain))

The rule BA is formulated in an entirely similar fashion. In this case, the second daughter is labelled by a derived category taking its argument from the left, and so on:

BA :   dtrs : (first : $\top$ $\wedge$ rest : (first : (cat : (side : left)) $\wedge$ rest : nil))

$\wedge$ (cat $\doteq$ (dtrs $\cdot$ rest $\cdot$ first $\cdot$ cat $\cdot$ range))

$\wedge$ ((dtrs $\cdot$ first $\cdot$ cat) $\doteq$ (dtrs $\cdot$ rest $\cdot$ first $\cdot$ cat $\cdot$ domain))

Using the translations of the combinatory rules given above, the translation of a categorial grammar $G = \langle N, T, P, S \rangle$ is defined as follows:

1. for $A \in \mathcal{C}(N)$,

    (a) if $A \in N$, then $\tau(A) = A$

    (b) if A is (B/C), then
$$\tau(A) = (\text{domain} : \tau(C) \wedge \text{range} : \tau(B) \wedge \text{side} : \text{right})$$

    (c) if A is $(B\backslash C)$, then
$$\tau(A) = (\text{domain} : \tau(C) \wedge \text{range} : \tau(B) \wedge \text{side} : \text{left})$$

2. $\tau(T) = \bigvee_{a \in T} a$

3. $\tau(F) = \bigvee_{a \in T} \left[\bigvee_{A \in F(a)} ((\text{cat} : \tau(A)) \wedge \text{dtrs} : (\text{first} : a \wedge \text{rest} : \text{nil})) \right]$

4. $\tau(G) = (\text{cat} : \tau(S)) \wedge \neg\text{DOM} : \neg(\text{FA} \vee \text{BA} \vee \tau(F) \vee \tau(T))$

Example 5.10 The translation of the categorial grammar of example 5.9 is given by the following description:

$$(\text{cat} : \text{S}) \wedge \neg\text{DOM} : \neg(\text{FA} \vee \text{BA} \vee \tau(F) \vee (Sam \vee Moira \vee knows))$$

where $\tau(F)$ is the disjunction:

$$(\text{cat} : \text{NP} \wedge \text{dtrs} : (\text{first} : Sam \wedge \text{rest} : \text{nil}))$$
$$\vee \quad (\text{cat} : \text{NP} \wedge \text{dtrs} : (\text{first} : Moira \wedge \text{rest} : \text{nil}))$$
$$\vee \quad (\text{cat} : \tau((\text{S}\backslash\text{NP})/\text{NP}) \wedge \text{dtrs} : (\text{first} : knows \wedge \text{rest} : \text{nil}))$$
$$\vee \quad (\text{cat} : \tau((\text{S}\backslash\text{NP})/\text{S}) \wedge \text{dtrs} : (\text{first} : knows \wedge \text{rest} : \text{nil}))$$

where $\tau((\text{S}\backslash\text{NP})/\text{NP})$ is given by:

$$(\text{range} : \tau(\text{S}\backslash\text{NP}) \wedge \text{domain} : \text{NP} \wedge \text{side} : \text{right})$$
$$= (\text{range} : (\text{range} : \text{S} \wedge \text{domain} : \text{NP} \wedge \text{side} : \text{left}) \wedge \text{domain} : \text{NP} \wedge \text{side} : \text{right})$$

(and similarly for $\tau((\text{S}\backslash\text{NP})/\text{S})$)

The basic categorial framework presented above may be modified in either (or both) of two different ways: by altering the definition of a category system, or by expanding the set of combinatory rules. For example, in the categorial system due to Ajdukiewicz, there is a single category formation operator $|$. A derived category is of the form $(A|B)$ and is *non-directional*:

the argument may be taken from either the left- or the right-hand side. Categories of this kind can easily be accommodated by defining the translation of a category $(A|B)$ as follows:

$$\tau(A|B) = (\text{domain} : \tau(B) \wedge \text{range} : \tau(A) \wedge \text{side} : (\text{left} \vee \text{right}))$$

(or perhaps more succinctly as $(\text{domain} : \tau(B) \wedge \text{range} : \tau(A))$ which simply omits any specification for **side**).

A number of researchers have investigated categorial grammars which make use of operations on categories in addition to the rules FA and BA. Two such operations are considered here as being of particular importance: *function composition* (or *partial combination*) and *type-raising* (or *lifting*). Both kinds of operation were included in the categorial system due to Lambek (1958, 1961). More recently, Steedman (1985, 1987) has proposed the use of function composition and type raising in order to handle the problem of discontinuous constituents and unbounded dependencies. The rules of *Forward Function Composition* (FC) and *Backward Function Composition* (BC) are presented below:

$$\text{FC:} \quad A/B \ \ B/C \ \Rightarrow \ A/C$$
$$\text{BC:} \quad B\backslash C \ \ A\backslash B \ \Rightarrow \ A\backslash C$$

Both rules combine two derived categories of the form $(A\omega B)$ (the 'principal category') and $(B\omega C)$ (the 'subsidiary category'). In order for function composition to go through, the domain of the principal category must be the same as the range of the subsidiary category, and function composition performs a kind of 'cancellation of the common term'. The result is a category whose domain is taken from that of the subsidiary category and whose range is taken from that of the principal category.

The operation of function composition provides a general mechanism for the description of 'incomplete' constituents. For example, an auxiliary verb such as *must* can be categorized as $(S\backslash NP)/(S_{inf}\backslash NP)$, signifying a function which maps (infinitival) verb phrases to verb phrases. Using simple function application, *must* can be combined as functor with *know Moira* as argument to yield *must know Moira* as result. On the other hand, the analysis is blocked if the object NP is missing, as for example in the relative clause *whom Sam must know __*. Using function composition however, *must* and *know* can be assembled into a single constituent having the category of transitive verb (i.e. a predicate missing an object NP). This is illustrated below:

$$
\left[
\begin{array}{ll}
\text{cat} & \left[\begin{array}{ll}\text{domain} & \boxed{1}\\ \text{range} & \boxed{2}\\ \text{side} & \text{right}\end{array}\right]\\
\text{dtrs} & \left\langle \left[\begin{array}{ll}\text{cat} & \left[\begin{array}{ll}\text{domain} & \boxed{3}\\ \text{range} & \boxed{2}\\ \text{side} & \text{right}\end{array}\right]\\ \text{dtrs} & \langle\ldots\rangle\end{array}\right], \left[\begin{array}{ll}\text{cat} & \left[\begin{array}{ll}\text{domain} & \boxed{1}\\ \text{range} & \boxed{3}\\ \text{side} & \text{right}\end{array}\right]\\ \text{dtrs} & \langle\ldots\rangle\end{array}\right]\right\rangle
\end{array}
\right]
$$

Figure 5.4: A representation of forward function composition

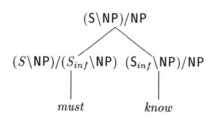

$$(S\backslash NP)/NP$$

$$(S\backslash NP)/(S_{inf}\backslash NP) \quad (S_{inf}\backslash NP)/NP$$

must   *know*

The following description captures the content of the rule FC considered as a node-admissibility condition. The rule BC is translated in an analogous way.

FC :   dtrs : (first : (cat : (side : right)))
$\wedge$ dtrs : (rest : (first : (cat : (side : right)) $\wedge$ rest : nil))
$\wedge$ dtrs : ((first · cat · domain) $\doteq$ (rest · first · cat · range))
$\wedge$ ((cat · domain) $\doteq$ (dtrs · rest · first · cat · domain))
$\wedge$ ((cat · range) $\doteq$ (dtrs · first · cat · range))
$\wedge$ (cat : (side : right))

This description is satisfied by feature structures of the general form shown in figure 5.4. Re-entrancy in the feature structure is used to ensure that the domain of the principal category (the first daughter) is identified with the range of the subsidiary category (the second daughter). Also, the

$$
\left[
\begin{array}{ll}
\text{cat} &
\left[
\begin{array}{ll}
\text{domain} &
\left[
\begin{array}{ll}
\text{domain} & \boxed{1} \\
\text{range} & \boxed{2} \\
\text{side} & \text{left}
\end{array}
\right] \\
\text{range} & \boxed{2} \\
\text{side} & \text{right}
\end{array}
\right] \\
\text{dtrs} &
\left\langle
\left[
\begin{array}{ll}
\text{cat} & \boxed{1} \\
\text{dtrs} & \langle \ldots \rangle
\end{array}
\right]
\right\rangle
\end{array}
\right]
$$

Figure 5.5: A representation of forward type raising

domain and range of the result category are identified with the domain and range of the subsidiary and principal categories respectively.

In contrast to the rules of function application and composition, which are binary operations on categories, type-raising is used to change the category assigned to a single expression. Applied to a category A, type-raising 'lifts' the category to a function which applies to an argument with domain A and range some category B and yields the category B as its result. As usual, there are forward and backward versions of the operation:

$$
\begin{array}{ll}
\text{FR:} & A \Rightarrow B/(B\backslash A) \\
\text{BR:} & A \Rightarrow B\backslash (B/A)
\end{array}
$$

Following Montague (1974), Steedman uses the rule of *Forward Raising* (FR) to re-analyse the category of subject NPs as $S/(S\backslash NP)$. That is, subjects are actually regarded as functions which may be combined with a predicate to yield a sentence. The translation of the rule FR into **NRRK** is presented next:

FR: dtrs : (first : ⊤ ∧ rest : nil)

∧ ((cat · domain · domain) $\doteq$ (dtrs · first · cat))

∧ cat : (side : right ∧ domain : (side : left) ∧ (range $\doteq$ (domain · range)))

The description FR licences representations of nodes having the general form of the feature structure shown in figure 5.5. It may be noted that the only restriction placed on the **range** of the node's category is that it should be identical to the **range** of the category's **domain**. This reflects the fact that the range category B in the type-raising rules given above is completely arbitrary: type-raising may 'lift' a category to any one of an infinite number of more complex categories of the indicated form. On the other hand, the category's **domain** will generally become instantiated through unification with an argument category to its right (e.g. if the 'raised' category occurs on the first daughter of a node admitted by function application). At this stage the **range** will also obtain a value.

5.2.5   Tree Adjoining Grammar

The Tree Adjoining Grammar (TAG) formalism was first introduced by Joshi, Levy and Takahashi (1975) and its formal and linguistic properties studied by Joshi (1985). A detailed examination of the linguistic relevance of TAG has been carried out by Kroch and Joshi (1985), while the formalism has been investigated from the point of view of both parsing and generation in a number of papers (Vijay-Shanker and Joshi (1985), Schabes and Joshi (1988), Joshi (1986)).

A TAG is a tree rewriting systems which is specified by providing a finite set of *elementary trees*. The elementary trees are understood as minimal, or basic structural descriptions for a given language, and are composed under a single operation of *adjoining* to derive more complex structures. There are two kinds of elementary trees: *initial trees*, which represent basic sentential forms, and *auxiliary trees*, which represent minimal recursive structures. An interesting property of the TAG formalism is that it allows for the factoring of recursion from the domain of syntactic dependencies such as subcategorization and agreement. Such dependencies are localized in the elementary trees and preserved under the adjoining operation. In principle, the adjoining operation may be used to insert an unbounded amount of material into a tree, giving rise to dependencies which hold over 'non-local' domains. The formal definition of TAG presented below follows that given by Weir (1988):

Definition 5.11 A *tree adjoining grammar* is a structure $G = \langle N, T, S, I, A \rangle$ where:

- N is a finite set of symbols (the *non-terminals*);

- T is a finite set of symbols disjoint from N (the *terminals*);

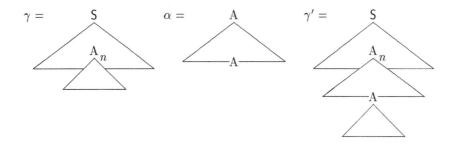

Figure 5.6: The adjoining operation in TAG

- $S \in N$ is a distinguished non-terminal (the *start symbol*);

- I is a finite set of constituent-structure trees with interior nodes labelled by elements of N, leaf nodes labelled by elements of T, and root node labelled by S (the *initial trees*);

- A is a finite set of constituent-structure trees with interior nodes labelled by elements of N, exactly one leaf node (the *foot node*) labelled by the same symbol that labels the root node; and all other leaf nodes labelled by elements of T (the *auxiliary trees*).

Each initial tree in I represents a basic sentential tree for the grammar G. The *adjoining* operation composes sentential trees with auxiliary trees to derive more complex sentential trees, and may be explained as follows. Suppose that γ is a sentential tree with some node n labelled by a non-terminal symbol A, and that α is an auxiliary tree with root node also labelled by A. Note that since α is an auxiliary tree it must have exactly one leaf node which is labelled by A (the foot node). To adjoin the auxiliary tree α to γ at the node n, the subtree rooted at node n is first removed and the auxiliary tree α inserted in its place. The excised subtree is then re-attached at the foot node of α to yield a new sentential tree γ'. The adjoining operation can be pictured as shown in figure 5.6.

The tree set $T(G)$ of a tree adjoining grammar G is defined as the set of all sentential trees which can be derived from the initial trees by repeated adjoining of the auxiliary trees. The (string) language $L(G)$ is the set of all strings which are the yield of some sentential tree in $T(G)$. The languages described by TAG are called *tree adjoining languages* (TAL). It was shown by Joshi, Levy and Takahashi (1975) that TAL properly contains the context-free languages, but is itself properly contained in the indexed languages. In fact, TAG belongs to a class of so-called *mildly context sensitive* (Joshi 1985) grammar formalisms which also include Linear Indexed Grammar (LIG) (see Gazdar (1988)), Head Grammar (HG) (Pollard (1984)) and Combinatory Categorial Grammar (CCG) (Steedman (1987)). The mildly context-sensitive grammars have been investigated in detail from the perspective of their strong generative capacity by Weir (1988). Vijay-Shanker and Weir have shown that the TAG, LIG, HG and CCG formalisms are equivalent in terms of their weak expressive power, and admit polynomial time recognition algorithms (Vijay-Shanker and Weir (1989, 1990a, 1990b)). The following example provides a more concrete illustration of the adjoining operation and derivations in TAG.

Example 5.12 Let $G = \langle N, T, S, I, A \rangle$ be a tree adjoining grammar such that:

- N is the set $\{\mathsf{S}, \mathsf{NP}, \mathsf{VP}, \mathsf{V}\}$;

- T is the set $\{Sam, Moira, knows\}$;

- $\mathsf{S} \in N$ is the start symbol;

- I contains the single initial tree γ shown in figure 5.7; and

- A contains the single auxiliary tree α of figure 5.7.

The string *Sam knows Moira* is the yield of the initial tree γ shown in figure 5.7. It follows that this string belongs to the language $L(G)$ described by the grammar of example 5.12[5]. The sentential tree γ' shown in figure 5.7 is derived from γ by adjoining the auxiliary tree α at the VP node. Thus, the string *Sam knows Sam knows Moira* also belongs to the language $L(G)$. The sentential tree γ' may of course undergo further adjoining with α.

It is now shown that a tree adjoining grammar G may be expressed as a description $\tau(G)$ in **NRRK**. The key to the translation presented below lies in the choice of representation for the elementary trees of G. In particular, the representation must allow for the adjoining operation to be simulated in terms of the accumulation of constraints on feature structures (i.e. in

---

[5] More generally TAGs may have associated constraints which make adjoining at certain nodes of an initial tree obligatory. In this case, the initial tree would not be regarded as belonging to the tree set of the grammar. Constraints on adjoining are discussed below.

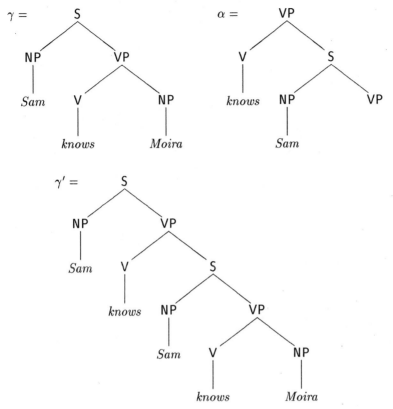

Figure 5.7: Sentential and auxiliary trees

terms of feature structure unification). First, it may be noted that the representation for parse trees used throughout this chapter is not suitable for this purpose. Consider for example the initial tree γ of figure 5.7. At first sight, it appears that this tree can be adequately described as follows (where **NPTree** and **VPTree** are assumed to be suitable descriptions of the **NP** and **VP** subtrees of γ):

(58) (cat : S ∧ dtrs : (first : NPTree ∧ rest : (first : VPTree ∧ rest : nil)))

Unfortunately, this will not do. Certainly, (58) describes a representation of the tree γ, but the structure of this tree is effectively fixed. There is no way in which conjoining additional descriptions can give rise to a tree having a different structure. An alternative means of representing information about elementary trees is therefore required, one which permits this information to be used in determining the *eventual* structure of a sentential tree. A suitable representation is described next.

Initial Trees: The initial trees of the grammar are represented in the following fashion. Each terminal node of an initial tree is encoded in the usual way by an atomic feature value. Each non-terminal node is also represented in much the same way as before, except that the list of daughter nodes appears as the value of a special feature label **idtrs** (for 'initial daughters'). For example, the initial tree γ of figure 5.7 may be represented by the following feature structure.

$$
\begin{bmatrix}
\text{cat} & \text{S} \\
\text{idtrs} & \left\langle \begin{bmatrix} \text{cat} & \text{NP} \\ \text{idtrs} & \langle Bill \rangle \end{bmatrix}, \begin{bmatrix} \text{cat} & \text{VP} \\ \text{idtrs} & \left\langle \begin{bmatrix} \text{cat} & \text{V} \\ \text{idtrs} & \langle knows \rangle \end{bmatrix}, \begin{bmatrix} \text{cat} & \text{NP} \\ \text{idtrs} & \langle Moira \rangle \end{bmatrix} \right\rangle \end{bmatrix} \right\rangle
\end{bmatrix}
$$

As will become clear, the idea is that the value of the feature label **idtrs** provides a constraint on the structure of the foot node of an auxiliary tree *after* adjoining. Only in the event that no adjoining takes place at a given node is the value of **idtrs** interpreted as the list of actual daughters for that node (i.e. the value of **dtrs**).

Auxilliary Trees: The representation of an auxiliary tree differs from that of an initial tree only in respect of the root and foot nodes. In the case of the root node, the list of daughters is represented in the usual way as the value of the feature label **dtrs**, while the value of **idtrs** is left unspecified. Similarly, the value of **idtrs** at the foot node of the tree is uninstantiated. However, the **idtrs** values of the two nodes are identified. This is illustrated by the feature structure shown below, which represents the auxiliary tree α of figure 5.7.

$$
\begin{bmatrix}
\text{cat} & \text{VP} \\
\text{dtrs} & \left\langle \begin{bmatrix} \text{cat} & \text{V} \\ \text{idtrs} & \langle knows \rangle \end{bmatrix}, \begin{bmatrix} \text{cat} & \text{S} \\ \text{idtrs} & \left\langle \begin{bmatrix} \text{cat} & \text{NP} \\ \text{idtrs} & \langle Bill \rangle \end{bmatrix}, \begin{bmatrix} \text{cat} & \text{VP} \\ \text{idtrs} & \boxed{1} \end{bmatrix} \right\rangle \end{bmatrix} \right\rangle \\
\text{idtrs} & \boxed{1}
\end{bmatrix}
$$

The effect of adjoining the auxiliary tree α at the VP node of γ can now be stated in terms of feature structure unification. Consider what happens when the representation of the auxiliary tree α is unified with the VP node in the feature structure representing the initial tree γ given previously. Two things occur. First, the feature structure representing the VP node of γ acquires the **dtrs** sequence of the auxiliary tree α. The resulting feature structure is therefore a locally well-formed representation of a non-terminal node of a constituent-structure tree, with category label VP and two daughters labelled V and S in that order. This corresponds to inserting the auxiliary tree at the VP node of γ. Second, the **idtrs** value of the feature structure representing the VP node of γ is unified with the **idtrs** value of the auxiliary tree's foot node. Consequently, all of the available information about the structure of this subtree is passed down to the foot node of the auxiliary tree. In effect, the VP subtree of γ has been attached at the foot node of α.

To complete the picture, it remains to state what happens at a node which does not undergo adjoining with an auxiliary tree. In this case, the node's **idtrs** value should become the **dtrs** sequence for the node. This can be achieved simply by unifying the representation of the node with a feature structure of the following form:

$$\begin{bmatrix} \text{dtrs} & \boxed{1} \\ \text{idtrs} & \boxed{1} \end{bmatrix}$$

The translation of a tree adjoining grammar $G = \langle N, T, S, I, A \rangle$ can now be defined. Each initial tree $\gamma \in I$ is associated with a description Init_γ in **NRRK** which describes the structure of this tree according to the representation outlined above. Likewise, each auxiliary tree $\alpha \in A$ is associated with a description Aux_α. The mapping τ is then given by:

- $\tau(T) = \displaystyle\bigvee_{a \in T} a$

- $\tau(I) = \displaystyle\bigvee_{\gamma \in I} \mathsf{Init}_\gamma$

- $\tau(A) = \displaystyle\bigvee_{\alpha \in A} \mathsf{Aux}_\alpha$

- $\tau(G) = \tau(I) \wedge \neg\mathsf{DOM} : \neg(\tau(A) \vee (\text{idtrs} \doteq \text{dtrs}) \vee \tau(T))$

The description $\tau(G)$ may be understood as follows. First, it may be noted that the initial trees are treated as constraints on the eventual structure of a parse tree for the grammar. The rest of the description then expresses a generalization which states that every node of a parse tree is either:

1. the result of unifying a node of an initial tree with an auxiliary tree (the adjoining operation);

2. the result of identifying the **idtrs** and **dtrs** values (no adjoining takes place); or

3. a terminal node which is labelled by some element of T.

In the first case, the node is locally well-formed, with a **dtrs** sequence acquired from the adjoined auxiliary tree in the manner described above. In the second case, the node is also locally well-formed having a **dtrs** sequence identical to the initial daughters sequence (**idtrs** value) of the node. Finally, each terminal node is well-formed. Intuitively then, the description $\tau(G)$ correctly characterizes a class of globally-well-formed representations of constituent-structure trees representing the parse trees of the grammar G.

In the foregoing account of the TAG formalism, the only constraint on adjoining is that the label of the node at which adjoining is performed should be identical to the label of the root and foot nodes of the adjoined auxiliary tree. In practice, the elementary trees of a grammar may involve additional local constraints on adjoining. Thus, a *selective adjoining* (SA) constraint associated with a node of an initial tree is an enumeration of a finite set of auxiliary trees which may be adjoined at that node. Alternatively, a node may be associated with a *null adjoining* (NA) constraint which states that adjoining cannot take place, or an *obligatory adjoining* (OA) constraint which indicates that adjoining is mandatory at that node.

Constraints on adjoining can be accounted for by providing additional statements about the nodes of the elementary trees. For example, if a node is associated with a NA constraint, then its description should include the statement (**idtrs** $\doteq$ **dtrs**). If the node has an OA constraint, on the other hand, then its description must state that ¬(**idtrs** $\doteq$ **dtrs**). There is a sense in which SA constraints are already present in the feature structure representation of initial and auxiliary trees. More specifically, adjoining will succeed (respectively, fail) if the feature structures representing the node at which adjoining is to take place, and the auxiliary tree to be adjoined at that node have compatible (respectively, incompatible) atomic **cat** values. Clearly, the adjoining operation can be made more sensitive than this simply by employing a more complex category system. For example, additional 'agreement' features would permit finer-grained distinctions to be made amongst the auxiliary trees which can be selected for adjoining at any given node.

A similar approach to TAGs has been proposed by Vijay-Shanker (Vijay-Shanker (1987), Vijay-Shanker and Joshi (1988)) who defines a new formalism, *Feature structure based TAG* (FTAG). In FTAG, each node n of an elementary tree is associated with two feature structures t_n and b_n. The idea is that the feature structure t_n encodes the relationship between the node n and its 'supertree' (the view of the node 'from the top') while b_n encodes the relationship between n and its descendants (the view of the node 'from the bottom'). Like the use of **idtrs** in the account of TAG provided here, the 'bottom' feature structure associated with a node provides a constraint on the structure which appears beneath the foot node of an auxiliary tree *after* adjoining. If adjoining is not performed, then both t_n and b_n hold (i.e. the two feature structures are unified). The two approaches share the advantage, noted above, that constraints on adjoining may be expressed naturally in terms of compatibility of feature structures. Vijay-Shanker also introduces a calculus for representing FTAG which extends Rounds-Kasper logic with the introduction of λ-abstraction and function application. Each auxiliary tree is viewed as a function over feature structures, and the adjoining operation corresponds to applying such a function to the 'bottom' feature structure of a node in an initial tree. In contrast, the present treatment of TAG considers a grammar as a single logical description which expresses a generalization about feature structures. The relationship between a sentential tree and a grammar is then given simply in terms of the model-theoretic satisfaction relation, and there is no need to extend the logic by introducing functions over feature structures.

5.3 Discussion

The preceding section has provided a number of extended examples of the way in which the language **NRRK** can be used to encode entire grammars. A grammar is represented by a logical description which captures a generalization about the local well-formedness of nodes in constituent-structure trees (represented in feature structures). The examples given in the previous section show how the descriptive devices employed in a number of different grammar formalisms can be expressed in a uniform logical language with a precise, model-theoretic semantics. While the details of the particular translations employed are to some extent arbitrary, they are nevertheless reasonably intuitive and remain faithful to the linguistic insights underlying the original grammar formalisms.

It is interesting to relate the **NRRK** encodings of the formalisms given in the previous section to the known formal properties of these systems. A first observation here is that there is a basic distinction to be drawn between those formalisms encoded without the use of path equations, and those for which path equations appear to be necessary, or provide the most 'direct' translation. Thus, the translations of the CFG and ID/LP grammar formalisms do not require the use of path equations, and it is well-known that the strings recognition problem for the class of languages described by these formalisms is decidable in polynomial time. In contrast, the recognition problem for the PATR formalism is undecidable[6]. Intuitively, this is because PATR allows path equations to be used to state arbitrary dependencies amongst the potentially unbounded structures associated with the nodes of a constituent-structure tree.

On the other hand, it is notable that the use of path equations *per se* does not imply that a formalism is undecidable. Consider for example the translation of the CG formalism. In this case, path equations are used to provide general statements of the combinatory rules (i.e. function application, function composition and type-raising). On closer inspection however, it is evident that (with the exception of the type-raising rule) the role of the path equations within a particular CG encoding is simply *abbreviatory*. That is to say, the path equations are actually being used to abbreviate a large, but finite number of rule instances.

Ignoring the type-raising rule for the moment, it is clear that while the category system of a categorial grammar G contains an unbounded number of derived categories, the number of 'useful' categories (i.e. those which can actually occur in the parse trees for G) is finite. To see this, it can be observed that the categorial lexicon F associates with each of a finite number of terminal symbols a finite number of categories. Moreover, 'closing' the set of all lexical categories under the operations of function application and function composition will in general yield a larger, but still finite set. This

---

[6]Without the 'off-line parsability condition' ((Kaplan and Bresnan 1982, p.266)

means that for a given grammar, the rules of function application and composition could in principle be encoded without the use of path equations, by expanding the rules out as a finite number of different rule instances.

The same argument does not go through for the rule of type-raising. As noted in section 5.2.4, type-raising can be used to 'lift' an arbitrary category to any one of an unbounded number of more complex categories. In this case however, the use of path equation in the **NRRK** statement of the rule is *essential* rather than abbreviatory because without further restriction, any one of the type-raised categories might appear in a parse tree for the grammar. On the other hand, it is interesting to note that in practice, type raising may be intended to apply only to a restricted set of categories. For example, Steedman (1985) limits its application to a small set of 'maximal' categories (e.g. NP, PP, VP, and S′). As a consequence of this stipulation, it is not possible for type raising to operate recursively, by applying to the output of previous invocations of the rule. Although such a restriction does not mean that the number of categories which can be obtained by type-raising is finite, it does seem likely that there will be only a finite number of 'useful' categories. Thus, in principle at least, the use of path equations to encode the rules of forward and backward type raising in this restricted sense may again be abbreviatory.

Consider finally the encoding of TAG given in section 5.2.5. In the TAG encoding, path equations are used to identify the idtrs values of the root and foot nodes in the representations of auxiliary trees. Unlike the translations of the rules of function application and composition in the encoding of CG, the use of path equations here is essential rather than abbreviatory. Intuitively, this is because the value of idtrs is used to keep track of the structure of the 'excised' subtree when adjoining takes place. In general however, there are an unbounded number of distinct subtrees which can occur as the value of idtrs and this implies that the representation of a given auxiliary tree cannot be viewed as abbreviating a finite number of different instances of the tree.

On the other hand, compared to the way in which path equations may be used in the PATR formalism, the use of path equations in the encoding of TAG is rather restrictive. Specifically, the encoding requires the use of path equations only in the descriptions of auxiliary trees, and then only to identify the idtrs values of the root and foot nodes of the tree. To see more clearly what is going on here, consider again the feature structure representation of the auxiliary tree α of figure 5.7, which is repeated below for convenience:

$$
\left[
\begin{array}{l}
\text{cat} \quad \text{VP} \\[4pt]
\text{dtrs} \quad \left\langle \left[\begin{array}{l} \text{cat} \quad \text{V} \\ \text{idtrs} \ \langle knows \rangle \end{array} \right], \left[\begin{array}{l} \text{cat} \quad \text{S} \\ \text{idtrs} \ \left\langle \left[\begin{array}{l} \text{cat} \quad \text{NP} \\ \text{idtrs} \ \langle Bill \rangle \end{array} \right], \left[\begin{array}{l} \text{cat} \quad \text{VP} \\ \text{idtrs} \ \boxed{1} \end{array} \right] \right\rangle \end{array} \right] \right\rangle \\[4pt]
\text{idtrs} \quad \boxed{1}
\end{array}
\right]
$$

This feature structure represents a locally well-formed node of a constituent structure tree, with a **VP** mother and two daughters labelled **V** and **S** respectively. The node can be pictured as shown below, where the notation $A \downarrow \sigma$ is used to abbreviate a feature structure with **cat** value A and **idtrs** value σ. Thus, the node's left daughter is associated with a feature structure having a **cat** value **V** and **idtrs** sequence $\langle knows \rangle$.

$$
\begin{array}{c}
\text{VP} \downarrow \boxed{1} \\
\diagup \quad \diagdown \\
\text{V} \downarrow \langle knows \rangle \quad \text{S} \downarrow \langle \text{NP} \downarrow \langle Sam \rangle, \text{VP} \downarrow \boxed{1} \rangle
\end{array}
$$

The important thing to note is that the **idtrs** value of the mother node is shared within the **idtrs** value of just one of the daughters (as indicated by the co-indexing box $\boxed{1}$). This is highly reminiscent of the use of stack information in *Linear* Indexed Grammar (LIG), where only one of the non-terminals on the right-hand side of a production can inherit the potentially unbounded stack from the non-terminal on the left-hand side. Consequently, stack information cannot be shared by different branches of a LIG derivation. It has been shown by Vijay-Shanker and Weir (1989, 1990a, 1990b) that as a result of this restriction it is possible to provide a polynominal time recognition algorithm for LIG. What the **NRRK** encoding of TAG reveals is that essentially the same restriction is built into the TAG formalism via the notion of an auxiliary tree and the adjoining operation.

To summarize, the language **NRRK** can be used to encode grammars expressed in a number of rather different formalisms, in a way which is intuitive and provides a basis for comparison. An inspection of the encodings given in this chapter shows that the formalisms differ with regard to the manner in which path equations are used to capture linguistic generalizations, and these differences can be related to the known formal properties of the formalisms.

Chapter 6

Conclusion

This book has been concerned with the application of formal logic to the study of grammar and the representation of linguistic information or knowledge. The work described in the preceding chapters belongs to an on-going programme of research in computational linguistics which has as its objective the formalization and analysis of concepts in grammar using tools and techniques developed in general logic. The use of logic is especially attractive in this context for at least two reasons. On the one hand, logic provides an invaluable analytic tool, allowing results from model-theory and proof-theory to be applied directly to the study of language and grammar. On the other, logic offers a sound basis for the declarative representation of linguistic knowledge with all the benefits that this confers. In particular, there is the promise that techniques for automated deduction developed in artificial intelligence can be applied to problems in natural language processing.

A central theme of the work described in this book is the idea that the relationship between a grammar and the objects is characterizes is essentially the same as the relationship between a logical formula and its models. Thus, a grammar can be viewed as a logical statement which has as its models well-formed linguistic structures. Much previous work on the logical formulation of linguistic knowledge (e.g. Definite Clause Grammar) has tended to emphasize a rather different view of the relationship between "knowledge of language" and linguistic structure. More specifically, a grammar is taken to be a system of logical statements which axiomatize certain properties of strings. From this point of view, the notion of grammaticality is subsumed under the more general notion of theoremhood, and linguistic structure corresponds closely to proof structure. In contrast, in the present

155

work grammaticality is viewed as satisfiability and linguistic structure as model structure. While both approaches support the appealing idea that language processing can be viewed as specialized inference within a logical language, the model-theoretic or 'structural' perspective adopted in the present work is held to be important for the following reasons.

First, it brings to the fore issues concerning the nature of linguistic information, and the kinds of mathematical structures needed to represent the linguistic objects that carry this information. The provision of precise, mathematical definitions of these representational structures is an important step in constructing adequate theories of natural language grammar. In much recent work, the mathematical structures chosen to represent linguistic objects are record- or frame-like data objects called feature structures, which provide for the encoding of linguistic information in terms of hierarchical sets of feature labels and associated values. A number of formal models of feature structures and their description languages was presented in chapter 2.

Second, in order to analyse and compare different approaches to grammar, it is fruitful to examine the kinds of informational structures that they characterize. Grammar formalisms (like programming languages and AI knowledge representation formalisms) employ a diverse range of novel notational devices. Such notational diversity can obscure deeper similarities between formalisms. In chapter 5.2 for example, it was observed that tree adjoining grammars embody a restriction on the sorts of informational dependencies that can arise in linguistic structures. This restriction is closely related to the use of the unbounded stack in Linear Indexed Grammar. Notationally, TAG and LIG are very different formalisms, but viewed in terms of the informational structures they characterize, it is possible to discern interesting similarities.

Third, from the perspective of computational linguistics, understanding the nature of the structures required to represent linguistic objects and information can lead to insights into the sorts of data structures and algorithms needed to process this information efficiently. Furthermore, it is difficult to see how the correctness of any implementation can be established without a precise account of the structures that represent linguistic objects and the way in which the grammar notation is used to describe these structures.

Fourth, a precise characterization of the structures which are used to model linguistic objects is important from the point of view of formalism design. Many different notational systems can be used to describe the same kinds of structures, but some may turn out to be more appropriate (linguistically or computationally) than others. Understanding the formal properties of these structures may suggest ways in which existing formalisms can be improved or extended.

In addition to these general observations, there are three specific contributions to the logical study of language and grammar contained in this book.

First, chapter 3.3 proposed a formalization of the linguistically useful device of functional uncertainty within the logical framework originally introduced by Rounds and Kasper. In the language of *Regular Rounds-Kasper logic* (**RRK**), descriptions of paths in feature structures are generalized to regular expressions over feature labels. As a consequence, the description language **RRK** can be used to express certain kinds of infinite disjunction. This has linguistic application in the treatment of unbounded dependencies in natural languages.

Second, chapter 4 further extended the language **RRK** with the addition of general description negation, and investigated the properties of the resulting language. It was shown that the combination of regular path expressions and negation makes it possible to write constraints on feature structures which apply to successively embedded levels of feature values. The language of *Regular Rounds-Kasper logic with Negation* (**NRRK**) is sufficiently expressive to capture generalizations about features and their values and can be used to provide general definitions of particular classes of structure.

Third, chapter 5.2 provided an investigation of the description language **NRRK** viewed as as a uniform framework for encoding grammars. It was shown that a grammar can be expressed as a logical description which captures a generalization about the well-formedness of nodes in constituent-structure trees (suitably encoded in feature structures). The relationship between a linguistic object and a grammar can then be viewed as that of model-theoretic satisfaction. It was shown that grammars written in a number of notationally rather different frameworks (simple Context-Free Grammar, ID/LP grammar, PATR Categorial Grammar and Tree Adjoining Grammar) may be encoded as descriptions in **NRRK** in a way which captures the linguistic intuitions underlying the original formalisms.

Investigation of the properties of the description languages **RRK** and **NRRK** also yielded a number of important formal results. These are summarized below, together with brief discussion where further work is required.

Section 3.3 presented a number of laws of logical equivalence for descriptions in **RRK**. Many of these laws are obtained by suitably generalizing the equivalences for Rounds-Kasper logic, while others are seen to arise from the interaction of the path operators and logical connectives. In general, determining logical equivalence for descriptions in **RRK** contains the equivalence problem for regular expressions as a subproblem, from which it follows that the logical equivalence problem for descriptions in **RRK** is PSPACE-hard. Further investigation is required in order to determine whether or not the logical equivalence problem for **RRK** is in PSPACE.

The main technical result concerning the language **RRK** is a partial decision procedure for the satisfiability problem for descriptions. It is notable that in contrast to Rounds-Kasper logic, the logical equivalence classes of **RRK** descriptions cannot be characterized in terms of the finite sets of subsumption-incomparable feature structures. Equivalently, there is no simple disjunctive normal form result for **RRK** analogous to that for Rounds-Kasper logic. Nevertheless, it has been shown that the satisfiability problem for **RRK** is decidable subject to an acyclicity condition on feature structures. The proof draws on an algorithm for solving functional descriptions with uncertainty sets developed by Kaplan and Maxwell (1988). The key to this algorithm lies in the observation that for any pair of conjoined function-application expressions there are only a finite and relatively small number of ways in which paths chosen from uncertainty sets can interact. Furthermore, these interactions can be effectively eliminated by isolating them in different disjuncts of a description. The result is a logically equivalent description which is 'free' in the sense that satisfiability is not dependent on a particular choice of paths.

Unfortunately, it was found that this technique is not immediately applicable to descriptions of feature structures expressed in the language **RRK**. This is because there is no guarantee that a given description in **RRK** is logically equivalent to a description which is 'free' in the required sense. For this reason, the proof given in section 3.4 proceeds indirectly. More precisely, it is shown that descriptions in **RRK** can be expressed in a language of equational constraints on feature structures to which the Kaplan-Maxwell algorithm may be directly applied.

It remains an open question whether or not the satisfiability problem for the description language **RRK** is decidable in the general case (i.e. without the acyclicity condition on feature structures). Clearly, it would be of interest for technical reasons to provide an answer to this question one way or another. Moreover, understanding the computational properties of cyclic feature structure descriptions may be important for practical reasons. Robust implementations of constraint-based grammar formalisms may need to tolerate cyclic structures, which can arise naturally as constraints are solved. On the other hand, the linguistic significance of cyclic structures is less clear. Although Johnson (1988, pp.19-20) suggests that cyclic structures may play a role in the treatment of relative clauses, constraint-based grammar formalisms generally do not make use of feature structures involving cycles. In many existing formalisms they are simply regarded as ill-formed or deviant in some way.

The ability of the language **NRRK** to express generalizations about features and their values has a precursor in the constraint language L_C (Category Logic), which was introduced by Gazdar et al. (1988) as part of a metatheoretical framework for studying the category systems of different grammar formalisms. Category logic employs two modal operators $\Box$ and $\Diamond$, which express universal and existential quantification over feature values. Section 4.3 investigated the formal relationship between the two languages and it was shown that L_C can be viewed as a restricted version of **NRRK**. More specifically, the modal operator $\Diamond$ of Category Logic is a special case of the functional uncertainty mechanism: for a given set of 'category valued' feature labels $\{f_1, f_2, \ldots, f_n\}$, the operator $\Diamond$ can be simulated by a regular path expression $(f_1 + f_2 + \ldots + f_n)^*$. Furthermore, from the equivalence $\Box\phi \Leftrightarrow \neg\Diamond\neg\phi$, it follows that the modal operator $\Box$ of Category Logic can also be expressed in **NRRK** in terms of regular path expressions and negation.

In section 4.4, it was demonstrated that the language **NRRK** can be used to simulate the computations of an arbitrary Turing machine. This shows that there can be no algorithm for deciding in general whether or not a description in **NRRK** has a satisfying feature structure. From a computational perspective, the undecidability of **NRRK** is not necessarily a fatal flaw. It may be noted for example, that a number of computationally inspired grammar formalisms (including Definite Clause Grammar and PATR) are known to be 'Turing-equivalent'. However, this does not make these formalisms unsuitable as a means of implementing grammars.

On the other hand, it is interesting to identify the source of this undecidability result. In fact, it has been shown the fragment of **NRRK** without path equations is a variant of *Deterministic Propositional Dynamic Logic*, for which a practical decision procedure has been given by Ben-Ari et al. (1982). Thus, the undecidability of **NRRK** resides in the possibility of writing descriptions of feature structures that express generalizations involving conditions on re-entrancy. For the purposes of encoding grammars, the elimination of path equations from the logic would limit the expressivity of the formalism too severely. The ability to express conditions on re-entrancy in feature structures accounts for much of the success of constraint-based approaches to grammar in providing concise descriptions of linguistic phenomena such as agreement and filler-gap dependencies. What this result does suggest however, is that it may be fruitful to investigate the computational properties of fragments of **NRRK** which place restrictions on the way path equations may be used to encode informational dependencies.

6.1   Closing Remarks

There are intimate connections between grammar and general logic. In studying the mathematical and computational properties of grammar formalisms, logic serves as an invaluable analytic tool. Above and beyond this however, logic also has an important role to play in the representation of linguistic knowledge and the investigation of language and grammar. Put more forcefully, it is both appropriate and beneficial to view grammar *as* logic.

The logical conception of grammar poses a challenge. In order to make it work, it is necessary to find logical systems that are suitable for representing and reasoning about 'knowledge of language'. The work described in this book contains one possible response to this challenge. A grammar is regarded simply as a logical description which expresses a generalization about the well-formedness of feature structures representing linguistic objects. In this final chapter, it has been argued that the model-theoretic approach to grammar provides an important direction for research into the nature of grammar and its connection with general logic.

Bibliography

Ades, A. E., and M. J. Steedman. 1982. On the order of words. *Linguistics and Philosophy*. 3:517–558.

Aho, A. V. 1968. Indexed grammars — An extension to context free grammars. *Journal of the ACM*. 15:647–671.

Aït-Kaci, H. 1984. *A New Model of Computation Based on a Calculus of Partially Ordered Type Structures*. PhD thesis, University of Pennsylvania, Pennsylvania.

Aït-Kaci, H., and R. Nasr. 1986. LOGIN: A logic programming language with built-in inheritance. *Journal of Logic Programming*. 13:185–215.

Aït-Kaci, H. 1986. An algebraic semantics approach to the effective resolution of type equations. *Theoretical Computer Science*. 45:293–351.

Ajdukiewicz, K. 1935. Die syntaktische Konnexität. *Studia Philosophica*. 1:1–27. English translation in: Polish logic 1920-1939, ed. by Storrs McCall, 207-231. Oxford:Oxford University Press.

Baader, F., H.-J. Bürckert, B. Nebel, W. Nutt, and G. Smolka. 1991. On the expressivity of feature logics with negation, functional uncertainty and sort equations. DFKI Report RR-91-01, DFKI, Saarbrücken.

Bar-Hillel, Y. 1953. A quasi-arithmetical notation for syntactic description. *Language*. 29:47–58.

Bar-Hillel, Y., C. Gaifman, and E. Shamir. 1964. On categorial and phrase structure grammars. In *Language and Information*. Reading, Mass.: Addison-Wesley.

Ben-Ari, M., J. Y. Halpern, and A. Pnueli. 1982. Deterministic propositional dynamic logic: Finite models, complexity, and completeness. *Journal of Computing and System Sciences.* 25:402–417.

Blackburn, P. 1991. Modal logic and attribute value structures. In M. de Rijke (Ed.), *Diamonds and Defaults*, Studies in Logic, Language and Information. Dordrecht: Kluwer.

Blackburn, P. 1992. Structures, languages and translations: the structural approach to feature logic. Research Paper HCRC/RP-33, HCRC Publications, University of Edinburgh, Edinburgh.

Blackburn, P., and E. Spaan. 1992. A modal perspective on the computational complexity of attribute value grammar. Logic Group Preprint Series No. 77, Department of Philosophy, Utrecht University, Utrecht.

Brachman, R. J., and J. G. Schmolze. 1985. An overview of the KL-ONE knowledge representation system. *Cognitive Science.* 9(2):171–216.

Calder, J. 1987. Typed unification for natural language processing. In E. Klein and J. van Benthem (Eds.), *Categories, Polymorphism and Unification*, 65–72. Edinburgh: Centre for Cognitive Science, University of Edinburgh.

Calder, J., E. Klein, and H. Zeevat. 1988. Unification categorial grammar: A concise, extendable grammar for natural language processing. In *Proceedings of COLING 88*, 83–86.

Carlson, L. 1988. Regular unification grammar. In *Proceedings of COLING 88*, 102–105.

Carpenter, B. 1990. Typed feature structures: Inheritance, (in)equality and extensionality. In W. Daelemans and G. Gazdar (Eds.), *Proceedings of the ITK Workshop: Inheritance in Natural Language Processing*, 9–18, Tilburg. Institute for Language Technology and Artificial Intelligence, Tilburg University.

Carpenter, B. 1992. *The Logic of Typed Feature Structures.* Cambridge Tracts in Theoretical Computer Science 32. Cambridge: Cambridge University Press.

Carpenter, B., C. Pollard, and A. Franz. 1991. The specification and implementation of constraint-based grammar formalisms. In *Proceedings of the Second International Workshop on Parsing Technologies*, 143–153, Cancun.

Chomsky, N. 1981. *Lectures on Government and Binding*. Dordrecht: Foris.

Chomsky, N. 1956. Three models for the description of language. *IRE Transactions on Information Theory*. IT-2:113–124.

Chomsky, N. 1973. Conditions on transformations. In S. R. Anderson and P. Kiparsky (Eds.), *A Festschrift for Morris Halle*, 232–286. New York: Holt, Rinehart and Winston.

Colmerauer, A. 1978. Metamorphosis grammars. In L. Bolc (Ed.), *Natural Language Communication with Computers*, 133–189. Berlin: Springer Verlag.

Dahl, V., and H. Abramson. 1984. On gapping grammars. In *Proceedings of the Second International Conference on Logic Programming*, 77–88, Uppsala. Ord & Form.

Dahl, V., and M. C. McCord. 1983. Treating coordination in logic grammars. *American Journal of Computational Linguistics*. 9:69–91.

Dawar, A., and K. Vijay-Shanker. 1989. A three-valued interpretation of negation in feature structure descriptions. In *Proceedings of the ACL. 27th Annual Meeting*, 18–24.

Dawar, A., and K. Vijay-Shanker. 1990. An interpretation of negation in feature structure descriptions. *Computational Linguistics*. 16(1):11–21.

Dörre, J., and A. Eisele. 1991. A comprehensive unification-based grammar formalism. DYANA Deliverable No. R3.1.B, Centre for Cognitive Science, University of Edinburgh, Edinburgh.

Dörre, J., and R. Seifert. 1991. Sorted feature terms and relational dependencies. IWBS Report No. 153, IBM Germany Science Center, Institute for Knowledge-Based Systems, Stuttgart.

Earley, J. 1970. An efficient context-free parsing algorithm. *Communications of the ACM*. 13(2):94–102.

Eisele, A., and J. Dörre. 1988. Unification of disjunctive feature structure descriptions. In *Proceedings of the ACL, 26th Annual Meeting*, 286–294.

Eisele, A., and J. Dörre. 1990. Disjunctive unification. IWBS Report No. 124, IBM Gemany Science Center, Institute for Knowledge-Based Systems, Stuttgart.

Emele, M., and R. Zajac. 1990. Typed unification grammars. In *Proceedings of COLING 90*, 1–6.

Fischer, M. J., and R. E. Ladner. 1977. Propositional modal logic of programs. In *Proceedings of the 9th ACM Symposium on Theory of Computation*, 286–284.

Fischer, M. J., and R. E. Ladner. 1979. Propositional dynamic logic of regular programs. *Journal of Computing and System Sciences*. 18:194–211.

Fitting, M. 1969. *Intuitionistic Logic, Model Theory, and Forcing*. Amsterdam: North-Holland.

Franz, A. 1990. A parser for HPSG. Report No. LCL-90-3, Laboratory for Computational Linguistics, Carnegie Mellon University, Pittsburgh.

Gazdar, G. 1988. Applicability of indexed grammars to natural languages. In U. Reyle and C. Rohrer (Eds.), *Natural Language Parsing and Linguistic Theories*. Dordrecht: D. Reidel.

Gazdar, G., E. Klein, G. K. Pullum, and I. A. Sag. 1985. *Generalized Phrase Structure Grammar*. Oxford: Basil Blackwell.

Gazdar, G., and G. K. Pullum. 1981. Subcategorization, constituent order, and the notion 'head'. In M. Moortgat, H. v.d. Hulst, and T. Hoekstra (Eds.), *The Scope of Lexical Rules*. Dordrecht: Foris.

Gazdar, G., and G. K. Pullum. 1982. Generalized phrase structure grammar: A theoretical synopsis. Indiana University Linguistics Club, Bloomington, Indiana.

Gazdar, G., G. K. Pullum, R. Carpenter, E. Klein, T. E. Hukari, and R. D. Levine. 1988. Category structures. *Computational Linguistics*. 14(1):1–19.

Halvorsen, P., and R. M. Kaplan. 1988. Projections and semantic descriptions in Lexical-Functional Grammar. In *Proceedings of the International Conference on 5th Generation Computer Systems*, 1116–1122.

Harel, D. 1984. Dynamic logic. In D. Gabbay and F. Guenther (Eds.), *The Handbook of Philosophical Logic, Vol. II*, 497–604. Dordrecht: D. Reidel.

Hellwig, P. 1988. Dependency unification grammar. In *Proceedings of COLING 88*, 195–198.

Höhfeld, M., and G. Smolka. 1988. Definite relations over constraint languages. LILOG Report No. 53, IBM Germany, Stuttgart.

Hopcroft, J. E., and J. D. Ullman. 1979. *Introduction to Automata Theory, Languages and Computation*. Reading, Mass.: Addison-Wesley.

Horrocks, G. 1987. *Generative Grammar*. Longman Linguistics Library. London and New York: Longman.

Johnson, D., and P. Postal. 1980. *Arc Pair Grammar*. Princeton, New Jersey: Princeton University Press.

Johnson, M. 1986. The LFG treatment of discontinuity and the double infinitive construction in Dutch. Report No. CSLI–86–65, CSLI, Stanford University, Stanford, California.

Johnson, M. 1988. *Attribute-Value Logic and The Theory of Grammar*. CSLI Lecture Notes 16. Chicago: Chicago University Press.

Johnson, M. 1990. Expressing disjunctive and negative feature constraints with classical first-order logic. In *Proceedings of the ACL, 28th Annual Meeting*, 173–179.

Johnson, M. 1991. Features and formulae. *Computational Linguistics*. 17(2):131–151.

Joshi, A. K. 1985. Tree Adjoining Grammars: How much context-sensitivity is required to provide reasonable structural descriptions. In D. Dowty, L. Karttunen, and A. Zwicky (Eds.), *Natural Language Processing*. New York: Cambridge University Press.

Joshi, A. K. 1986. The relevance of tree adjoining grammars to generation. Paper presented at the *3rd International Workshop on Natural Language Generation*, Nijmegen.

Joshi, A. K., L. S. Levy, and M. Takahashi. 1975. Tree adjunct grammars. *Journal of Computing and System Sciences.* 10(1).

Kaplan, R. M. 1989. Three seductions of computational psycholinguistics. In P. Whitelock et al. (Eds.), *Linguistic Theory and Computer Applications*, 149–188. London: Academic Press.

Kaplan, R. M., and J. Bresnan. 1982. Lexical-Functional Grammar: A formal system for grammatical representation. In J. Bresnan (Ed.), *The Mental Representation of Grammatical Relations.* Cambridge Mass.: MIT Press.

Kaplan, R. M., and J. T. Maxwell. 1988. An algorithm for functional uncertainty. In *Proceedings of COLING 88*, 297–302.

Kaplan, R. M., and A. Zaenen. 1986. Long-distance dependencies, constituent structure and functional uncertainty. In M. Baltin and A. S. Kroch (Eds.), *Alternative Conceptions of Phrase Structure*, 17–42. Chicago: Chicago University Press.

Kaplan, R. M., and A. Zaenen. 1988. Functional uncertainty and functional precedence in continental west Germanic. In *Proceedings of ÖGAI–88*, 114–123.

Karttunen, L. 1984. Features and values. In *Proceedings of COLING 84*, 28–33.

Karttunen, L. 1986. Radical lexicalism. In M. Baltin and A. S. Kroch (Eds.), *Alternative Conceptions of Phrase Structure*, 43–65. Chicago: Chicago University Press.

Kasami, T. 1965. An efficient recognition and syntax algorithm for context-free languages. Technical Report AF-CRL-65-758, Air Force Cambridge Research Laboratory, Bedford, Mass.

Kasper, R. T. 1987a. *Feature Structures: A Logical Theory with Application to Language Analysis.* PhD thesis, University of Michigan, Michigan.

Kasper, R. T. 1987b. A unification method for disjunctive descriptions. In *Proceedings of the ACL, 25th Annual Meeting*, 235–242.

Kasper, R. T. 1988. Conditional descriptions in functional unification grammar. In *Proceedings of the ACL, 26th Annual Meeting*, 233–240.

Kasper, R. T., and W. C. Rounds. 1986. A logical semantics for feature structures. In *Proceedings of the ACL, 24th Annual Meeting*, 257–266.

Kasper, R. T., and W. C. Rounds. 1990. The logic of unification in grammar. *Linguistics and Philosophy*. 13(1):35–58.

Kay, M. 1979. Functional grammar. In *5th Annual Meeting of the Berkeley Linguistics Society*, 142–158.

Kay, M. 1985. Parsing in functional unification grammar. In *Natural Language Parsing: Psychological, Computational, and Theoretical Perspectives*, chapter 7, 251–278. Cambridge: Cambridge University Press.

Keller, B. 1992. Formalisms for grammatical knowledge representation. *Artificial Intelligence Review*. 6:365–381.

King, P. 1989. *A Logical Formalism for Head-Driven Phrase Structure Grammar*. PhD thesis, University of Manchester, Manchester.

Kleene, S. C. 1952. *Introduction to Metamathematics*. New York: Van-Nostrand.

Kowalski, R. A. 1974. Logic for problem solving. DCL Memo 75, Department of Artificial Intelligence, University of Edinburgh, Edinburgh.

Kracht, M. 1989. On the logic of category definitions. *Computational Linguistics*. 15(2):111–113.

Kripke, S. A. 1965. Semantical analysis of intuitionistic logic I. In J. Crossley and M. Dummett (Eds.), *Formal Systems and Recursive Functions*, 92–130. Amsterdam: North-Holland.

Kroch, A. S., and A. K. Joshi. 1985. Linguistic relevance of tree adjoining grammars. Technical Report MS-CIS-85-18, Department of Computer and Information Science, University of Pennsylvania, Pennsylvania.

Lambek, J. 1958. The mathematics of sentence structure. *American Mathematical Monthly*. 65:154–170.

Lambek, J. 1961. On the calculus of syntactic types. In R. Jakobson (Ed.), *Twelfth Symposium in Applied Mathematics*, 166–178, Providence, Rhode Island. American Mathematical Society.

Langholm, T. 1989. How to say no with feature structures. COSMOS Report 13, Mathematics Institute, University of Oslo, Oslo.

Leśniewski, S. 1929. Grundzüge eines neuen Systems der Grundlagen der Mathematik. *Fundamenta Mathematicae.* 14:1–81.

McCawley, J. 1968. Concerning the base component of a transformational grammar. *Foundations of Language.* 4:243–269. Reprinted in J. D. McCawley. 1973. *Grammar and Meaning*, pp. 35–58, Taishukan: Tokyo.

McCord, M. C. 1985. Modular logic grammars. In *Proceedings of the ACL, 23rd Annual Meeting*, 104–117.

Meyer, A. R., and L. J. Stockmeyer. 1973. Word problems requiring exponential time. In *Fifth ACM Symposium on Theory of Computing*, 1–9.

Minsky, M. 1975. A framework for representing knowledge. In P. H. Winston (Ed.), *The Psychology of Computer Vision*, 211–277. New York: McGraw-Hill.

Montague, R. 1974. The proper treatment of quantification in ordinary English. In R. H. Thomason (Ed.), *Formal Philosophy: Selected papers of Richard Montague*, 188–221. New Haven: Yale University Press.

Moortgat, M. 1987. Generalized categorial grammar. In F. G. Droste (Ed.), *Mainstreams in Linguistics.* Amsterdam: Benjamins.

Moshier, D. 1988. *Extensions to Unification Grammar for the Description of Programming Languages.* PhD thesis, University of Michigan, Ann Arbor.

Moshier, D., and W. C. Rounds. 1987. A logic for partially specified data structures. In *Fourteenth ACM Symposium on Principles of Programming Languages*, 156–167.

Netter, K. 1986. Getting things out of order (an LFG proposal for the treatment of German word order). In *Proceedings of COLING 86*, 494–496.

Oehrle, R. T., E. Bach, and D. Wheeler (Eds.). 1988. *Categorial Grammars and Natural Language Structures.* Studies in Linguistics and Philosophy 32. Dordrecht: D. Reidel.

Partee, B., A. ter Meulen, and R. E. Wall. 1990. *Mathematical Methods in Linguistics*. Studies in Linguistics and Philosophy 30. Dordrecht: Kluwer Academic Publishers.

Pereira, F. C. N. 1981. Extraposition grammars. *Computational Linguistics*. 7(4):243–256.

Pereira, F. C. N. 1983. *Logic for Natural Language Analysis*. PhD thesis, University of Edinburgh, Edinburgh. Reprinted as Technical Note 275, January 1983, Artificial Intelligence Center, SRI International, Menlo Park, California.

Pereira, F. C. N. 1987. Grammars and logics of partial information. In *Proceedings of the 4th International Conference on Logic Programming*, 989–1013.

Pereira, F. C. N., and S. M. Shieber. 1984. The semantics of grammar formalisms seen as computer languages. In *Proceedings of COLING 84*, 655–726.

Pereira, F. C. N., and D. Warren. 1980. Definite clause grammars for language analysis: A survey of the formalism and a comparison with augmented transition networks. *Artificial Intelligence*. 13:231–278.

Pereira, F. C. N., and D. Warren. 1983. Parsing as deduction. In *Proceedings of the ACL, 21st Annual Meeting*, 137–144.

Pollard, C. 1984. *Generalized Phrase Structure Grammars, Head Grammars and Natural Language*. PhD thesis, Stanford University, Stanford.

Pollard, C., and I. A. Sag. 1987. *Information-Based Syntax and Semantics Volume 1: Fundamentals*. CSLI Lecture Notes 13. Chicago: Chicago University Press.

Pollard, C. in press. Sorts in unification-based grammar formalisms and what they mean. In M. Pinkal and B. Gregor (Eds.), *Unification in Natural Language Analysis*. Cambridge, Mass.: MIT Press.

Popowich, F. 1988. *Reflexives and Tree Unification Grammar*. PhD thesis, Centre for Cognitive Science, University of Edinburgh, Edinburgh.

Popowich, F. 1989. Tree unification grammar. In *Proceedings of the ACL, 27th Annual Meeting*, 228–236.

Pullum, G. K. 1982. Free word order and phrase structure rules. In J. Puste-jovsky and P. Sells (Eds.), *Proceedings of the 12th Annual Meeting of the North Eastern Linguistic Society*, 209–220.

Pullum, G. K., and G. Gazdar. 1982. Natural languages and context-free languages. *Linguistics and Philosophy*. 4:471–504.

Ramsay, A. 1987. Restrictions on disjunctive unification. In *Natural Language Processing, Unification and Grammar Formalisms*, 9–14, Stirling. Proceedings of on an Alvey/SERC-sponsored workshop, University of Stirling.

Reape, M. 1991. An introduction to the semantics of unification-based grammar formalisms. DYANA Deliverable R3.2.A, Centre for Cognitive Science, University of Edinburgh, Edinburgh.

Ross, J. R. 1967. *Constraints on Variables in Syntax*. PhD thesis, Massachusetts Institute of Technology, Cambridge, Mass.

Ross, J. R. 1986. *Infinite Syntax*. Norwood, New Jersey: Ablex.

Rounds, W. C. 1988. LFP: A logic for linguistic description and an analysis of its complexity. *Computational Linguistics*. 14(4):1–9.

Rounds, W. C., and R. T. Kasper. 1986. A complete logical calculus for record structures representing linguistic information. In *IEEE Symposium on Logic and Computer Science*.

Rounds, W. C., and A. Manaster-Ramer. 1987. A logical version of functional grammar. In *Proceedings of the ACL, 25th Annual Meeting*, 89–96.

Saiki, M. 1986. A new look at Japanese relative clauses: A Lexical-Functional Grammar approach. *Descriptive and Applied Linguistics*. 19:219–230.

Schabes, Y., and A. K. Joshi. 1988. An Earley-type parsing algorithm for tree adjoining grammars. In *Proceedings of the ACL, 26th Annual Meeting*, 258–269.

Scott, D. 1982. Domains for denotational semantics. In *ICALP 82*, Aarhus, Denmark.

Segerberg, K. 1977. A completeness theorem in the modal logic of programs. *Notices of the American Mathematical Society*. 24(6):A–552.

Sells, P. 1985. *Lectures on Contemporary Syntactic Theories.* CSLI Lecture Notes 3. Chicago: Chicago University Press.

Shieber, S. M. 1984a. The design of a computer language for linguistic information. In *Proceedings of COLING 84*, 363–366.

Shieber, S. M. 1984b. Direct parsing of ID/LP grammars. *Linguistics and Philosophy.* 7:135–154.

Shieber, S. M. 1985. Using restriction to extend parsing algorithms for complex-feature-based formalisms. In *Proceedings of the ACL, 23rd Annual Meeting*, 82–93.

Shieber, S. M. 1986a. *An Introduction to Unification-Based Approaches to Grammar.* CSLI Lecture Notes 4. Chicago: Chicago University Press.

Shieber, S. M. 1986b. A simple reconstruction of GPSG. In *Proceedings of COLING 86*, 211–215.

Shieber, S. M. 1988. Separating linguistic analyses from linguistic theories. In U. Reyle and C. Rohrer (Eds.), *Natural Language Parsing and Linguistic Theories*, 33–68. Dordrecht: D. Reidel.

Shieber, S. M., H. Uszkoreit, J. Robinson, and M. Tyson. 1983. The formalism and implementation of PATR II. In B. Grosz and M. Stickel (Eds.), *Research on Interactive Acquisition and Use of Knowledge.* Menlo Park, California.: Artificial Intelligence Center, SRI International.

Smolka, G. 1988. A feature logic with subsorts. LILOG Report No. 33, IBM Germany, Stuttgart.

Smolka, G. 1989. Feature constraint logics for unification grammars. IWBS Report No. 93, IBM Germany Science Centre, Institute for Knowledge-Based Systems, Stuttgart.

Steedman, M. J. 1985. Dependency and coordination in the grammar of Dutch and English. *Language.* 61:523–568.

Steedman, M. J. 1987. Combinatory grammars and parasitic gaps. *Natural Language and Linguistic Theory.* 5:403–439.

Tomita, M. 1986. *Efficient Parsing for Natural Language: A Fast Algorithm for Practical Systems.* Boston: Kluwer Academic Publishers.

Uszkoreit, H. 1986. Categorial unification grammar. In *Proceedings of COL-ING 86*, 187–194.

Vijay-Shanker, K. 1987. *A Study of Tree Adjoining Grammars*. PhD thesis, University of Pennsylvania, Pennsylvania.

Vijay-Shanker, K., and A. K. Joshi. 1985. Some computational properties of tree adjoining grammars. In *Proceedings of the ACL, 23rd Annual Meeting*, 82–93.

Vijay-Shanker, K., and A. K. Joshi. 1988. Feature structures based tree adjoining grammars. In *Proceedings of COLING 88*, 714–719.

Vijay-Shanker, K., and D. J. Weir. 1989. The recognition of Combinatory Categorial Grammars, Linear Indexed Grammars, and Tree Adjoining Grammars. In *International Workshop of Parsing Technologies*, 172–181, Pittsburgh.

Vijay-Shanker, K., and D. J. Weir. 1990a. Polynomial parsing of Combinatory Categorial Grammars. In *Proceedings of the ACL, 28th Annual Meeting*, 1–8.

Vijay-Shanker, K., and D. J. Weir. 1990b. The recognition of Combinatory Categorial Grammars and Linear Indexed Grammars. In M. Tomita (Ed.), *Current Issues in Parsing Technology*. Boston: Kluwer Academic Publishers.

Wall, R. 1972. *Introduction to Mathematical Linguistics*. Englewood Cliffs, New Jersey: Prentice-Hall.

Weir, D. J. 1988. *Characterizing Mildly Context-Sensitive Grammar Formalisms*. PhD thesis, University of Pennsylvania, Pennsylvania.

Woods, W. A. 1970. Transition network grammars for natural language analysis. *Communications of the ACM*. 13:591–606.

Younger, D. H. 1967. Recognition and parsing of context-free languages in time n^3. *Information and Control*. 10(2):189–208.

Zajac, R. 1992. Inheritance and constraint-based grammar formalisms. *Computational Linguistics*. 18(2):159–182.

Zeevat, H., E. Klein, and J. Calder. 1987. Unification categorial grammar. In N. Haddock, E. Klein, and G. Morrill (Eds.), *Categorial Grammar, Unification Grammar and Parsing*, Edinburgh Working Papers in Cognitive Science, Vol. 1., 195–233. Edinburgh: Centre for Cognitive Science, University of Edinburgh.

CSLI Publications

Reports

The following titles have been published in the CSLI Reports series. These reports may be obtained from CSLI Publications, Ventura Hall, Stanford, CA 94305-4115.

Coordination and How to Distinguish Categories Ivan Sag, Gerald Gazdar, Thomas Wasow, and Steven Weisler CSLI-84-3

Belief and Incompleteness Kurt Konolige CSLI-84-4

Equality, Types, Modules and Generics for Logic Programming Joseph Goguen and José Meseguer CSLI-84-5

Lessons from Bolzano Johan van Benthem CSLI-84-6

Self-propagating Search: A Unified Theory of Memory Pentti Kanerva CSLI-84-7

Reflection and Semantics in LISP Brian Cantwell Smith CSLI-84-8

The Implementation of Procedurally Reflective Languages Jim des Rivières and Brian Cantwell Smith CSLI-84-9

Parameterized Programming Joseph Goguen CSLI-84-10

Shifting Situations and Shaken Attitudes Jon Barwise and John Perry CSLI-84-13

Completeness of Many-Sorted Equational Logic Joseph Goguen and José Meseguer CSLI-84-15

Moving the Semantic Fulcrum Terry Winograd CSLI-84-17

On the Mathematical Properties of Linguistic Theories C. Raymond Perrault CSLI-84-18

A Simple and Efficient Implementation of Higher-order Functions in LISP Michael P. Georgeff and Stephen F. Bodnar CSLI-84-19

On the Axiomatization of "if-then-else" Irène Guessarian and José Meseguer CSLI-85-20

The Situation in Logic–II: Conditionals and Conditional Information Jon Barwise CSLI-84-21

Principles of OBJ2 Kokichi Futatsugi, Joseph A. Goguen, Jean-Pierre Jouannaud, and José Meseguer CSLI-85-22

Querying Logical Databases Moshe Vardi CSLI-85-23

Computationally Relevant Properties of Natural Languages and Their Grammar Gerald Gazdar and Geoff Pullum CSLI-85-24

An Internal Semantics for Modal Logic: Preliminary Report Ronald Fagin and Moshe Vardi CSLI-85-25

The Situation in Logic–III: Situations, Sets and the Axiom of Foundation Jon Barwise CSLI-85-26

Semantic Automata Johan van Benthem CSLI-85-27

Restrictive and Non-Restrictive Modification Peter Sells CSLI-85-28

Institutions: Abstract Model Theory for Computer Science J. A. Goguen and R. M. Burstall CSLI-85-30

A Formal Theory of Knowledge and Action Robert C. Moore CSLI-85-31

Finite State Morphology: A Review of Koskenniemi (1983) Gerald Gazdar CSLI-85-32

The Role of Logic in Artificial Intelligence Robert C. Moore CSLI-85-33

Applicability of Indexed Grammars to Natural Languages Gerald Gazdar CSLI-85-34

Commonsense Summer: Final Report Jerry R. Hobbs, et al CSLI-85-35

Limits of Correctness in Computers Brian Cantwell Smith CSLI-85-36

The Coherence of Incoherent Discourse Jerry R. Hobbs and Michael H. Agar CSLI-85-38

A Complete, Type-free "Second-order" Logic and Its Philosophical Foundations Christopher Menzel CSLI-86-40

Possible-world Semantics for Autoepistemic Logic Robert C. Moore CSLI-85-41

An Architecture for Tuning Rules and Cases Yoshio Nakatami and David Israel CSLI–92–173

The Linguistic Information in Dynamic Discourse Megumi Kameyama CSLI–92–174

Epsilon Substitution Method for Elementary Analysis Grigori Mints and Sergei Tupailo CSLI–93–175

Information Spreading and Levels of Representation in LFG Avery D. Andrews and Christopher D. Manning CSLI–93–176

1992 Annual Report CSLI–93–177

Lecture Notes

The titles in this series are distributed by the University of Chicago Press and may be purchased in academic or university bookstores or ordered directly from the distributor at 11030 South Langley Avenue, Chicago, IL 60628 (USA) or by phone 1-800-621-2736, (312)568-1550.

A Manual of Intensional Logic. Johan van Benthem, second edition, revised and expanded. Lecture Notes No. 1. 0-937073-29-6 (paper), 0-937073-30-X (cloth)

Emotion and Focus. Helen Fay Nissenbaum. Lecture Notes No. 2. 0-937073-20-2 (paper)

Lectures on Contemporary Syntactic Theories. Peter Sells. Lecture Notes No. 3. 0-937073-14-8 (paper), 0-937073-13-X (cloth)

An Introduction to Unification-Based Approaches to Grammar. Stuart M. Shieber. Lecture Notes No. 4. 0-937073-00-8 (paper), 0-937073-01-6 (cloth)

The Semantics of Destructive Lisp. Ian A. Mason. Lecture Notes No. 5. 0-937073-06-7 (paper), 0-937073-05-9 (cloth)

An Essay on Facts. Ken Olson. Lecture Notes No. 6. 0-937073-08-3 (paper), 0-937073-05-9 (cloth)

Logics of Time and Computation. Robert Goldblatt, second edition, revised and expanded. Lecture Notes No. 7. 0-937073-94-6 (paper), 0-937073-93-8 (cloth)

Word Order and Constituent Structure in German. Hans Uszkoreit. Lecture Notes No. 8. 0-937073-10-5 (paper), 0-937073-09-1 (cloth)

Color and Color Perception: A Study in Anthropocentric Realism. David Russel Hilbert. Lecture Notes No. 9. 0-937073-16-4 (paper), 0-937073-15-6 (cloth)

Prolog and Natural-Language Analysis. Fernando C. N. Pereira and Stuart M. Shieber. Lecture Notes No. 10. 0-937073-18-0 (paper), 0-937073-17-2 (cloth)

Working Papers in Grammatical Theory and Discourse Structure: Interactions of Morphology, Syntax, and Discourse. M. Iida, S. Wechsler, and D. Zec (Eds.) with an Introduction by Joan Bresnan. Lecture Notes No. 11. 0-937073-04-0 (paper), 0-937073-25-3 (cloth)

Natural Language Processing in the 1980s: A Bibliography. Gerald Gazdar, Alex Franz, Karen Osborne, and Roger Evans. Lecture Notes No. 12. 0-937073-28-8 (paper), 0-937073-26-1 (cloth)

Information-Based Syntax and Semantics. Carl Pollard and Ivan Sag. Lecture Notes No. 13. 0-937073-24-5 (paper), 0-937073-23-7 (cloth)

Non-Well-Founded Sets. Peter Aczel. Lecture Notes No. 14. 0-937073-22-9 (paper), 0-937073-21-0 (cloth)

Partiality, Truth and Persistence. Tore Langholm. Lecture Notes No. 15. 0-937073-34-2 (paper), 0-937073-35-0 (cloth)

Attribute-Value Logic and the Theory of Grammar. Mark Johnson. Lecture Notes No. 16. 0-937073-36-9 (paper), 0-937073-37-7 (cloth)

The Situation in Logic. Jon Barwise. Lecture Notes No. 17. 0-937073-32-6 (paper), 0-937073-33-4 (cloth)

The Linguistics of Punctuation. Geoff Nunberg. Lecture Notes No. 18. 0-937073-46-6 (paper), 0-937073-47-4 (cloth)

Anaphora and Quantification in Situation Semantics. Jean Mark Gawron and Stanley Peters. Lecture Notes No. 19. 0-937073-48-4 (paper), 0-937073-49-0 (cloth)

Propositional Attitudes: The Role of Content in Logic, Language, and Mind. C. Anthony Anderson and Joseph Owens. Lecture Notes No. 20. 0-937073-50-4 (paper), 0-937073-51-2 (cloth)

Literature and Cognition. Jerry R. Hobbs. Lecture Notes No. 21. 0-937073-52-0 (paper), 0-937073-53-9 (cloth)

Situation Theory and Its Applications, Vol. 1. Robin Cooper, Kuniaki Mukai, and John Perry (Eds.). Lecture Notes No. 22. 0-937073-54-7 (paper), 0-937073-55-5 (cloth)

The Language of First-Order Logic (including the Macintosh program, Tarski's World). Jon Barwise and John Etchemendy, second edition, revised and expanded. Lecture Notes No. 23. 0-937073-74-1 (paper)

Lexical Matters. Ivan A. Sag and Anna Szabolcsi, editors. Lecture Notes No. 24. 0-937073-66-0 (paper), 0-937073-65-2 (cloth)

Tarski's World 4.0. Jon Barwise and John Etchemendy. Lecture Notes No. 25. 1-881526-27-5 (paper)

Situation Theory and Its Applications, Vol. 2. Jon Barwise, J. Mark Gawron, Gordon Plotkin, and Syun Tutiya, editors. Lecture Notes No. 26. 0-937073-70-9 (paper), 0-937073-71-7 (cloth)

Literate Programming. Donald E. Knuth. Lecture Notes No. 27. 0-937073-80-6 (paper), 0-937073-81-4 (cloth)

Normalization, Cut-Elimination and the Theory of Proofs. A. M. Ungar. Lecture Notes No. 28. 0-937073-82-2 (paper), 0-937073-83-0 (cloth)

Lectures on Linear Logic. A. S. Troelstra. Lecture Notes No. 29. 0-937073-77-6 (paper), 0-937073-78-4 (cloth)

A Short Introduction to Modal Logic. Grigori Mints. Lecture Notes No. 30. 0-937073-75-X (paper), 0-937073-76-8 (cloth)

Linguistic Individuals. Almerindo E. Ojeda. Lecture Notes No. 31. 0-937073-84-9 (paper), 0-937073-85-7 (cloth)

Computer Models of American Speech. M. Margaret Withgott and Francine R. Chen. Lecture Notes No. 32. 0-937073-98-9 (paper), 0-937073-97-0 (cloth)

Verbmobil: A Translation System for Face-to-Face Dialog. Martin Kay, Mark Gawron, and Peter Norvig. Lecture Notes No. 33. 0-937073-95-4 (paper), 0-937073-96-2 (cloth)

The Language of First-Order Logic (including the Windows program, Tarski's World). Jon Barwise and John Etchemendy, third edition, revised and expanded. Lecture Notes No. 34. 0-937073-90-3 (paper)

Turing's World. Jon Barwise and John Etchemendy. Lecture Notes No. 35. 1-881526-10-0 (paper)

Syntactic Constraints on Anaphoric Binding. Mary Dalrymple. Lecture Notes No. 36. 1-881526-06-2 (paper), 1-881526-07-0 (cloth)

Situation Theory and Its Applications, Vol. 3. Peter Aczel, David Israel, Yasuhiro Katagiri, and Stanley Peters, editors. Lecture Notes No. 37. 1-881526-08-9 (paper), 1-881526-09-7 (cloth)

Theoretical Aspects of Bantu Grammar. Mchombo, editor. Lecture Notes No. 38. 0-937073-72-5 (paper), 0-937073-73-3 (cloth)

Logic and Representation. Robert C. Moore. Lecture Notes No. 39. 1-881526-15-1 (paper), 1-881526-16-X (cloth)

Meanings of Words and Contextual Determination of Interpretation. Paul Kay. Lecture Notes No. 40. 1-881526-17-8 (paper), 1-881526-18-6 (cloth)

Language and Learning for Robots. Colleen Crangle and Patrick Suppes. Lecture Notes No. 41. 1-881526-19-4 (paper), 1-881526-20-8 (cloth)

Hyperproof. Jon Barwise and John Etchemendy. Lecture Notes No. 42. 1-881526-11-9 (paper)

Mathematics of Modality. Robert Goldblatt. Lecture Notes No. 43. 1-881526-23-2 (paper), 1-881526-24-0 (cloth)

Feature Logics, Infinitary Descriptions, and Grammar. Bill Keller. Lecture Notes No. 44. 1-881526-25-9 (paper), 1-881526-26-7 (cloth)

Tarski's World 4.0. Jon Barwise and John Etchemendy. Lecture Notes No. 45. 1-881526-28-3 (paper)

Other CSLI Titles Distributed by UCP

Agreement in Natural Language: Approaches, Theories, Descriptions. Michael Barlow and Charles A. Ferguson, editors. 0-937073-02-4 (cloth)

Papers from the Second International Workshop on Japanese Syntax. William J. Poser, editor. 0-937073-38-5 (paper), 0-937073-39-3 (cloth)

The Proceedings of the Seventh West Coast Conference on Formal Linguistics (WCCFL 7). 0-937073-40-7 (paper)

The Proceedings of the Eighth West Coast Conference on Formal Linguistics (WCCFL 8). 0-937073-45-8 (paper)

The Phonology-Syntax Connection. Sharon Inkelas and Draga Zec (Eds.) (co-published with The University of Chicago Press). 0-226-38100-5 (paper), 0-226-38101-3 (cloth)

The Proceedings of the Ninth West Coast Conference on Formal Linguistics (WCCFL 9). 0-937073-64-4 (paper)

Japanese/Korean Linguistics. Hajime Hoji, editor. 0-937073-57-1 (paper), 0-937073-56-3 (cloth)

Experiencer Subjects in South Asian Languages. Manindra K. Verma and K. P. Mohanan, editors. 0-937073-60-1 (paper), 0-937073-61-X (cloth)

Grammatical Relations: A Cross-Theoretical Perspective. Katarzyna Dziwirek, Patrick Farrell, Errapel Mejías Bikandi, editors. 0-937073-63-6 (paper), 0-937073-62-8 (cloth)

The Proceedings of the Tenth West Coast Conference on Formal Linguistics (WCCFL 10). 0-937073-79-2 (paper)

On What We Know We Don't Know. Sylvain Bromberger. 0-226-075400 (paper), (cloth)

The Proceedings of the Twenty-fourth Annual Child Language Research Forum. Eve V. Clark, editor. 1-881526-05-4 (paper), 1-881526-04-6 (cloth)

Japanese/Korean Linguistics, Vol. 2. Patricia M. Clancy, editor. 1-881526-13-5 (paper), 1-881526-14-3 (cloth)

Arenas of Language Use. Herbert H. Clark. 0-226-10782-5 (paper), (cloth)

Japanese/Korean Linguistics, Vol. 3. Sonja Choi, editor. 1-881526-21-6 (paper), 1-881526-22-4 (cloth)

The Proceedings of the Eleventh West Coast Conference on Formal Linguistics (WCCFL 11). 1-881526-12-7 (paper)

Books Distributed by CSLI

The Proceedings of the Third West Coast Conference on Formal Linguistics (WCCFL 3). 0-937073-44-X (paper)

The Proceedings of the Fourth West Coast Conference on Formal Linguistics (WCCFL 4). 0-937073-43-1 (paper)

The Proceedings of the Fifth West Coast Conference on Formal Linguistics (WCCFL 5). 0-937073-42-3 (paper)

The Proceedings of the Sixth West Coast Conference on Formal Linguistics (WCCFL 6). 0-937073-31-8 (paper)

Hausar Yau Da Kullum: Intermediate and Advanced Lessons in Hausa Language and Culture. William R. Leben, Ahmadu Bello Zaria, Shekarau B. Maikafi, and Lawan Danladi Yalwa. 0-937073-68-7 (paper)

Hausar Yau Da Kullum Workbook. William R. Leben, Ahmadu Bello Zaria, Shekarau B. Maikafi, and Lawan Danladi Yalwa. 0-93703-69-5 (paper)

Ordering Titles Distributed by CSLI

Titles distributed by CSLI may be ordered directly from CSLI Publications, Ventura Hall, Stanford, CA 94305-4115 or by phone (415)723-1712, (415)723-1839. Orders can also be placed by FAX (415)723-0758 or e-mail (pubs@csli.stanford.edu).

All orders must be prepaid by check or Visa or MasterCard (include card name, number, and expiration date). California residents add 8.25% sales tax. For shipping and handling, add $2.50 for first book and $0.75 for each additional book; $1.75 for first report and $0.25 for each additional report.

For overseas shipping, add $4.50 for first book and $2.25 for each additional book; $2.25 for first report and $0.75 for each additional report. All payments must be made in U.S. currency.

Overseas Orders

The University of Chicago Press has offices worldwide which serve the international community.

Canada: David Simpson, 164 Hillsdale Avenue East, Toronto, Ontario M4S 1T5, Canada. Telephone: (416) 484-8296.

Mexico, Central America, South America, and the Caribbean (including Puerto Rico): EDIREP, 5500 Ridge Oak Drive, Austin, Texas 78731 U. S. A. Telephone: (512)451-4464.

United Kingdom, Europe, Middle East, and Africa (except South Africa): International Book Distributors, Ltd., 66 Wood Lane End, Hemel Hempstead HP4 3RG, England. Telephone: 0442 231555. FAX: 0442 55618.

Australia, New Zealand, South Pacific, Eastern Europe, South Africa, and India: The University of Chicago Press, Foreign Sales Manager, 5801 South Ellis Avenue, Chicago, Illinois 60637 U.S.A. Telephone: (312)702-0289. FAX: (312)702-9756.

Japan: Libraries and individuals should place their orders with local booksellers.

Booksellers should place orders with our agent: United Publishers Services, Ltd., Kenkyu-sha Building, 9 Kanda Surugadai 2-chome, Chiyoda-ku, Tokyo, Japan. Telephone: (03)291-4541.

China (PRC), Hong Kong, and Southeast Asia: Peter Ho Hing Leung, The America University Press Group, P.O. Box 24279, Aberdeen Post Office, Hong Kong.

Korea and Taiwan (ROC): The American University Press Group, 3-21-18-206 Higashi-Shinagawa, Shinagawa-ku, Tokyo, 140 Japan. Telephone: (813)450-2857. FAX: (813)472-9706.